Business
Letters
Made Easy™

D0308433

Business Letters Made Easy
Edited by David Crosby

Text Copyright 1997 Wyvern Publications Limited
Format Copyright 1999 Lawpack Publishing Limited

© 2005 Lawpack Publishing Limited

Lawpack Publishing Limited
76–89 Alscot Road
London SE1 3AW

www.lawpack.co.uk

ISBN 1 904053 87 4

Exclusion of Liability and Disclaimer

Table of contents

Acknowledgements   xii
Introduction   xiii
Index of letters by type   xv

1 Managing suppliers   1

   Quotations
      Friendly request for a quotation   4
      Formal request for a quotation   5

   Quotations – querying
      Querying a price   6
      Refusing a price change   7

   Orders
      Placing an order and requesting delivery   8
      Placing an order and clarifying terms   9
      Amending delivery instructions   10
      Amending the order quantity   11
      Ticking off a supplier for not sticking to the order   12
      Disputing a supplier's terms and conditions   13

   Invoices and statements
      Requesting a credit note – incorrect items received   14
      Querying invoices   15
      Disputing a carriage charge   16
      Requesting a refund of delivery charges   17

   Requests, enquiries and instructions
      Requesting further information about a product   18
      Requesting consultancy information   19
      Advising existing suppliers of a change in terms and
         conditions   20
      Advising a supplier of delivery instructions   21

Negotiating arrangements
Explaining why a new system is required 22
Informing a supplier of changed terms and conditions 23
Negotiating a rate with a supplier 24
Turning down a supplier 25
Firing a strong warning shot at a supplier 26

Errors
Returning an incorrect consignment 27
Returning a non-conforming consignment 28

Making complaints – friendly and firm approaches
Gentle complaint to a good supplier – keeping him on
  his toes 29
Friendly complaint about repeated missing items 30
Complaining about repeatedly missing items 31
Complaining that the quality of service is deteriorating 32
Demanding that defective work be made good 33
Non-delivery of goods – initial letter 34
Non-delivery of goods – second letter 35

Making complaints – using a stronger tone
Getting a too-persistent sales representative off
  your back 36
Letter of complaint about the quality of a product 37
Complaining about a service that fell well below acceptable
  standards 38
Complaining that a verbal assurance has been broken 39
Firm letter to a supplier over a dispute 40
Stern reply to a negative response regarding a refund 41

2 Managing customers 43

Giving quotations
Providing a quote, ex-works 45
Quoting and advising a potential customer 46
Correcting a pricing error, informally 47
Correcting a pricing error 48

Responding to enquiries and orders
Welcoming a new customer, informally 49
Welcoming a new customer 50

Responding to an international enquiry and outlining terms   51
Requesting an international client to issue a letter of credit   52
Playing one client off against another   53
Querying an order with a customer   54
Confirming packing list details with an international
    customer   55
Acknowledging an order – goods temporarily out of stock   56
Telling a customer it's too late to amend an order   57

Making apologies
Apologising to a person receiving unwanted mail   58
Notifying a customer that corrective action has been taken   59
Replying to a complaint about poor service   60
Apologising to a customer for a delay in supplying a
    product   61
Apologising for a missed appointment   62
Making a gentle apology to an established customer   63
Explaining an apparent quality defect   64

Apologies with a hint of grovelling
Apologising for breaking a verbal assurance   65
Apologising to a customer for items that have not arrived   66

Handling awkward customers
Handling a customer who is trying it on   67
Handling a very rude customer   68
Denying liability following a complaint   69
Denying a potential breach of contract   70

Refusing customers
Advising a customer that new orders cannot be supplied   71
Refusing to accept that a carriage charge be deducted   72
Negotiating an amendment to an order   73
Refusing a customer a refund – outside the time period   74

Thanking customers
Responding to a letter of appreciation   75
Thank-you letter for hospitality   76
Thanking a satisfied customer   77
Thanking a good client, slightly cheekily   78
Thanking a business associate for a referral   79

Keeping customers informed
Appointment of a new General Manager   80
Personal announcement to a customer about your new
   position   81
Reawakening a business relationship   82
Surveying customer attitudes   83
Using a customer-service exercise to revive a lapsed
   customer   84

3 Sales and marketing management   85

Sales letters that sell
Inviting the customer to visualise   87
Using the lure of large potential gains   88
Using a force-free trial to increase response   89
Using curiosity to arouse interest   90
Seeking new business with a personalised letter   91
Outlining services on offer   92
Using a testimonial to gain interest   93
Selling on enthusiasm, immediacy and personal attention 94
Telling a story to grab attention   95
Encouraging a customer to renew a subscription   96
Following up a meeting to solicit new business   97

Requesting an agency
Declining a distributor's offer   98
Asking for an agency   99
Accepting an agency – outlining the terms   100
Declining an agency but offering distribution   102

Managing an agent's performance and conduct
Thanking an agent for obtaining some business   103
Motivating an agent with an extra discount for higher sales 104
Complaining to an agent who is acting beyond his powers 105
Reprimanding an agent who is working for a competitor   106
Explaining why agency powers have been exceeded   107
Dismissing an agent for working for a competitor   108

Handling queries about an agent's commission
Recommending that prices be reduced   109
Responding to a request for lower prices   110

Asking for more commission 111
Negotiating a request for more commission 112

Notifying agents of changes
Notifying an agent of revised prices 113
Notifying a distributor about a need for a surcharge 114

Managing public relations
Friendly letter to the media about the loss of a key person 115

Dealing with advertising agencies
Confirming an advertisement to an agency 116
Note to an agency about the incorrect position of an
  advertisement 117
Refusing one offer to advertise and accepting another 118
Making a very low offer to advertise 119

4 Debt collection and credit control 121

Demands for payment
Gently reminding a customer about payment not received 123
Requesting confirmation of when items will be paid for 124
Reminding a customer about credit terms and requesting
  payment 125
Chasing up a commission payment 126

Stronger demands for payment
Notifying that an account is overdue and requesting
  payment 127
Requesting payment within seven days 128
Requesting more timely payment 129
Appealing to a customer's sense of fair play to obtain
  payment 130

Final demands for payment
Notifying that an account is seriously overdue 131
Requesting payment from a company which seems to be
  going under 132
Asking for payment in full – keeping up the pressure 133
Announcing court proceedings in seven days 134

Granting credit
Opening an account for a customer 135

Notifying a new trading account   136
Notifying a buyer about a discount for prompt payment   137
Announcing a credit surcharge on all accounts   138

Refusing credit
Sending a proforma invoice   139
Sending a proforma invoice, due to a poor record of
  payment   140
Complaining about credit terms not being adhered to   141
Writing off a debt and refusing to supply a company   142

Handling queries and disputes
Enclosing a copy of an invoice requested   143
Rejecting an invitation to 'contra' invoices   144
Informing a customer that a statement has already been
  paid   145

Responding to requests for payment
Advising that immediate payment is on its way   146
Advising an international customer that payment is on
  its way   147

Involving the lawyers
Asking for a quotation from solicitors   148

5 Employing people   149

Interviews and offers
Asking a candidate to attend an interview   151
Confirming an interview appointment   152
Acknowledging a job application   153
Rejecting a speculative job application   154
Rejecting a candidate after an interview   155
Rejecting a candidate who came very close to being
  appointed   156
Making an offer of employment   157

References
Asking for a reference   158
Replying to a request for a reference   159
Giving a qualified reference   160

Resignations
Resigning from a job   161

Terminating contracts
Terminating a consultant's contract, due to a disability   162

Warnings and dismissal
First written warning to an employee (for breaching the
    safety code)   163
Final written warning to an employee (for breaching the
    safety code)   164
Dismissing an employee (for breaching the safety code)   165
Summary dismissal   166

General announcements and notices
Announcing a bonus   167
Advising employees of an intention to relocate   168
Notifying staff about the resignation of an employee   169

Notices to individual employees
Notifying an employee of her entitlement to sick pay   170
Refusing to allow a leave of absence with pay   171
Notifying an employee about a company loan   172
Confirming to an employee the termination of her
    employment   173

Maternity and other leave
Notifying an employee of her entitlement to maternity pay 174
Confirming that an employee is not entitled to receive
    maternity pay   175
Wishing an employee a speedy recovery   176

Motivating staff
Motivating an employee whose performance has
    deteriorated   177
Using a promotion to motivate an employee   178
Motivating a team to achieve a goal   179

Offering congratulations
Announcing a performance award   180
Appreciating an employee's special effort   181
Congratulating the winner of a business award   182

Health and safety
Reminding staff about the health and safety policy   183
Reporting a death to the Health and Safety Executive   184

Holiday policy
Announcing extra holiday entitlement   185
Announcing the carrying over of outstanding holiday
     entitlement   186

Offering sincere condolences
Offering condolences to a bereaved wife   187
Offering condolences to the parents on the sudden loss
     of a son   188

6 Banking, insurance and property   189

Managing an account
Opening a current account   191
Cancelling a cheque   192
Notifying a bank about a change of signature for cheques   193
Closing an account   194

Loans and overdrafts
Declining an offer to open an account   195
Following up an application for a business loan   196
Informing a bank of your positive current position   197
Informing a bank of your deteriorating position   198

Insurance
Requesting insurance   199
Asking an insurance broker for a revised quotation   200

Property
Asking for a quote to survey a property   201
Instructing a surveyor to inspect a property   202
Making an offer on a property to an estate agent   203
Confirming an offer to an estate agent   204

Finance documentation
Asking the bank to pay on the presentation of a letter of
     credit   205

7 Business and the community 207

Requests and invitations
    Accepting a request for a donation 209
    Invitation to present an award at a ceremony 210
    Offering support for a community venture 211
    Accepting an invitation to speak at a meeting 212

Declining requests and invitations
    Declining a request for a donation – pre-existing
      commitment 213
    Declining a request for a donation – criterion not met 214
    Declining a request to speak at a meeting 215
    Declining a request to serve on a local committee 216

Objections – making and handling
    Responding to local residents about a potential disruption 217
    Objecting to a planning application 218

Appendix 1 219
Appendix 2 233
Appendix 3 243

Index 253

Acknowledgements

The Publisher would like to thank the customers who contributed letters to this Guide, including: David Lambert of APTECH, Peter Le Conte of Van der Windt Packaging (UK) Ltd, DR Radia of NRG Victory Reinsurance Ltd, Eddie Mander of GCS, DRE Clark of the AEC Group of Companies Ltd and Martin Oates of BSG Products. Special thanks also to Vic Blake of Cambridge for his contributions to the work.

Introduction

Rattle out business letters in a fraction of the time

It is difficult to compose, write and sign a business letter in under 20 minutes. Many letters, if you think about it, can take 30 or 40 minutes, or even an hour each, just to get sorted. The morning post can be the start of a frustrating, time-consuming irritation for many managers.

It doesn't have to be that way. All the letters in this book may be copied straight from the page, and some will require only a slight amendment. With other letters, you may want to take a phrase here or a paragraph there and slot it into the rest of your letter. The important thing to remember is that the 'thinking' has already been done for you – so, those difficult situations, where you can't quite get the right words together, can now be banished ... forever.

Your time is expensive – this book could save you £££s

When a typical letter can cost a business about £15 to send out, mostly in the time of the manager composing it, anything that can bring this cost down will make a big difference. With 199 letters in this Made Easy Guide (each costing a fraction of this amount), it is easy to see how many pounds you can save by slicing hours off your letter writing time.

Angry letters, friendly letters, diplomatic letters, letters that get results

Identifying how subtle tones in a letter are achieved using different phrases is not always easy to pinpoint. What makes, for example, the tone in a letter of complaint either friendly, neutral, angry, diplomatic or strong? To help you find the answer, each letter in this book comes with its own incisive commentary, many of which highlight the specific words and phrases that alter the tone. The commentaries also clarify the meaning that is implicit in the words chosen, and demonstrate how a recipient will perceive and interpret those phrases, helping you to get exactly what you want.

Finding the letter you want is easy

The Guide has a comprehensive Contents page, which groups the letters by topic (Managing Suppliers, Managing Customers, etc.). Each topic is then subdivided into further categories, for example, under Managing Suppliers you will find (amongst others) Quotations, Orders, Invoices and statements, etc. Each letter is also numbered for ease of reference.

But what if you want to look up all the letters concerned with, say, negotiating? All you have to do is turn to the Index of Letters by Type on page xv, where a comprehensive list of these letters (and other types) will be found. For a final catch-all, there is a comprehensive topic index at the end of the work.

No matter what letter you have to write, *Business Letters Made Easy* will repay you, not only in time saved, but also in helping you to clinch deals, get debts paid quickly, obtain better prices and persuade people to your way of thinking. Whatever the letter, I wish you every success.

Index of letters by type

This index is designed to be used with the Contents and the main Index at the end of the book. The Contents gives a good overview of the letters concerned with suppliers, customers, employees and so on. But if you have to write a complaining letter (and want to compare these kinds of letters), it is difficult to find them easily by examining the Contents. However, if you look up *Complaining* in this index, you will find a list of the letters featured that are concerned with this topic and their page number.

Accepting
100 Accepting an agency – outlining the terms
209 Accepting a request for a donation
212 Accepting an invitation to speak at a meeting

Acknowledging
56 Acknowledging an order – goods temporarily out of stock
153 Acknowledging a job application

Advising
20 Advising existing suppliers of a change in terms and conditions
21 Advising a supplier of delivery instructions
46 Quoting and advising a potential customer
71 Advising a customer that new orders cannot be supplied
146 Advising that immediate payment is on its way
147 Advising an international customer that payment is on its way
168 Advising employees of an intention to relocate

Amending (see also Correcting)
10 Amending delivery instructions

11   Amending the order quantity
57   Telling a customer it's too late to amend an order
73   Negotiating an amendment to an order

Announcing
80   Appointment of a new General Manager
81   Personal announcement to a customer about your new position
134 Announcing court proceedings in seven days
138 Announcing a credit surcharge on all accounts
167 Announcing a bonus
180 Announcing a performance award
185 Announcing extra holiday entitlement
186 Announcing the carrying over of outstanding holiday entitlement

Apologising
58   Apologising to a person receiving unwanted mail
61   Apologising to a customer for a delay in supplying a product
62   Apologising for a missed appointment
63   Making a gentle apology to an established customer
65   Apologising for breaking a verbal assurance
66   Apologising to a customer for items that have not arrived

Appealing
130 Appealing to a customer's sense of fair play to obtain payment

Appreciating (see also Congratulating; Thanking)
75   Responding to a letter of appreciation
181 Appreciating an employee's special effort

Asking (see also Requesting)
33   Demanding that defective work be made good
99   Asking for an agency
111 Asking for more commission
133 Asking for payment in full – keeping up the pressure
148 Asking for a quotation from solicitors
151 Asking a candidate to attend an interview
158 Asking for a reference
200 Asking an insurance broker for a revised quotation
201 Asking for a quote to survey a property

205 Asking the bank to pay on the presentation of a letter of credit

Cancelling (see also Terminating)
192 Cancelling a cheque
194 Closing an account

Chasing (see also Reminding)
34 Non-delivery of goods – initial letter
35 Non-delivery of goods – second letter
126 Chasing up a commission payment

Clarifying (see also Explaining)
9 Placing an order and clarifying terms

Complaining (see also Objecting)
29 Gentle complaint to a good supplier – keeping him on his toes
30 Friendly complaint about repeated missing items
31 Complaining about repeatedly missing items
32 Complaining that the quality of service is deteriorating
37 Letter of complaint about the quality of a product
38 Complaining about a service that fell well below acceptable standards
39 Complaining that a verbal assurance has been broken
60 Replying to a complaint about poor service
69 Denying liability following a complaint
105 Complaining to an agent who is acting beyond his powers
141 Complaining about credit terms not being adhered to

Confirming
55 Confirming packing list details with an international customer
116 Confirming an advertisement to an agency
124 Requesting confirmation of when items will be paid for
152 Confirming an interview appointment
173 Confirming to an employee the termination of her employment
175 Confirming that an employee is not entitled to receive maternity pay
204 Confirming an offer to an estate agent

Congratulating (see also Appreciating; Thanking)
182 Congratulating the winner of a business award

Consoling

176 Wishing an employee a speedy recovery
187 Offering condolences to a bereaved wife
188 Offering condolences to the parents on the sudden loss of a son

Correcting (see also Amending)

27 Returning an incorrect consignment
47 Correcting a pricing error, informally
48 Correcting a pricing error
59 Notifying a customer that corrective action has been taken

Declining (see also Denying; Refusing)

98 Declining a distributor's offer
102 Declining an agency but offering distribution
195 Declining an offer to open an account
213 Declining a request for a donation – pre-existing commitment
214 Declining a request for a donation – criterion not met
215 Declining a request to speak at a meeting
216 Declining a request to serve on a local committee

Denying (see also Declining; Refusing)

69 Denying liability following a complaint
70 Denying a potential breach of contract

Dismissing

108 Dismissing an agent for working for a competitor
165 Dismissing an employee (for breaching the safety code)
166 Summary dismissal

Disputing

13 Disputing a supplier's terms and conditions
16 Disputing a carriage charge
40 Firm letter to a supplier over a dispute

Enclosing

143 Enclosing a copy of an invoice requested

Encouraging (see also Motivating)

96 Encouraging a customer to renew a subscription

Explaining (see also Clarifying)

22   Explaining why a new system is required

64   Explaining an apparent quality defect

107 Explaining why agency powers have been exceeded

Following up

97   Following up a meeting to solicit new business

196 Following up an application for a business loan

Giving

160 Giving a qualified reference

Handling

67   Handling a customer who is trying it on

68   Handling a very rude customer

Informing and telling (see also Notifying; Reporting)

23   Informing a supplier of changed terms and conditions

57   Telling a customer it's too late to amend an order

95   Telling a story to grab attention

145 Informing a customer that a statement has already been paid

197 Informing a bank of your positive current position

198 Informing a bank of your deteriorating position

Instructing

202 Instructing a surveyor to inspect a property

Inviting

87   Inviting the customer to visualise

144 Rejecting an invitation to 'contra' invoices

210 Invitation to present an award at a ceremony

212 Accepting an invitation to speak at a meeting

Motivating (see also Encouraging)

104 Motivating an agent with an extra discount for higher sales

177 Motivating an employee whose performance has deteriorated

178 Using a promotion to motivate an employee

179 Motivating a team to achieve a goal

Negotiating

24 Negotiating a rate with a supplier
53 Playing one client off against another
73 Negotiating an amendment to an order
112 Negotiating a request for more commission

Notifying (see also Informing and telling; Reporting)

59 Notifying a customer that corrective action has been taken
113 Notifying an agent of revised prices
114 Notifying a distributor about a need for a surcharge
115 Friendly letter to the media about the loss of a key person
117 Note to an agency about the incorrect position of an advertisement
127 Notifying that an account is overdue and requesting payment
131 Notifying that an account is seriously overdue
136 Notifying a new trading account
137 Notifying a buyer about a discount for prompt payment
161 Resigning from a job
169 Notifying staff about the resignation of an employee
170 Notifying an employee of her entitlement to sick pay
172 Notifying an employee about a company loan
174 Notifying an employee of her entitlement to maternity pay
193 Notifying a bank about a change of signature for cheques

Objecting (see also Complaining)

218 Objecting to a planning application

Offering

98 Declining a distributor's offer
119 Making a very low offer to advertise
157 Making an offer of employment
187 Offering condolences to a bereaved wife
188 Offering condolences to the parents on the sudden loss of a son
195 Declining an offer to open an account
203 Making an offer on a property to an estate agent
204 Confirming an offer to an estate agent
211 Offering support for a community venture

Opening

135 Opening an account for a customer

191 Opening a current account

Outlining
51 Responding to an international enquiry and outlining terms
92 Outlining services on offer

Placing
8 Placing an order and requesting delivery
9 Placing an order and clarifying terms

Querying
6 Querying a price
15 Querying invoices
54 Querying an order with a customer

Quoting
4 Friendly request for a quotation
5 Formal request for a quotation
45 Providing a quote, ex-works
46 Quoting and advising a potential customer
148 Asking for a quotation from solicitors
200 Asking an insurance broker for a revised quotation
201 Asking for a quote to survey a property

Recommending
109 Recommending that prices be reduced

Refusing (see also Declining; Denying)
7 Refusing a price change
72 Refusing to accept that a carriage charge be deducted
74 Refusing a customer a refund – outside the time period
118 Refusing one offer to advertise and accepting another
142 Writing off a debt and refusing to supply a company
171 Refusing to allow a leave of absence with pay

Rejecting
25 Turning down a supplier
144 Rejecting an invitation to 'contra' invoices
154 Rejecting a speculative job application
155 Rejecting a candidate after an interview

156   Rejecting a candidate who came very close to being appointed

Reminding (see also Chasing)
123   Gently reminding a customer about payment not received
125   Reminding a customer about credit terms and requesting payment
183   Reminding staff about the health and safety policy

Replying (see also Responding)
41   Stern reply to a negative response regarding a refund
60   Replying to a complaint about poor service
159   Replying to a request for a reference

Reporting (see also Informing and telling; Notifying)
184   Reporting a death to the Health and Safety Executive

Reprimanding
12   Ticking off a supplier for not sticking to the order
26   Firing a strong warning shot at a supplier
36   Getting a too-persistent sales representative off your back
106   Reprimanding an agent who is working for a competitor

Requesting (see also Asking)
4   Friendly request for a quotation
5   Formal request for a quotation
8   Placing an order and requesting delivery
14   Requesting a credit note – incorrect items received
17   Requesting a refund of delivery charges
18   Requesting further information about a product
19   Requesting consultancy information
52   Requesting an international client to issue a letter of credit
110   Responding to a request for lower prices
112   Negotiating a request for more commission
124   Requesting confirmation of when items will be paid for
125   Reminding a customer about credit terms and requesting payment
128   Requesting payment within seven days
129   Requesting more timely payment
132   Requesting payment from a company which seems to be going under
143   Enclosing a copy of an invoice requested

159   Replying to a request for a reference
199   Requesting insurance
209   Accepting a request for a donation
213   Declining a request for a donation – pre-existing commitment
214   Declining a request for a donation – criterion not met
215   Declining a request to speak at a meeting
216   Declining a request to serve on a local committee

Responding (see also Replying)
41   Stern reply to a negative response regarding a refund
51   Responding to an international enquiry and outlining terms
75   Responding to a letter of appreciation
89   Using a force-free trial to increase response
110   Responding to a request for lower prices
217   Responding to local residents about a potential disruption

Returning
27   Returning an incorrect consignment
28   Returning a non-conforming consignment

Reviving
82   Reawakening a business relationship
84   Using a customer-service exercise to revive a lapsed customer
96   Encouraging a customer to renew a subscription

Seeking
91   Seeking new business with a personalised letter

Selling
94   Selling on enthusiasm, immediacy and personal attention

Sending
139   Sending a proforma invoice
140   Sending a proforma invoice, due to a poor record of payment

Surveying
83   Surveying customer attitudes

Terminating (see also Cancelling)
162   Terminating a consultant's contract, due to a disability

173 Confirming to an employee the termination of her employment

Thanking (see also Appreciating; Congratulating)
76   Thank-you letter for hospitality
77   Thanking a satisfied customer
78   Thanking a good client, slightly cheekily
79   Thanking a business associate for a referral
103 Thanking an agent for obtaining some business

Using
84   Using a customer-service exercise to revive a lapsed customer
88   Using the lure of large potential gains
89   Using a force-free trial to increase response
90   Using curiosity to arouse interest
93   Using a testimonial to gain interest
178 Using a promotion to motivate an employee

Warning
26   Firing a strong warning shot at a supplier
163 First written warning to an employee (for breaching the safety code)
164 Final written warning to an employee (for breaching the safety code)

Welcoming
49   Welcoming a new customer, informally
50   Welcoming a new customer

CHAPTER 1

Managing suppliers

What you'll find in this chapter

✔ Quotations
✔ Quotations – querying
✔ Orders
✔ Invoices and statements
✔ Requests, enquiries and instructions
✔ Negotiating arrangements
✔ Errors
✔ Making complaints – friendly and firm approaches
✔ Making complaints – using a stronger tone

Suppliers often need to be held on a tight rein. Whether you need to query a quotation, place an order, negotiate a special arrangement, or simply want to make a complaint using a stern reproach, this chapter offers ideas and solutions designed to keep your suppliers firmly under your control. Just a few of the highlights are featured here.

Need to negotiate a rate with a supplier?

Suppliers may suggest a rate that is not feasible. Letter 21 shows how to clinch a deal without overstretching your budget.

Need to negotiate a better price?

Suppliers may sometimes be tempted to nudge their prices up above the competition. If you want to keep them on their toes, try letter 4 to negotiate a keen quotation.

Need to sell a new idea to a supplier?

Sometimes you may need to change the way you want suppliers to do things for you. If a supplier has been doing it in a certain way for you for a long time, you will need to sell the idea and persuade him to accept that you want it done differently. Letter 19 shows how to bring him around to your way of thinking.

Do you need to fire a strong warning shot at a supplier?

It is a common trick for a supplier to agree a competitive price but then for that price to creep up over a period. Letter 23 shows how to adopt a polite but firm stance that demonstrates to your supplier just how far you are prepared to go.

Stand up to unreasonable terms and conditions

Don't let suppliers get away with unreasonable terms and conditions. And don't fall into the trap of thinking they won't try to enforce them. Sort them out when placing your order and stand up for your rights. Remember, you are the customer. Letter 10 illustrates it in practice.

Don't shy away from changing your terms and conditions

If things are not going the way you want them to, you may have to change the terms and conditions with a supplier. Don't shy away from it just because other terms were agreed previously. Letter 20 shows how to present new terms to a supplier so that they are readily accepted and there is no quibble about them.

Making a stern reproach

When complaining, make sure that you strike the right note to produce the desired response. Too harsh, and you risk alienating your suppliers. Too soft, and they may walk all over you. Seven different letters portray some of the options available to you.

QUOTATIONS
Letter 1: Friendly request for a quotation

The supplier here has a good existing relationship with the customer. There is no need to specify delivery instructions as the supplier knows where the parts are to be sent. The specification, though, remains clearly set out.

It is a good idea to give the date by when you want the quote – this helps bring it to the top of the supplier's priorities. If he then gives you the quote after the date requested, you will be able to come down harder on him. Otherwise, you could be greeted with excuses such as 'I didn't realise it was so urgent'.

Fenner & Sons

16 George Street, Woodbridge,
Suffolk IP3 7KL
Tel: (01394) 198423
Fax: (01394) 198444
Registered in England: 91221299
VAT No: 919129075 80

Mr J M Hibberd
Sales Manager
Pecklacks (Metals) Ltd
Drovers Lane
Slough
SL42 3RG

31 May 2005

Dear Jim,

I am delighted to say that our sales are ahead of expectations and so we are boosting our production. Consequently, we need more parts urgently (within ten days of placing the order). The parts are:

Item	Part No:	Unit:	Quantity:
1.5" Aluminium Trunking	B14375	3 metre	10
Lock Nuts	J388851	each	60
2" Mild Steel Bolts	J388232	each	60
Closing Strip	B13650	3 metre	10
Steel Brackets	C18724	each	27
Steel Brackets	C18725	each	3

We shall be making our decision on Thursday 16 June, so please let me have your prices by that date.

Yours sincerely,

Patrick Thompson
Production Manager

QUOTATIONS
Letter 2: Formal request for a quotation

This is a standard request for a quotation. It is brief and to the point and the formality is appropriate for a new supplier. Note the specification of part numbers accompanying each item. This avoids any ambiguity about what items are to be supplied, particularly with the steel brackets, of which there are two different types.

Fenner & Sons

16 George Street, Woodbridge,
Suffolk IP3 7KL
Tel: (01394) 198423
Fax: (01394) 198444
Registered in England: 91221299
VAT No: 919129075 80

Mr J M Hibberd
Sales Manager
Pecklacks (Metals) Ltd
Drovers Lane
Slough
SL42 3RG

31 May 2005

Dear Mr Hibberd,

Please supply a quotation for the following:

Item	Part No:	Unit:	Quantity:
1.5"Aluminium Trunking	B14375	3 metre	10
Lock Nuts	J388851	each	60
2" Mild Steel Bolts	J388232	each	60
Closing Strip	B13650	3 metre	10
Steel Brackets	C18724	each	27
Steel Brackets	C18725	each	3

Delivery will be to Cardiff and we are looking for a delivery date within ten days of placing our order.

We would appreciate your quotation by fax and at the latest by Thursday 16 June.

Yours sincerely,

Patrick Thompson
Production Manager

QUOTATIONS – QUERYING
Letter 3: Querying a price

Price is often a sensitive issue between suppliers and customers. Here, a customer clearly senses that she is not being treated as well as she was by another branch of the same printing firm.

It is important not to jump to immediate conclusions and accuse the supplier of foul play. There may, after all, be a perfectly valid excuse.

The style of the two short sentences in the second paragraph ('I have just one query. The price.') puts the reader on the spot but stops short of making an accusation.

Hart & Tucker Ltd
19 Green Street, Maidstone, Kent ME41 1TJ
Telephone: (01622) 109109
Facsimile: (01622) 108106
Reg. No: England 96223978 VAT No: 91210674

Ms Sally Patterson
Sales Manager
Colourfast Printing
245 Downfields Ind. Est.
Maidstone
Kent
ME3 3ED

23 May 2005

Dear Ms Patterson,

Your Quotation: SL 3490
Thanks for your quotation for printing 2,000 booklets.

I have just one query. The price.

As you know, I used to deal with your Halstead branch prior to our relocation last month. Three months ago, we placed an identical order for a related project. The extent is the same, the paper quality is the same and the quantity is the same. So why is your price 25 per cent higher?

Yours sincerely,

Jean Oilson
Production Manager

QUOTATIONS – QUERYING
Letter 4: Refusing a price change

Where a customer has an existing agreement with a supplier and the supplier has chosen to forget or ignore a substantive term, a stern letter is called for. This one has the backing of the agreement which has been broken and the negotiating power that a better price can be obtained elsewhere.

The supplier has no option but to back down or face losing the business. If the customer had not obtained a more competitive quote, then the last sentence, which threatens to transfer the business, should be omitted. It wouldn't carry the same weight and a supplier may take it for what it would be – just an idle threat.

SIMPSON & MARTIN

39 TOP STREET
STOKE-ON-TRENT
ST2 3DR, UNITED KINGDOM
Tel: (01782) 156232 Fax: (01782) 120899
Reg. No: England 96223978 VAT No: 91210674

Mr T Edwards
Sales Director
Bond & Bond Paper Merchants
12–16 Little Lane
Great Langdale
Ambleside
Cumbria
CU2 7BT

6 Oct 2005

Dear Tony,

Your Quotation No. TE/219785

Thanks for your quotation for supplying 30 reams of 85gsm paper. I am aware the price of paper has been escalating recently, but, frankly, I am not at all happy with this price or your suggestion for remedying the situation.

We had an explicit agreement that your prices would remain unchanged until the end of the calendar year. I took this to mean that all goods **ordered** before the end of the calendar year would be supplied at that year's rate. The fact that the order cannot be supplied until the New Year is, frankly, not our problem.

Incidentally, I have received a quotation from a direct competitor of yours at Make-it Paper who has offered to guarantee your **original** price for the next six months.

In the light of this, may I suggest that you reconsider your quotation to us. If you are unable to match Make-it Paper's price, then I regret that we shall have no option but to transfer our business.

Yours sincerely,

Mike Moy
Senior Buyer

ORDERS
Letter 5: Placing an order and requesting delivery

This is a simple letter to accompany a purchase order for a supplier with whom a credit account has not been opened.

Sending a cheque with the order should result in prompt service. Although the delivery details and date by when the goods are required should already be on the purchase order, it does no harm to spell them out in a letter as well. It also gives you the opportunity to confirm special instructions, as with the packing specifications here.

 ## WILSON SMITH LTD
A wholly owned subsidiary of The Wilson Group PLC
16 Willow Walk, Retford, Nottingham NG6 8WS
Tel: (01777) 121211 Fax: (01777) 121233
Reg. No: England 1212298762

Mr H Johnson
Sales Executive
P & J Electrical
Nuffield Ind. Est.
Morton, Retford
Nottingham
NG23 5TG

12 September 2005

Dear Mr Johnson,

OUR ORDER NO. 10743
Please find our cheque to the value of £1,123.60 to cover our order no. 10743. We require delivery on or by Thursday 20 October 2005. Please ensure the items are packed in double-walled boxes, shrink-wrapped on pallets.

Delivery address:

Howlett & Son Ltd
Burston Industrial Estate
16 Garrard Street
Greenwich
London SE14

Please advise us of the delivery date as soon as possible.

Many thanks for your co-operation.

Yours sincerely,

Penny Taylor
Buyer

ORDERS
Letter 6: Placing an order and clarifying terms

The service here is critical to the buyer. She needs the disk back urgently and is placing the order on the understanding it will be returned on a specified day. Note how she doesn't simply say she is enclosing a cheque but breaks down the charge into its various components showing how the amount is arrived at. The implication in this letter is 'if anything is different from what is specified here, I expect you to let me know'.

SIMPSON
& MARTIN

39 TOP STREET
STOKE-ON-TRENT
ST2 3DR, UNITED KINGDOM
Tel: (01782) 156232 Fax: (01782) 120899
Reg. No: England 96223978 VAT No: 91210674

Ms Jenny Croft
Sales Co-ordinator
CJB Services
Highfield House
Standish Industrial Estate
Wigan
WN7 9OE

23 February 2005

Dear Jenny,

Disk Conversion
Following our telephone conversation today, I enclose a copy of the Apple Mac Disk (Word 3.0) which I would like converted to Word for Windows 3.1.

I understand the charge for this is £10 plus £20 for the express service plus VAT. I therefore have pleasure in enclosing a cheque for £35.25.

I understand the express service means you will send the disk back the same day it is received by 1st class post. On this basis, I look forward to receiving the disk back on Friday 25 February.

As we shall be needing this service again, I would be grateful if you could arrange for an account to be opened.

Yours sincerely,

Nina Rose
Publications Assistant

ORDERS
Letter 7: Amending delivery instructions

However much you plan, last-minute changes will often occur. A supplier may have already booked a carrier to deliver goods to one place and then someone else decides they should go to a different location. The opening in this letter helps to defuse any irritation that a supplier may feel, especially when he realises that the change is due to circumstances beyond your control.

Wright & Simpson

157 Colder Way
Basingstoke
Hants RG21 5TG
Tel: (01256) 125907
Fax: (01256) 190986

Mr J Matthews
Sales Manager
Bull (Prints) Limited
Tillman's Trading Estate
Bristol
BS21 2LG

23 June 2005

Dear Julian,

Re: Our Order No. 11978

I am sorry if this messes you around, but our client has just notified us that they would like their order delivered into a different warehouse. The goods should now be sent to:

Hobbles (Cambridge) Limited
Eagle Trading Estate
Colchester Road
Basildon
Essex
B4 9UO

I hope this doesn't cause you too much inconvenience.

Many thanks for your co-operation.

Yours sincerely,

Edward Wright

Partners: EG Wright MA & FA Simpson

ORDERS
Letter 8: Amending the order quantity

If you do make a mistake, it is best to sort it out as soon as possible. This letter would be written to a supplier who is well known to you.

The unconventional opening contains an element of surprise, signifying that it is not just a piece of routine correspondence but something that demands immediate attention. The friendly tone also sets the scene for the supplier to forgive you for overlooking something so simple and, importantly, tells him immediately that it is not his fault.

 WILSON SMITH LTD
A wholly owned subsidiary of The Wilson Group PLC
16 Willow Walk, Retford, Nottingham NG6 8WS
Tel: (01777) 121211 Fax: (01777) 121233
Reg. No: England 1212298762

Facsimile Message

To: RPP Holdings plc
F.A.O.:   Bob Taylor
From: Tom Greate
Date: 23 August 2005
No. of Pages: 1

Dear Bob,

Wilson Smith Quality Manual
Oops! We've made a real clanger.

Don has just created a sample of the contents for our quality manual, which he has inserted into the ringbinder – only to discover that the binder is too small. It seems that someone here interpreted the extent of 350 *leaves* as 350 *pages*.

Is it too late to change the order? I tried to call you but your phone was continuously engaged, so I am faxing this to you instead.

Please call me back urgently so we can discuss this.

Yours sincerely,

Tom Greate
Quality Manager

ORDERS
Letter 9: Ticking off a supplier for not sticking to the order

The tone of this curt letter is designed to bring the supplier sharply into line. You need to be a little careful to ensure you are not overreacting to the situation. It would be appropriate for a supplier who had ignored similar requests in the past.

The last comment '...I look forward to continuing our business relationship on a more organised note' is in danger of putting the reader's back up as it sounds like a personal attack – even if it is not intended that way. It could be rephrased as 'I trust our purchase order instructions will be rigidly adhered to in future', which apportions no blame but gets the same message across.

 RPP Holdings Plc
35/38 New Road, Paignton, Devon TQ3 4UU
Tel: 01803 175653 Fax: 01803 187908
Reg. No: England 1976143

Mr J Patel
Sales Co-ordinator
Charles Bright Limited
63 Crow Lane
Brentwood
Essex
CM15 2AM

28 September 2005

Dear Mr Patel,

Our Purchase Order No. R467985
Thank you for your latest delivery, received today.

I would like to draw to your attention a very important point, which has been missed with the processing of this order.

On the purchase order, it is stated that your delivery note must be marked for the attention of Thomas Jones and, more importantly, contain our purchase order number. This is vital to us when we are receiving hundreds of items a day.

As this is a new request from us, we shall not be delaying payment as stated on the order, but please bear this arrangement in mind for future business.

I hope you will appreciate the necessity behind this instruction and I look forward to continuing our business relationship on a more organised note.

Yours sincerely,

Nina Lynch
Purchasing Manager

ORDERS
Letter 10: Disputing a supplier's terms and conditions

When you start trading with a new company, it is important to check on and agree the terms and conditions of supply. It is no use the supplier sending his quotation, listing his terms and conditions of supply, and then you sending your purchase order with its terms and conditions of purchase, and hoping that will do. What happens later on if there is a dispute? It is far better to clarify conflicting terms at the outset.

One of the commonest areas that is open to misinterpretation is what is meant by 30 days' credit. Is it literally 30 days from the date of the invoice? Or is the interpretation that the buying company makes here correct? Make sure you are clear about what is meant.

There are two phrases to note here: '...subject to...', which is very useful when you want to qualify a particular term, and '...we reserve the right to...', which is handy when you want the option, but not the obligation, to do something.

IDENDEN INDUSTRIES
A division of Idenden Plc
Porter House, Hull HU7 4RF, England

Tel 01482 119087 Fax 01482 119088
Registered in England No: 1218943

Mr G Glover
Sales Manager
Christian Engineering
Rochdale Road
Middleton
Manchester
M24 5TH

14 July 2005

Dear Gordon,

PURCHASE ORDER NO. 298745
Here is our Purchase Order No. 298745 for the boxes. Please let your accounts people know that they must quote this purchase order number on all invoices and correspondence, otherwise payment will be delayed.

Please also note the following points regarding the terms and conditions:

Clause 4 Terms
Your payment terms of 30 days are subject to the timing of our payment runs. We settle all invoices at the end of the month in which they fall due for payment. An invoice dated 25 August, for example, will be paid on 30 September, as will an invoice dated 5 August. Accordingly, we cannot accept your interest on overdue accounts as some may appear to be overdue when they are not.

Clause 13 Quantity
We are not prepared to pay a premium to ensure delivery of the exact order quantity so we must accept that there may be some slight variation. However, we reserve the right to return over-deliveries rather than pay for them, if they are not needed.

Clause 19 Intellectual Property
I do not accept this clause as written. Any copyright you own, you will continue to own. Any copyright we own, we will continue to own. Your work on our behalf does not entitle you to copyright on anything we have designed.

Clause 21 Title & Risk in the Goods
We do not accept clause (b). It is your responsibility to ensure safe delivery of the goods to us. We will not become liable to pay for any goods that do not reach us in satisfactory condition.

Finally, I enclose the customer credit application form duly completed and signed. It is subject to the contents of this letter.

Yours sincerely,

Michael Preston
Marketing Manager

INVOICES AND STATEMENTS
Letter 11: Requesting a credit note – incorrect items received

Someone has processed an order incorrectly and the wrong goods have been sent out. A common enough mistake. This letter explains to the person in accounts exactly what the position is and why payment is not being made against the invoice. It ends on a reassuring note, saying to him when payment for other outstanding items will be made.

B & R HENDERSONS LTD
Marlows Road, Aberdeen AB20 5GT
Tel: 01224 267855 Fax: 01224 267977
Reg. No: 16497811 VAT No: 7387945

Frank O'Neil
Accounts Manager
Benton Copleys
Roundtree House
Kennet
Newmarket
CB8 7LP

25 April 2005

Dear Frank,

Your Invoice No. 143880
I have received your statement requesting payment of Invoice No. 143880 for £156.77, dated 29 July.

I understand that the items received against this invoice were sent in error and the goods ordered are out of stock at your warehouse.

Please could you arrange for a credit note to be issued for the full amount of £156.77. We shall be settling the remaining invoices at the end of this month.

Yours sincerely,

David Barker
Purchasing Manager

INVOICES AND STATEMENTS
Letter 12: Querying invoices

Occasionally the wrong goods may be sent to the wrong company – or someone has circumvented normal procedures when buying them. Although the goods probably aren't intended for your company, it is best to check first with the supplier, just in case. Asking for the supplier's reference should help get to the bottom of the story. It would be more embarrassing to return the goods, only to find that someone high up had placed the order but not told anyone! Discretion is the better part of valour.

 WILSON SMITH LTD

A wholly owned subsidiary of The Wilson Group PLC
16 Willow Walk, Retford, Nottingham NG6 8WS
Tel: (01777) 121211 Fax: (01777) 121233
Reg. No: England 1212298762

Mr Trevor Goodge
Sales Manager
Idenden Industries
Porter House
Hull
HU7 4RF

15 June 2005

Dear Trevor,

Your Invoice No. 85903

I have received in the post this morning your Invoice No. 85903 for £300.80 for 40 high-pressure seal rings.

We have no record of placing this order and your invoice omits to provide a reference. All our orders must be made on a valid purchase order and signed by an authorised signatory. I have checked with my colleagues to see if anyone has ordered these items and accidentally omitted to draft a purchase order but no one recalls placing such an order.

Before we return the goods to you, please could you let me know what reference you have for this order and I will look into the matter further for you.

Yours sincerely,

Jim Bone
Purchasing Manager

INVOICES AND STATEMENTS
Letter 13: Disputing a carriage charge

Carriage charges are often a source of contention. Companies supplying goods are aware that it costs a lot of money to deliver them. Equally, the business placing the order wants to keep the price as low as possible.

Some invoices may carry a carriage charge, added automatically when they are produced. This could explain how this 'error' occurred – or it could be a case of the supplier trying it on. Either way, a short letter, backed up with the knowledge that you had specified that carriage be included in the quote, should put matters straight. 'I was surprised...' sets a gentle but firm tone for the reader.

Thomas King & Palmer Ltd
serving the world

24 Fuller Road, Welling,
Kent DA16 7JP
Tel: (01322) 100132
Fax: (01322) 100178

Reg. No: England 1212298762
VAT No: 92905643

Henry Fuller
Sales Manager
Savill Plastics Ltd
Saxon Way
Hitchin
Herts
HN7 5TG

23 June 2005

Dear Henry,

Your Invoice No. 29783
Thank you for your Invoice No. 29783 for £7,800.

I was surprised to see a carriage charge included for £69. Your original quotation (no. LM89753) made no mention of an additional charge for delivery. As our purchase order specified that the goods be delivered carriage paid, I was led to believe that this was included in your quotation.

Please could you send us a credit note for the full amount of the carriage.

Yours sincerely,

Alan Scott
Purchasing Manager

INVOICES AND STATEMENTS
Letter 14: Requesting a refund of delivery charges

Note the tone used to handle the unexpected charge here. The letter offers no thanks to the company for sending the invoice but uses the more neutral 'I have received...'. This forewarns the reader that all may not be well.

The second paragraph has a more demonstrative tone, with useful emphatic expressions such as: '...no mention was made...' and the firm '...referred expressly to the fact...'. Remember, if you use the term 'expressly', the point must have been definitely stated (preferably in writing) and not implied.

Charles Cunningham Ltd
29 Baker Street, LONDON N34 6GH, England
Tel: (020) 7015 1290 Fax: (020) 7015 1271
Reg. No: England 1104398135 VAT No: 82108643

Adams Office Supplies
Brentwood Road
Fulham
London
SW6 8JM

22 March 2005

Dear Sir/Madam,

Your Invoice No. DL67501
I have received your invoice for the departmental shredder which was ordered. I note that the invoice amount includes a delivery charge of £25.50.

When we placed our order, no mention was made by your sales representative of this charge and our Purchase Order No. WR15498 referred expressly to the fact that delivery was to be included within the price quoted. This was not queried prior to receipt of the shredder.

I look forward to receiving a credit note for the full amount of £25.50.

Yours faithfully,

Joan Smith
Office Manager

REQUESTS, ENQUIRIES AND INSTRUCTIONS
Letter 15: Requesting further information about a product

Product catalogues are not always clear and often omit information that a customer wants. In this letter, the potential customer has four pieces of information that he needs to know before making a decision to buy.

When faced with a number of questions, setting them out as a numbered list helps the reader to assimilate quickly what information is being asked for. The writer could just as easily have presented the items as bullet points, but it is easier for a respondent to refer to a number in a reply (especially in long lists) than to have to explain which point is being talked about.

Grange & Turner Ltd
32 WESTBOURN ROAD, WITNEY, OXON OX6 7HY

Telephone (01993) 107888
Fax (01993) 107843

Reg. No: England 13078453
VAT No: 75698764

Mr E Thomas
Sales Administrator
Starbright Office Supplies
Wilmslow Road
Didcot
Oxon
OX7 5GH

20 March 2005

Dear Mr Thomas,

Fax Machines
I have received your catalogue of fax machines. Before I decide which model to purchase, please could you advise me about the facilities for the Sharp UX3500 and Panasonic UF321 machines:

1. What is the automatic feed capacity of each machine?

2. Will both machines accept A3 size paper?

3. What is the print resolution of the Sharp model?

4. When the catalogue refers to transmission speed in seconds, is this the speed it takes for one A4 sheet of paper to be transmitted?

Yours sincerely,

John Sand
Office Manager

REQUESTS, ENQUIRIES AND INSTRUCTIONS
Letter 16: Requesting consultancy information

Not everything can be bought off the shelf by simply quoting a product name and price. With professional services, there will be a process of exploring what is required before agreeing terms. This letter seeks a consultant to help implement the ISO 9000 standard.

The writer could have given more details about the size of the company – how many employees there are, size of turnover, breakdown of the activities and so on. But equally, these will occur in the course of the subsequent telephone conversation. It may even be preferable to arouse the reader's curiosity – a useful tactic to ensure a swift response.

It is always useful to say how you got hold of his name. If it was a referral and you are competing for attention, naming your common source can help to build a rapport. Note the close. Thanking the recipient before he has even responded is a convenient way of putting an obligation on him to reply.

Grange & Turner Ltd

32 WESTBOURN ROAD, WITNEY, OXON OX6 7HY

Telephone (01993) 107888
Fax (01993) 107843

Reg. No: England 13078453
VAT No: 75698764

Mr Tom Patterson
Managing Partner
T P Consultancy
234 Slade Street
Milton Keynes
MK43 7PL

7 August 2005

Dear Mr Patterson,

We are a small company specialising in business-to-business direct marketing. We are coming under increasing pressure from our clients to implement the BS EN ISO 9000 specification. We would therefore be interested to find out exactly what this would involve, in terms of man hours, cost and procedures.

Your name was passed to me by the Association of Quality Management Consultants as someone who is registered to advise in this area. I would be most grateful if you would agree to visit us and give us an introduction to the requirements, which I understand would be free of charge.

If you are available, please would you ring me at the above number to fix a mutually convenient time.

Thank you for your kind attention. I look forward to hearing from you.

Yours sincerely,

William Barker
Marketing Director

REQUESTS, ENQUIRIES AND INSTRUCTIONS
Letter 17: Advising existing suppliers of a change in terms and conditions

Terms and conditions of supply should regularly be reviewed by companies. Sometimes they will need to be amended; if they do, a letter like this will be sufficient. Don't forget to include the date from when the new terms apply.

If the change is more significant than the one shown here – for example, changing payment terms to 60 days' from 30 days' – you should get written confirmation from the supplier that he agrees to the change, to avoid subsequent disputes. This could be done by asking him to countersign an enclosed copy of the letter and return it to you.

GKT Products Ltd, Unit 10, Castleway Lane, Alloway, Ayr, KA7 4BE
Telephone (01292) 177900 Fax (01292) 199855   Reg. No: 17964583 VAT No: 679845

The Sales Manager
SLP Engineering
27 Vine Street
Penrith
Cumbria
CA9 3FV

3 June 2005

Dear Sir/Madam,

Amendment to Terms and Conditions
I am writing to advise you of a change in our terms and conditions, which affects all orders placed with us from 1 July.

All delivery notes accompanying goods supplied to us must contain the correct purchase order number. This will enable us to match up the relevant paperwork more quickly and prevent any delays in payment to you.

Thank you for your co-operation in this matter.

Yours faithfully,

Jean Hardcastle
Accounts Manager

REQUESTS, ENQUIRIES AND INSTRUCTIONS
Letter 18: Advising a supplier of delivery instructions

Delivery instructions often need to be given after an order has been placed. If more than one order from your company is going through the supplier at any one time, you need to make sure the original purchase order number is given, to avoid confusion.

Delivery instructions should also give a contact name and be marked for the attention of a named person. It can be all too easy for goods to be delivered to a company and for the person who placed the order to be the last to find out, because none of the accompanying documentation gives his name.

RPP Holdings Plc
35/38 New Road, Paignton, Devon TQ3 4UU
Tel: 01803 175653 Fax: 01803 187908
Reg. No: England 1976143

Jane Summers
Marketing Executive
Corrugated Card & Packaging Ltd
Unit 8, London Road Ind. Est.
Truro
Cornwall
TR9 7KM

27 July 2005

Dear Jane,

Purchase Order Number 548792
Please arrange for the consignment of 500 cardboard boxes to be delivered to our Middleton warehouse. The address is:

Unit 4
The Middleton Business Park
Angles Lane
Middleton
MD3 4XZ

The consignment should be marked for the attention of Mr Jeff Holmes, our Warehouse Manager.

Yours sincerely,

Helen Meeting
Supplies Manager

NEGOTIATING ARRANGEMENTS
Letter 19: Explaining why a new system is required

A supplier is questioning a new procedure that has been forced upon him. Here the supplier's customer is persuading the supplier to accept the change of policy. Note how it is being 'sold' to the supplier, not as something new but as something which he should have been doing anyway: '...it should be little more than an extension of what your current practices are'. This is a neat argument, against which there is little defence.

B & R HENDERSONS LTD
Marlows Road, Aberdeen AB20 5GT
Tel: 01224 267855 Fax: 01224 267977
Reg. No: 16497811 VAT No: 7387945

Robert Noyes
Sales Manager
NPB Manufacturing Ltd
4 Manor Close
Warrington
WA3 3HY

20 August 2005

Dear Robert,

Re: Progress Sheets

Thank you for your recent faxes, and I apologise for the delay in replying.

First of all, I would like to reassure you that our policy of demanding progress sheets, properly signed and dated, is designed to protect both you and other suppliers involved in the manufacturing process. With this system in place, if a problem arises at any stage in the process, we will have a better idea of where the fault might lie. It also aims to catch any hitches at the start of the process, rather than on the day that our goods are meant to be delivered. All we are doing is formalising the procedure that we have always asked our subcontractors and printers to follow (see our letter dated 24 June) but that, in practice, has not been carried out.

It is not intended to be a sword hanging over anyone's head – it should be little more than an extension of what your current practices are. All our suppliers have been asked to comply with this new policy, since everyone has experienced problems in the past.

I hope this explains our reason for implementing the system satisfactorily and trust that you will be able to co-operate with its operation. Should you be uncertain about any aspect of it, please do not hesitate to give us a call.

Yours sincerely,

Roger McIntyre
Manager

NEGOTIATING ARRANGEMENTS
Letter 20: Informing a supplier of changed terms and conditions

You may at some time need to revise your systems if you find that they are not working well. Note how the suggestion here starts off relatively softly '...below is what we propose' and 'We would be very grateful for your co-operation...', aiming to win the supplier over.

However, the implementation of a 'stick' element in '...we will be adding a penalty clause...' noticeably gives the supplier no choice, even though the first part sounds as if the supplier has a say in the matter. This is confirmed by the closing line, which doesn't ask for his reaction but simply presents it as a fait accompli.

Grange & Turner Ltd

32 WESTBOURN ROAD, WITNEY, OXON OX6 7HY

Telephone (01993) 107888
Fax (01993) 107843

Reg. No: England 13078453
VAT No: 75698764

Terry Coles
Sales Manager
C & D Print Services
33 Top Street
Aldermaston
Reading
RG7 8JU

22 November 2005

Dear Terry,

Re: Deliveries

As you know, we deal with a number of different printers and print suppliers. Over the last year or so all have had at least one problem, due to insufficiently labelled deliveries.

We have tried to suggest systems to help both printer and supplier to prevent this problem, but on the whole, we have been politely ignored (or conveniently forgotten), once the immediate problem is over.

So we now feel that we have to insist that a good system for recording deliveries is adhered to by both suppliers and printers and below is what we propose.

All boxes of printed matter should in future be labelled as follows:

1. Sample of the contents on top of the box.
2. On the side of the box:
   - Quantity of items in the box
   - Scratch code of the item
   - Promotion code
   There should be no other codes, which may cause confusion on the boxes.
3. On the dispatch note: total quantity of each item, by scratch code.

Our suppliers to whom you send items will be required to count in the boxes and confirm that the quantity supplied matches the dispatch note, and that there are sufficient boxes as indicated by the Job Sheet supplied by us. They will also be required to fax us a confirmation of the quantity received and any shortfall. This will also ensure that any problems are noted in good time, to prevent delivery being delayed.

We would be very grateful for your co-operation in this, which is designed to protect all of us. To assist with its compliance, we will be adding a penalty clause, with immediate effect, that a failure to label the boxes and count them in to the mailing house correctly will result in delay of payment of 30 days beyond our normal credit terms with you.

Thank you for your assistance in this matter.

Yours sincerely,

Helen Mace
Production Manager

NEGOTIATING ARRANGEMENTS
Letter 21: Negotiating a rate with a supplier

If a supplier suggests a rate for a job that is not feasible, it may be better to go back to him with a fixed figure that you are prepared to spend and see if an agreement can be reached.

The friendly tone will reassure the supplier that the intention is sincere and it is not simply a question of trying to tie him down on price. The rhetorical question at the end 'Are you game?' acts as a challenge and is designed to clinch the deal.

Thomas King
& Palmer Ltd
serving the world

24 Fuller Road, Welling,
Kent DA16 7JP
Tel: (01322) 100132
Fax: (01322) 100178

Reg. No: England 1212298762
VAT No: 92905643

Mr D R West
67 Millers Lane
Tackley
Oxford
OX6 3AG

26 May 2005

Dear David,

Corporate Newsletter

Thanks for your fax of 9 May. Sorry that I have sat on it for so long – particularly as my need is so urgent!!

While a daily charge sounds logical, I am uncomfortable with it because neither of us knows how long these things are going to take to produce. And anyway, some will take longer than others, depending on the available resources.

So, I have an alternative suggestion to make which, I think, is fair.

We put £350 *per newsletter* on the table to write it. So, following a thorough discussion and briefing, you do what you feel is reasonable for that amount of money. The intention is not to squeeze a quart out of a pint pot. It is to see what we can achieve within that sort of budget. Are you game?

I look forward to hearing from you.

Kind regards

Yours sincerely,

Kay Mitchell
Marketing Manager

NEGOTIATING ARRANGEMENTS
Letter 22: Turning down a supplier

Declining a supplier politely is not always easy. This letter strikes an agreeable but firm tone. The politeness of the decline is helped by going for the understatement: '...it does not fit comfortably...', which contrasts with the firmer 'Thanks but no thanks', which is refreshingly frank and leaves no doubt about the decision, so nobody's time is wasted.

What goes unsaid is often as important as what is said. Note how the customer does not offer any hope for the future – a clear sign that the products the supplier produces are unsuitable for this market.

Grange & Turner Ltd

32 WESTBOURN ROAD, WITNEY, OXON OX6 7HY

Telephone (01993) 107888
Fax (01993) 107843
Reg. No: England 13078453
VAT No: 75698764

Mr A French
Sales Administrator
Squeeky-Kleen
45 Todd Square
Glasgow
G20 5XA

28 September 2005

Dear Mr French,

Squeeky-Kleen

Thank you for your letter of 12 September and for the samples of your innovative cleaning product.

At the moment, it does not fit comfortably with our catalogue plans for the next six months and I am afraid I must say 'Thanks but no thanks'.

If you are thinking of doing any direct mail of your own on the product, we do have a strong mailing list of corporate customers who have bought related items. If you are interested in renting these, do give me a call.

Yours sincerely,

Brian Reed
Marketing Manager

NEGOTIATING ARRANGEMENTS
Letter 23: Firing a strong warning shot at a supplier

This letter is designed to send a strong message. It tries to make the supplier face up to the reality of the situation.

It starts off gently but firmly: 'The unfortunate fact of the matter...'. Note how the additional expense is very slightly exaggerated (or made to appear more serious) by adding the words '...up to £400...', £400 being the worst case, not the average case.

A polite but firm stance is maintained to the end '...we will probably have to agree to part company', the 'probably' leaving the door open for further negotiations but signalling at the same time how far you are prepared to go.

Hart & Tucker Ltd
19 Green Street, Maidstone, Kent ME41 1TJ
Telephone: (01622) 109109
Facsimile: (01622) 108106
Reg. No: England 96223978 VAT No: 91210674

Terry Coles
Sales Manager
C & D Print Services
33 Top Street
Aldermaston
Reading
RG7 8JU

22 September 2005

Dear Terry,

Re: Your Charges

Thank you for your letter of 12 September and for taking the trouble to clarify the situation for me. I am sorry that I had to ask you to do this because our files had got into such a mess.

I can see that I must accept the invoices raised on promotions 102 and 109 as having been agreed. However, I believe that Claire is still waiting for a breakdown of your invoice for order 118. We are not satisfied that there was £300 of origination work required when we sent you all new film and we are also disputing the charge for the amendments.

Next year

The unfortunate fact of the matter is that with these carriage and origination charges, as well as the higher base price of £1,100, it has cost us up to £400 a month *more* to put work through you rather than through our other printers. And we have no control over the variables – we don't know whether carriage is going to be £200 or £500 for the year. We don't know whether the proofs are going to be £90 or £500 a time.

There is no question about the quality of your work. It is comparable with the quality we receive from our other suppliers. But the price you charge for our jobs is simply too high.

I am afraid that, unless you can find a way to do our printing profitably for a flat rate of £1,100, we will probably have to agree to part company.

Yours sincerely,

Tony Green
Marketing Director

ERRORS
Letter 24: Returning an incorrect consignment

When the wrong goods are sent, you want the error to be corrected quickly. Here someone has inverted the numbers 60 and 30 for the quantity and size. A simple request to have them changed should be sufficient. The invoice will have mentioned the correct quantity and size, so this doesn't need to be changed. It should, however, be referred to in the letter, so the company can identify it on its system easily. Note how the writer tries to avoid the confusion by putting the quantity (sixty) in words and the size (30) in numbers.

If you do return goods to a company, always send them separately from a letter asking for replacements. Returns often get put to one side to be dealt with later – sometimes weeks later. It could be disastrous if your letter requesting corrective action is held up amongst the returns.

IDENDEN INDUSTRIES
A division of Idenden Plc
Porter House, Hull HU7 4RF, England

Tel 01482 119087 Fax 01482 119088
Registered in England No: 1218943

Ms Elizabeth Taylor
Sales Co-ordinator
Litson & Fulton Ltd
Unit 8 Clifton Ind. Est.
Clifton Road
Liverpool
L9 6DD

24 October 2005

Dear Elizabeth,

Our Purchase Order No. YTL8906

Yesterday, we received sixty 30mm clips for high-velocity piping, which were supplied against your Invoice No. LP1018 dated 20 October.

Our Purchase Order No. YTL8906 clearly asked for thirty 60mm clips. I would be grateful if you could supply the correct items to us by return.

The 30mm clips are being returned to you under separate cover.

Yours sincerely,

Stuart O'Neil
Purchasing Manager

ERRORS
Letter 25: Returning a non-conforming consignment

Which style should be used in letters: 'I' or 'we'?

If you are writing on behalf of your company and you want the letter to sound as if it has the full weight of your organisation behind you, opt for 'we' and 'our'. If you are writing in your own right, then 'I' and 'my' is preferable.

In practice, there is very little to choose between the two styles, although 'we' and 'our' can, in some situations, sound a touch formal. It may also be that the person writing doesn't want to take personal responsibility for what is being said in the letter.

IDENDEN INDUSTRIES
A division of Idenden Plc
Porter House, Hull HU7 4RF, England

Tel 01482 119087 Fax 01482 119088
Registered in England No: 1218943

Ms Elizabeth Taylor
Sales Co-ordinator
Litson & Fulton Ltd
Unit 8 Clifton Ind. Est.
Clifton Road
Liverpool
L9 6DD

24 October 2005

Dear Elizabeth,

Our Order No. YTL8906

Today, your carrier attempted to deliver thirty 60mm clips for high-velocity piping, in response to our Order No. YTL8906.

We examined the clips and found they do not correspond with samples we received from you on 18 October, and we therefore refused to accept them.

The carrier was instructed to return them to you. We look forward to receiving correct, replacement goods as soon as possible, and your confirmation of this.

Yours sincerely,

Stuart O'Neil
Purchasing Manager

MAKING COMPLAINTS – FRIENDLY AND FIRM APPROACHES
Letter 26: Gentle complaint to a good supplier – keeping him on his toes

This letter aims to present a complaint under the guise of good humour. Its tone opts for a midway between the formal and very casual. It succeeds in building a rapport with the reader, which will make him want to come back and put the window right.

Helen Meeting is unconcerned exactly when it will be done because she knows she can rely on John Fuller to fix the problem. The letter suggests a trust between the two which more formal business letters don't imply.

 RPP Holdings Plc
35/38 New Road, Paignton, Devon TQ3 4UU
Tel: 01803 175653 Fax: 01803 187908
Reg. No: England 1976143

John Fuller
Works Manager
RG Fuller & Sons
53 Jackson Way
Tiverton
Devon
TV7 4HG

1 October 2005

Dear John,

Thanks for coming to put the additional window in our office. It has really helped to lighten up the room. However, there is one minor point I want to raise with you.

For some reason, the part of the window that opens doesn't seem to want to stay in its correct position and has shuffled itself along, so that one side is scraping against the frame while the other side has an unusually large gap. Fine for a bit of ventilation in the summer months but not so pleasant when we have a howling gale!

Could you call round some time next week to have a look at it and encourage it back to its proper position? Give me a call to let me know when you are coming.

Yours sincerely,

Helen Meeting
Office Manager

MAKING COMPLAINTS – FRIENDLY AND FIRM APPROACHES
Letter 27: Friendly complaint about repeated missing items

This fairly unconventional letter should be reserved for people with whom you have built up a good relationship and have a clear understanding.

A jokey response like this (particularly when it is in a complaint setting) should score you many points with your supplier. Its aim is to evoke a positive reaction in the reader so that he feels more inclined to respond favourably to your request. Its danger, which you should be aware of, is that your supplier takes you for granted and thinks that, because you are taking a light-hearted approach, you are prepared to put up with the poor service.

Note how a more casual tone is created by using abbreviated phrases and terms: 'Thanks for' instead of the more formal 'Thank you for' and 'ASAP' in place of 'as soon as possible'.

RPP Holdings Plc
35/38 New Road, Paignton, Devon TQ3 4UU
Tel: 01803 175653 Fax: 01803 187908
Reg. No: England 1976143

Jane Summers
Marketing Executive
Corrugated Card & Packaging Ltd
Unit 8
London Road Ind. Est.
Truro
Cornwall
TR9 7KM

1 October 2005

Dear Jane,

Purchase Order Number 548792
Thanks for your delivery of the cardboard boxes received yesterday.

Once again, gremlins appear to have intervened and kidnapped 49 cardboard boxes out of the consignment. We are waiting for the ransom demand. Or perhaps they were hijacked by homeless people looking for a new cardboard duvet for the night?

Please, please, please supply us with the missing items ASAP.

Yours sincerely,

Helen Meeting
Office Manager

MAKING COMPLAINTS – FRIENDLY AND FIRM APPROACHES
Letter 28: Complaining about repeatedly missing items

When mistakes are repeatedly being made, customers are justified in raising their hackles. The tone of the letter is one of irritation. But it doesn't seek to blame. Instead it points out the need to improve matters because everyone is suffering. Ranting and railing on its own is often pointless – it may feel good, but it is usually better to suggest a constructive solution, or at least, as here, to sit down and talk about the issues.

RPP Holdings Plc
35/38 New Road, Paignton, Devon TQ3 4UU
Tel: 01803 175653 Fax: 01803 187908
Reg. No: England 1976143

Jane Summers
Marketing Executive
Corrugated Card & Packaging Ltd
Unit 8
London Road Ind. Est.
Truro
Cornwall
TR9 7KM

12 December 2005

Dear Jane,

Purchase Order Number 548792
We received your delivery of 500 cardboard boxes yesterday.

When our Warehouse Manager checked the number of boxes that had been supplied, he discovered that 49 were missing. As you know this is the fifth time in a row that there has been a shortfall in the delivery. This causes us inconvenience, you extra expense and both of us aggravation. Could I suggest that you set up a meeting between us and your Warehouse Manager to discuss what can be done to improve matters? If deliveries do not then improve, I regret we shall have to consider turning to a more reliable supplier.

In the meantime, please arrange for the balance to be supplied as soon as possible.

Yours sincerely,

Helen Meeting
Office Manager

MAKING COMPLAINTS – FRIENDLY AND FIRM APPROACHES
Letter 29: Complaining that the quality of service is deteriorating

The aim of this letter is to fire a warning shot at the supplier and shake him into changing his attitude towards you.

Clearly, the supplier has taken your company's business for granted for too long. The poor performance is made to sound worse when contrasted against the 'impeccable' service that you received at the outset. The catalogue of general mistakes is then supported by a specific incident that has finally broken your faith in the supplier.

If the supplier has the will, he will make the changes, but if he doesn't make amends, then the customer leaves no doubt that his business will go elsewhere: '...we shall have no option...' emphasises how far you are prepared to go. It is a useful phrase that is very handy in negotiations. Beware of using it lightly, though: if you say it, make sure you are prepared to carry it out.

B & R HENDERSONS LTD
Marlows Road, Aberdeen AB20 5GT
Tel: 01224 267855 Fax: 01224 267977
Reg. No: 16497811 VAT No: 7387945

Mr Andrew McBride
Manager
Scottish Stationery Supplies
45 High Road
Aberdeen
AB19 2EW

26 July 2005

Dear Andrew,

I am writing to express my growing dissatisfaction with the service we are receiving from Scottish Stationery Supplies.

For the first year, the service you gave us was impeccable. Since then, though, we have noticed a gradual deterioration. The goods are frequently out of stock or taking longer for you to supply; you do not respond to our requests as speedily as before and the number of incorrect items delivered has increased. This was compounded this morning when, for the second time in a row, you supplied us with five boxes of C5 instead of C6 envelopes.

It is essential that all our suppliers give us the best possible service. We shall be monitoring the situation closely over the coming weeks, but if a significant improvement is not noticeable we shall have no option but to seek an alternative supplier.

Yours sincerely,

Tina Vail
Office Manager

MAKING COMPLAINTS – FRIENDLY AND FIRM APPROACHES
Letter 30: Demanding that defective work be made good

When asking for repairs to be done, you need to emphasise how serious the situation is. Here, the work seemed satisfactory when it was done, but within a short period it is clear that all is not well.

This letter leaves the request to put it right until the end. Blame is not apportioned directly (it could be the fault of the type of cement used), but note the use of the phrase '...come and remedy the defective work...', which implies heavily that the supplier is being held responsible.

SIMPSON
& MARTIN

39 TOP STREET
STOKE-ON-TRENT
ST2 3DR, UNITED KINGDOM
Tel: (01782) 156232 Fax: (01782) 120899
Reg. No: England 96223978 VAT No: 91210674

Mr R Henderson
JKB Builders
16 Ponts Hill
Wysall
Stoke-on-Trent
ST4 5HT

23 September 2005

Dear Mr Henderson,

39 Top Street, Stoke-on-Trent

A week ago you arranged for a three-foot-high boundary wall to be repaired outside our property.

The work was completed to our specification, but this morning it was noticed that the mortar used to bind the bricks together has cracked, to such an extent that it is not only flaking away, but several of the bricks are now in danger of becoming loose.

Would you kindly arrange for someone to come and remedy the defective work as soon as possible?

Yours sincerely,

John Good
Managing Director

MAKING COMPLAINTS – FRIENDLY AND FIRM APPROACHES
Letter 31: Non-delivery of goods – initial letter

The delays that have occurred here are not serious and the customer did not make it a condition of the contract that time should be of the essence. To start issuing threats of taking your business elsewhere, therefore, would not fit the circumstances. Nevertheless, the customer is being inconvenienced. A plea for the supplier to give it 'your most urgent attention' should be sufficient to get the wheels moving.

Taylor Taylor & Shaw
Benton House, Clifton, Bristol BS16 7LJ
Tel: (0117) 1089254   Fax: (0117) 1089211

Mr N Stacey
N Stacey & Co Ltd
Amber House
Grant Mill
Bristol
BS6 4RE

16 September 2005

Dear Mr Stacey,

Our Purchase Order No. AB46972 Dated 6 September

On 6 September, we placed an order with your company for a portable air conditioner (model no. A132487). Our Purchase Order No. is AB46972.

When the order was placed, I was informed that you were temporarily out of stock of this item, but that you had more on order and we could expect delivery within one week.

When I contacted your office on 13 September, I was told that the air conditioner would arrive the next day. Three days have now passed and there is still no sign of a delivery or an explanation from yourselves.

Please give this matter your most urgent attention.

Yours sincerely,

AW Taylor

Partners: AW Taylor & GS Taylor

MAKING COMPLAINTS – FRIENDLY AND FIRM APPROACHES
Letter 32: Non-delivery of goods – second letter

The delay has now become unacceptable and it is fully justifiable to threaten to cancel the order.

When writing letters like this, it is a good ploy to make use of certain emotional triggers, such as 'You will understand that, as a business, we put a high premium on reliability'. This is designed to provoke the response 'but so do we'. If it has the right effect, the supplier will pull out all the stops to deliver the item on time or, at the very least, to tell the customer what the situation is immediately.

Taylor Taylor & Shaw
Benton House, Clifton, Bristol BS16 7LJ
Tel: (0117) 1089254   Fax: (0117) 1089211

Mr N Stacey
N Stacey & Co Ltd
Amber House
Grant Mill
Bristol
BS6 4RE

28 September 2005

Dear Mr Stacey,

Re: Our Order No. AB46972, Dated 6 September

I wrote to you on 16 September, chasing the above order for a portable air conditioner model no. A132487.

In spite of my letter and several phone calls, this order is still outstanding and is now very urgently required.

When placing the order on 6 September, we were told there would be a delay of only four days. Four weeks have now passed without an explanation from yourselves. Please telephone me on receipt of this letter with a new and definite date for delivery.

You will understand that, as a business, we put a high premium on reliability. If I do not receive your call, or if further delays are expected, this order will be cancelled and our business will be taken elsewhere.

Yours sincerely,

AW Taylor

Partners: AW Taylor & GS Taylor

MAKING COMPLAINTS – USING A STRONGER TONE
Letter 33: Getting a too-persistent sales representative off your back

This letter is strongly worded but wisely stops short of using anger to make its impact felt.

Showing that you have already considered several times whether to complain adds weight to your justification in complaining now. It tells the reader that you are not overreacting but that your patience has been tested.

The overall message is clear: the salesperson's behaviour is reflecting badly on his company, and has reached such a state that you want nothing whatever to do with it.

If the writer had been tempted to show his anger, it would have undermined his credibility and inclined the reader to take the matter less seriously.

IDENDEN INDUSTRIES
A division of Idenden Plc
Porter House, Hull HU7 4RF, England

Tel 01482 119087 Fax 01482 119088
Registered in England No: 1218943

Mr L Hines
Managing Director
Banks & Banister Ltd
The Old Exchange
Cambridge Road
Brampton
Cumbria
CA4 7MK

17 April 2005

Dear Mr Hines,

John Higgins

I had hoped that I would not have to write to you about the activities of your company representative John Higgins, but his behaviour finally leaves me no option.

He has persistently called our office in an attempt to sell us one of your photocopiers. He has been told repeatedly that we have no requirements for any photocopiers and that we are very happy with our existing supplier. Today, he called my secretary and claimed that he was a close friend so that he would be put through. I regard this behaviour as totally unprofessional. His only success to date has been to increase my resolve that we shall never buy anything from your company.

I trust that we shall not hear from Mr Higgins again, nor any other representative from your company.

Yours sincerely,

David Rex
Director

MAKING COMPLAINTS – USING A STRONGER TONE
Letter 34: Letter of complaint about the quality of a product

If a supplier suddenly goes very quiet following a complaint, you need to try to open the channels of communication again.

Although it will be irritating to you, and you may be feeling very annoyed, your letter should retain a tone of calm professionalism. There will be plenty of time to vent your feelings later. Your goal now is to force the supplier to respond. Reminding him that you are withholding payment should be sufficient to make him react.

SIMPSON & MARTIN

39 TOP STREET
STOKE-ON-TRENT
ST2 3DR, UNITED KINGDOM
Tel: (01782) 156232 Fax: (01782) 120899
Reg. No: England 96223978 VAT No: 91210674

Mr F Benson
Benson Envelopes
Unit 5 Longacre Ind. Est.
Stoke-on-Trent
ST5 7VB

30 August 2005

Dear Mr Benson,

Our Purchase Order No. AB54673
I am extremely disappointed that I find myself having to write to you yet again.

I wrote to you on 9 August concerning a consignment of 50,000 C5 envelopes (printed one colour on front only) which we received from you on 6 August. A copy of my letter is enclosed. I remind you that we are withholding payment as the goods are defective.

Since then, a week has passed and I have received no reply from you, nor the replacement envelopes. I have telephoned several times but my calls have not been returned.

Please telephone me on receipt of this letter to let me know when we can expect to receive the replacement order.

Yours sincerely,

Vera Young
Marketing Production Manager

MAKING COMPLAINTS – USING A STRONGER TONE
Letter 35: Complaining about a service that fell well below acceptable standards

The disasters relayed in this letter reach the status of a catastrophe. Presenting the individual complaints as a list makes them appear far worse. Each one has been identified and will have to be accounted for. No amount of apology could undo the wrong. The strength of feeling is conveyed in the evocative phrase 'shambolic disaster'.

Hotels and restaurants live by their reputations and the manager will be well aware of the damage if his receives a bad name. He may not be too concerned if the writer doesn't eat there again, but he will be concerned if lots of people are deterred from trying out the hotel.

PARKER
Glass Ltd

Unit 27 Willow Park
Christchurch, Dorset BH23 6MM
Tel: 01202 109111
Fax: 01202 109112

Reg. No: England 962578762
VAT No: 9120564

Mr P Hoat
Manager
Wayside Hotel
Riverside Walk
Christchurch
Dorset
BO4 2DD

24 July 2005

Dear Mr Hoat,

Lunch at the Wayside Hotel on 22 July
Yesterday, I entertained three very important potential clients at your hotel, which, as your staff will confirm, I have visited on many occasions over the last two years.

It gives me no pleasure to say that the occasion was a shambolic disaster from start to finish.

1. It took a full 15 minutes from placing our drinks order to being served with them – not a pleasant experience when all of us were parched.

2. We were not invited to take our seat in the dining room for a full 45 minutes after arriving.

3. The cold soup was spiced to a degree that was unbearable. No warning was given of this either in the menu or by the waiter.

4. One of the starters did not arrive until ten minutes after the others were served.

5. There was an unacceptable gap of 20 minutes between our finishing the starters and the main course arriving.

6. Two of the waiters, although not discourteous, did not show the attentiveness that is expected from a hotel of your class.

Had I realised that we would receive this kind of treatment I would not have entertained such important guests at your hotel. You have my assurance that I will not be entertaining or recommending anyone to eat there in future.

Yours sincerely,

Frank Crasson

MAKING COMPLAINTS – USING A STRONGER TONE
Letter 36: Complaining that a verbal assurance has been broken

A verbal assurance is still a contract and one that has been broken here. The letter veers towards an angry tone when it uses the phrase 'I was therefore astounded...', but elsewhere retains its sense of measured annoyance.

Good phrases to remember to use when an agreement has been breached is the one '...failure to comply with our terms...' and '...seeking recompense for any losses that we incur...'. It should be sufficient to put the wind up them.

Kelso Limited
16 Abbots Road, Luton, Bedfordshire MK44 7YT
Tel: (01234) 136953 Fax: (01234) 136422
Registered in England No: 9126719 VAT No: 91523489 76

Mr Hardy
Sales Manager
Cambridge Cutters Ltd
Gratton Road
Cambridge
CB1 1MJ

2 December 2005

Dear Mr Hardy,

Our Order No. 64987
I was given your verbal assurance on Tuesday that you would have no problem in completing the cutting processes requested for the folder order placed with you last week and delivering them to us on the Wednesday, in time for us to complete our processes. The order was booked in well in advance and we delivered the items to you at the time agreed.

I was therefore astounded to find that not only had you not completed the processes and returned the order to us by yesterday, but that we were not kept informed why the order would not be completed on time.

As your failure to comply with our terms will mean that our client will seek compensation from us for untimely delivery, we shall deduct any losses that we incur from your invoice.

Yours sincerely,

John Piggott
Sales Director

MAKING COMPLAINTS – USING A STRONGER TONE
Letter 37: Firm letter to a supplier over a dispute

Here is an abundance of effective phrases to use in situations where you want to be firm about an issue: '...not of merchantable quality...'; '...do not have a moral leg to stand on'; '...really should know better...'; 'It was not we who caused this problem'; 'It is time this matter was brought to a close'; '...in full and final settlement...'. These are all strong phrases that add weight to the claim being made and will convince the other side that you mean business.

Thomas King
& Palmer Ltd
serving the world

24 Fuller Road, Welling,
Kent DA16 7JP
Tel: (01322) 100132
Fax: (01322) 100178

Reg. No: England 1212298762
VAT No: 92905643

Mr S K Robinson
Sales Director
Wright & Robinson Ltd
43 Knights Drive
Kenilworth
Warwickshire
CV10 4ZN

13 June 2005

Dear Mr Robinson,

Our Purchase Order No. 346987; Your Invoice No. 120786
Further to your fax to our Accounts Manager of 11 April, regarding the dispute on this transaction, I shall deal with this matter. I am very sorry that you find yourself in the middle of this dispute.

As you know, quite simply, the list of names was not of merchantable quality as presented.

As you are also aware, the timings on mailings are always tight. Every mailer has to commit to print before the lists can be run. The stark alternative to reworking the list to make as much of it as possible mailable was to dump the mailing pieces prepared for the list. We would have needed a great deal more than a full credit to compensate for that. Reworking the list was the only option.

The list suppliers may not like our solution, but they do not have a moral leg to stand on. A list in this condition simply should not have been represented as a mailing list. As a regular mailer of international lists, we know what constitutes acceptable product, and this clearly did not. The list suppliers really should know better than to maintain that the original list rental should be paid in full. It was not we who caused this problem.

It is time this matter was brought to a close. We have always explained we are willing to pay the balance. Our final offer is therefore £112.55 plus VAT in full and final settlement, made up as on the attached sheet. We will pay this on receipt of the credit note for £708.77 plus VAT.

I look forward to hearing from you.

Yours sincerely,

Arthur French
Marketing Director

MAKING COMPLAINTS – USING A STRONGER TONE
Letter 38: Stern reply to a negative response regarding a refund

Occasionally, a supplier will not play ball and may attempt to put up a fight. He may have decided (for whatever reason) that your business is not worth retaining.

Matters here are coming to a head. The supplying company is attempting to wriggle out of the complaint, but the customer is having none of it and knows that the law is on her side.

The phrase 'We have now decided to take legal advice...with a view to recovery of our money...' and '...instructions will be issued to our solicitors to proceed against you' are designed to leave the supplier in no doubt that he must pay up or face legal action.

GKT Products Ltd, Unit 10, Castleway Lane, Alloway, Ayr, KA7 4BE
Telephone (01292) 177900 Fax (01292) 199855   Reg. No: 17964583 VAT No: 679845

Mr Paul Newman
Marketing Executive
Computer & Stationery Supplies
Parkside Business Park
Oakham
Leicester
LE4 7HJ

28 April 2005

Dear Mr Newman,

Our Order 219784
I refer to your letter of 22 April 2005 about a consignment of faulty computer disks that we received from you on 5 April.

In your letter you claim that these disks are of the highest quality and would, therefore, have left your premises in perfect condition. You presume, therefore, that they must have been mishandled in some way by us and that the fault is, therefore, ours. You also state that these disks were supplied at a special promotional discount and that discounted goods are not subject to replacement or refund. This point, you maintain, would have been made clear to us at the time of purchase.

I must point out to you that we have many years' experience and our staff are highly trained and know very well how to handle and store computer disks. We can assure you that these disks **were** faulty at the time we received them. We do not doubt your company's ability to handle such equipment but feel particularly aggrieved that you feel free to doubt ours. On this point alone, we have decided to have no more dealings with your company.

On the matter of the special promotional discount, you can be assured that at no time was any caveat given to us regarding refunds. You will also be aware that the Sale of Goods Act 1979 states quite clearly that faulty goods **are** subject to refund or replacement. A simple disclaimer on your part does not alter the law in any way.

We have now decided to take legal advice on this matter, with a view to recovery of our money and you are advised that, unless a full refund is received from you within three days, instructions will be issued to our solicitors to proceed against you.

As stated, we will be having no further dealings with your company.

Yours sincerely,

Betty Davis
Purchasing Manager

CHAPTER 2

Managing customers

What you'll find in this chapter

✔ Giving quotations
✔ Responding to enquiries and orders
✔ Making apologies
✔ Apologies with a hint of grovelling
✔ Handling awkward customers
✔ Refusing customers
✔ Thanking customers
✔ Keeping customers informed

The customer is king. But knowing that doesn't make it any easier when you have an awkward one to manage, or mistakes happen that need to be sorted out. There can be few matters less pleasant than an irate customer, and few more gratifying than one who is satisfied. The letters in this chapter provide a wealth of ideas for keeping relations with customers on an even keel and, when the waters turn choppy, what you can do to calm them down again.

Saying sorry

It sounds simple, but how many customers genuinely believe what you say? Saying sorry sincerely, so that a customer decides to stay with you rather than move to your competition, is an art. Letters 59 and 60 are examples of those that genuinely worked.

What if they are trying it on?

Sometimes, you may find yourself up against a customer who is being economical with the truth. You can't openly accuse him of lying, so how do you handle it? Letter 61 shows how.

Handling awkward customers

Difficult customers need to be handled carefully. Don't just ignore them even if they are rude, as in letter 62. And don't let them steamroller their way with you – be firm, as in letter 64.

The easiest source of new business?

Your existing customers are your easiest source of new business. They have used you once and, if they enjoyed the experience, they will come back to you again, and again. Taking the time and trouble to thank them may not seem a profitable use of your time but it will reap rewards. Letters 69–73 give plenty of ideas.

Don't forget your lapsed customers

These ones are well worth trying to revive. You won't get them all back, but just a few will make the effort worthwhile. See letters 76 and 78.

GIVING QUOTATIONS
Letter 39: Providing a quote, ex-works

'Ex-works' is a term that commonly occurs in quotations and means that the supplier makes the goods available from his premises. Unless stated otherwise, the purchaser is expected to arrange collection of the goods and organise any export licences and other documentation that may be required, as well as transportation. The purchaser assumes the full risk of damage to the goods, once the goods are in his control. For a precise understanding of the term ex-works (and other shipping terms), it is recommended that you consult a copy of the Incoterms, which can be obtained from the International Chamber of Commerce (see www.iccwbo.org/ index_incoterms.asp).

Note again, the helpful advice that the supplier is giving: what additional costs will have to be borne; the fact it will be cheaper to transport the items by sea rather than air and when he is going to be unavailable.

 WILSON SMITH LTD

A wholly owned subsidiary of The Wilson Group PLC
16 Willow Walk, Retford, Nottingham NG6 8WS
Tel: (01777) 121211 Fax: (01777) 121233
Reg. No: England 1212298762

Mr Winston Pathmanathan
Director
Kuantan Industries
5 Ipoh Street
5100 Kuala Lumpur
Malaysia

20 July 2005

Dear Winston,

I am pleased to quote you ex-works prices for the items, as requested. All are in excellent working order, but, in some cases, I am offering you an alternative for new items. I cannot give you the total price until I know exactly what you require, as we will have to add inland haulage, packing and freight charges. Please let me know whether you want the items sent by sea or air freight. Given the bulk of some of them, sea would be cheaper.

1. Photocopiers @ £940.00 each.

2. IBM typewriters – second-hand Golf Ball @ £90.00 each. New modern electronic @ £360.00 each.

3. Olympia manual typewriters – second-hand @ £105.00 each. New @ £300.00 each.

4. Fax machines – we can supply new or reconditioned second-hand @ £375.00 each. Obviously, the second-hand ones are sturdier machines with more functions than the new ones for the same price.

Please contact me as soon as possible, to let me know your requirements, as I shall be away on annual leave for two weeks from 5 to 22 August.

I look forward to hearing from you shortly.

Yours sincerely,

James Smith
Marketing Director

GIVING QUOTATIONS
Letter 40: Quoting and advising a potential customer

This quotation is to a customer whom the supplier already knows. It doesn't have the formality of a quotation form. The supplier knows that the customer probably doesn't want more than 100kg and so doesn't bother to provide the figures but leaves the option open. He also ends the letter confidently, expecting the order.

Note how the supplier is using his skill to advise the customer on what he believes will be the best option, given the specification that has been asked for. This kind of service will be appreciated and the customer may be more inclined to place an order because he knows his requirements will be looked after.

If the customer had to choose between one supplier who offered a straight quote and this supplier who is offering a quote and helpful advice, it is easy to see which one he is likely to opt for.

 WILSON SMITH LTD

A wholly owned subsidiary of The Wilson Group PLC
16 Willow Walk, Retford, Nottingham NG6 8WS
Tel: (01777) 121211 Fax: (01777) 121233
Reg. No: England 1212298762

Mr G Benn
Sales Manager
Drake & Huggins Ltd
Orchard Road
Saffron Walden
Essex
CB21 6HN

19 August 2005

Dear Gordon,

I confirm our faxed quotation for yellow ruling powder at £6.00 per kg. If you require more than 100kg, we can offer you better prices.

I enclose the standard colour range. Please note that although we are able to produce a lemon yellow, this appears rather dull. I have therefore excluded it, as I believe your client specified it should be bright. Also, the royal blue and black print up much more strongly than in the sample shown, as these prints have been produced on the wrong paper. I am getting some more drawn up on the correct substrate and will forward them to you as soon as they are available.

I look forward to hearing from you and, of course, to receiving your order.

Yours sincerely,

John Wilson
Sales Director

GIVING QUOTATIONS
Letter 41: Correcting a pricing error, informally

Here a situation has arisen where a quoted price is significantly lower than it is in reality. The difference is so great that the customer may already realise it is a simple typographical error. Nevertheless, the supplier wants to retain the goodwill of the customer.

Making light of it in this way is not always appropriate: it all depends on how well you know your customer. Here, they get on very well, so the tone is fitting.

Passing the blame on to an imaginary 'gremlin' also cleverly diverts the attention away from the real cause of the mistake – yourself, perhaps.

The exclamation mark in brackets in the last sentence lightens what might otherwise be a rather solemn sentence.

BELLS OF BASILDON

Bells of Basildon Ltd, Unit 12, Way Park, Basildon SS12 6DE
Tel: 01268 109 9954 Fax: 01268 109 5576 Reg. No: England 13078453 VAT No: 75698764

Mr J Bracket
Purchasing Manager
A S Charlwood Ltd
87 Main Street
Brentwood
Essex
CH7 8DC

16 June 2005

Dear Jim,

What can I say? Sorry.

It seems a gremlin got into our word processor and decided to move the decimal point over a little too far. The price should, of course, have been £2,545 and not £254.50. We are doing our best to control the beast but it still occasionally steps out of line.

I hope, in spite of the apparent tenfold increase (!), that the price is still acceptable.

Yours sincerely,

Terry Monk
Estimator

GIVING QUOTATIONS
Letter 42: Correcting a pricing error

A supplier here has misquoted a price. It may be that the customer thought he was going to be getting a bargain of a better model at a lower price. The customer's reaction is bound to be one of disappointment, especially as he is being asked to pay almost another £200.

The supplier, concerned that this may be enough to deter the customer, works hard to retain the business by taking the opportunity of pointing out the additional features of the more expensive model.

To draw the sting of the higher price, the supplier offers a nice surprise to the customer – a small free item – which will go a long way towards retaining the goodwill of the customer, which will far outweigh the cost of the pointer.

H J KINGSLEY (NORWICH) LTD
Kingsley House, Morris Street, Norwich NR6 7JM
Tel: (01603) 117097 Fax: (01603) 117099 Reg. No: England 12086215 VAT No: 8793519

Mr W Johns
General Manager
Gurteen & Parker
Unit 7 Meadowview Ind. Est.
Norwich
NR2 4ED

15 February 2005

Dear Mr Johns,

Nobo 90 Overhead Projector
Thank you for your letter querying the price of the Nobo 90 Overhead Projector.

I confirm the price of this item is £595 (excluding VAT) and not £409 as previously stated. It seems that the person who took your original call misheard the model number. I apologise for this error. However, as I am sure you have already discovered, the Nobo 90 has the advantages of being both more compact and lighter than the Nobo 99, as well as having better-quality lenses. All Nobo models come with a 12-month, on-site guarantee.

I am sorry if this oversight has caused you any inconvenience. As a token of our appreciation of your custom, we are pleased to offer you a free telescopic pointer with your order.

Yours sincerely,

Marilyn Morris
Sales Director

RESPONDING TO ENQUIRIES AND ORDERS
Letter 43: Welcoming a new customer, informally

Too many businesses take new customers for granted, even though they are like gold dust.

A letter of welcome should take the opportunity to give the customer the confidence that she has chosen the right company and is in safe hands.

Note how the business creates a good impression in the mind of the customer, by offering an additional service free of charge as a 'nice surprise'.

Expressions worth noting here are: '...a long and happy association...' and 'Should we fall short of your high expectations...', which emphasise how much trouble your business is prepared to take to help, and leaves the customer feeling comfortable with choosing you.

IDENDEN INDUSTRIES
A division of Idenden Plc
Porter House, Hull HU7 4RF, England

Tel 01482 119087 Fax 01482 119088
Registered in England No: 1218943

Mrs J Holmes
Holmes and Barker Associates
23 Holly Bush Lane
Stretham
Cambs
CB8 4JK

16 August 2005

Dear Mrs Holmes,

Interior fittings for 23 Holly Bush Lane
Many thanks for your order received today.

We are delighted that you have chosen us to supply you with interior fittings for your new premises. I hope that you will be pleased with the results of our work, but, should you have any quibble, however small, please contact me and I will ensure that it is attended to immediately.

As part of our welcome pack for new clients, your order entitles you to have a free consultation, with a recommendation of how the workspace can be designed to the ergonomic advantage of your employees. This service is completely free to all customers placing their first order with us before the end of the year. If you would like to take advantage of this limited offer, please complete and return the enclosed card.

We look forward to a long and happy association with your business. Should we fall short of your high expectations in any matter, please contact me personally.

Yours sincerely,

Stuart Jones
Sales Manager

RESPONDING TO ENQUIRIES AND ORDERS
Letter 44: Welcoming a new customer

Taking the trouble to welcome new customers is a good opportunity to offer thanks for their custom.

Here, the business has to get the customer to sign an agreement – potentially tricky – as it is an opportunity for the customer to decide that she doesn't want the service after all.

Instead of stressing that the customer is now committing herself to the agreement, the writer cunningly puts himself into the shoes of the customer, when he says these are '...our promises '(and your rights...' a careful choice of phrase, designed to make the customer feel like a winner.

Note also how the process is made to seem so easy:'...simply sign both copies...'.

IDENDEN INDUSTRIES
A division of Idenden Plc
Porter House, Hull HU7 4RF, England

Tel 01482 119087 Fax 01482 119088
Registered in England No: 1218943

Mrs J Holmes
Holmes and Barker Associates
23 Holly Bush Lane
Stretham
Cambs
CB8 4JK

16 August 2005

Dear Mrs Holmes,

Your Order No: BYR 99854WE
Thank you for your order.

We have arranged for an engineer to call at your premises to fit your boiler on the morning of 6 September 2005, if this is convenient for you.

We note that you have opted for our full-service agreement to cover maintenance of the boiler and any spare parts. I enclose a service agreement, listing the conditions under which maintenance and parts will be supplied, together with a copy of our 12-month guarantee, which sets out our promises (and your rights if we fail to live up to any of them).

Please check all the details. If you are happy with them, simply sign both copies of the agreement and return one to us in the return envelope provided.

If you have any queries, please do not hesitate to call us on 01482 119087, from 9am to 5pm, Monday to Saturday.

We look forward to welcoming you as a customer.

Yours sincerely,

Robert Patterson
Account Manager

RESPONDING TO ENQUIRIES AND ORDERS
Letter 45: Responding to an international enquiry and outlining terms

This letter is to a potential new client. With international clients, you need to be more careful about payment terms. Here, the supplier is indicating that payment must be by a guaranteed method, such as an Irrevocable Letter of Credit, which is a written undertaking between the buyer's bank and the exporter to pay. The documents and conditions must be precisely in order. The smallest mistake can delay payment.

Thomas King
& Palmer Ltd
serving the world

24 Fuller Road, Welling,
Kent DA16 7JP
Tel: (01322) 100132
Fax: (01322) 100178

Reg. No: England 1212298762
VAT No: 92905643

N Kiyeyo (Graphic Arts) Limited
Kiyeyo House
10 Santa Maria Street
Valletta
Malta

25 August 2005

Dear Sirs,

Many thanks for your fax of 21 August and your interest in our products.

I have pleasure in enclosing two copies of our brochure, outlining our main products. As you can appreciate, the diversity of requirements in the printing and graphic arts industries precludes us from listing all of the available items. We would, of course, be very pleased to quote and supply against specific requests.

Our terms of payment are normally Irrevocable Letter of Credit, confirmed on a prime UK bank or prepayment in pounds sterling. However, we have learned that our own bankers, the Co-operative Bank Plc, are a correspondent bank to the Bank of Valletta and we would, therefore, accept a 30-day bank draft or faxed guarantee of payment bank-to-bank.

We are solely an export company and, therefore, you can feel confident in our ability to deal with shipping, export packing and documentation. We are also aware of the special requirements of hot and/or dusty environments and many of our products are specifically formulated to cope with these conditions.

I would like you to thank Mr Bernard Thomas for his prompt introduction and I very much look forward to dealing with you in the future.

Yours faithfully,

Helen Smith
International Sales

RESPONDING TO ENQUIRIES AND ORDERS
Letter 46: Requesting an international client to issue a letter of credit

A buyer is interested in purchasing some reconditioned machines. The supplier will only agree to sell them provided that payment is made by a documentary letter of credit. The supplier starts the ball rolling by issuing a proforma invoice requesting payment by letter of credit. Until the letter of credit is in place, the supplying company will not commence work on the goods, giving the buyer an incentive to complete the paperwork quickly.

IDENDEN INDUSTRIES
A division of Idenden Plc
Porter House, Hull HU7 4RF, England

Tel 01482 119087 Fax 01482 119088
Registered in England No: 1218943

Mr Hailu Indieka
Director
IMTU
PO Box 1120
Addis Ababa
Ethiopia

28 February 2005

Dear Mr Indieka,

Proforma Nos. 11938665 and 11938667
Many thanks for your letter of 16 February.

I enclose proformas for the KORD 64 machines, which we currently have on our books. I would like to advise you that upon receipt of your letter of credit for whichever machine you think is preferable, our engineers will commence work in stripping down and refurbishing. This work will take approximately three weeks.

I trust that you find our offers of interest and look forward to receiving your letter of credit shortly.

Yours sincerely,

John Foster
International Sales

RESPONDING TO ENQUIRIES AND ORDERS
Letter 47: Playing one client off against another

Just occasionally, you may find yourself in the happy position of having two customers competing for the same item, as here. It may not happen very often, but it can do wonders for concentrating the customer's mind on the buying decision.

Here, the supplier signals that he is going to accept the higher bidder. A word of warning, though: don't play this game unless you have someone else who is seriously interested – otherwise it could backfire on you badly. You should also bear in mind that the loser may feel ill will towards you. If you think a longer-term relationship may be jeopardised, it would be better to accept the first offer and tell the second client that the item is already sold.

 WILSON SMITH LTD

A wholly owned subsidiary of The Wilson Group PLC
16 Willow Walk, Retford, Nottingham NG6 8WS
Tel: (01777) 121211 Fax: (01777) 121233
Reg. No: England 1212298762

Mr Winston Pathmanathan
Director
Kuantan Industries
5 Ipoh Street
5100 Kuala Lumpur
Malaysia

30 November 2005

Dear Winston,

Re: Chambon Machine
As requested, I enclose the specification and photograph of the Chambon machine, which we have on offer.

We currently have a potential buyer from Ghana, who is interested and has offered £50,000 ex-works. We are prepared to accept this offer and he will be looking at the machine next week, unless you are seriously interested and make a better offer. Please 'phone or fax me quickly, before I close the deal with this client.

I look forward to hearing from you.

Yours sincerely,

John Wilson
Sales Director

RESPONDING TO ENQUIRIES AND ORDERS
Letter 48: Querying an order with a customer

Occasionally, customers may place an order but omit a fundamental piece of information or, as here, misunderstand how many items are in a packet. The more technical the item being requested, the more likely this is to occur.

Here, the supplier is asking the customer to confirm what is required. It can be dangerous to make assumptions about an order when it is not clear. The last thing this supplier would want to do is to send out the wrong items and find them coming flooding back, especially when the customer is being asked to pay in advance of receiving the items.

Don't forget, even if the customer is in the wrong, it still puts you in a bad light.

 WILSON SMITH LTD

A wholly owned subsidiary of The Wilson Group PLC
16 Willow Walk, Retford, Nottingham NG6 8WS
Tel: (01777) 121211 Fax: (01777) 121233
Reg. No: England 1212298762

Mr Winston Pathmanathan
Director
Kuantan Industries
5 Ipoh Street
5100 Kuala Lumpur
Malaysia

8 February 2005

Dear Winston,

Many thanks for your letter of 13 January.

Unfortunately, I think you have made a number of errors in your request, which has prevented me from sending you the proforma invoices.

1. On all the plates you have requested 'Packets'. SORD, KORD and ROLAND plates are packed 25 per packet and M1850 and G201 are 100 per packet. This would mean, for example, 1,250 KORD plates costing $6,787.50 and 5,000 1850 plates costing $7,250.00. If this is correct, your total consignment would cost about $65,000.

2. There are two sizes of ROLAND 3 plate, as specified in my letter of 15 October. Which size is required?

3. Do you require Negative or Positive plates for M1850 and GTO?

I would be grateful if you could answer these queries by return, so that we can process your order for you as soon as possible.

Yours sincerely,

James Smith
Marketing Director

RESPONDING TO ENQUIRIES AND ORDERS
Letter 49: Confirming packing list details with an international customer

A packing list has gone astray and a client has asked for a confirmation of what it contained.

The 'tare' is the weight of the container in which the goods are carried (without the goods).

The marks identify how the container has been labelled for shipping purposes, to help with identification.

IDENDEN INDUSTRIES
A division of Idenden Plc
Porter House, Hull HU7 4RF, England

Tel 01482 119087 Fax 01482 119088
Registered in England No: 1218943

Mr A Ngwako
Mellpack Industries Limited
PO Box 1121
Addis Ababa
Ethiopia

23 April 2005

Dear Abraham,

IDR No. RID 92 203425/001

I confirm that the packing list details, which we sent to you on 10 April, contained the following information:

Shipped on Board Vessel Veronique Delmas 9 April 2005
BOL No. 4014 – Container No. PACG 000761-0

1 x 20ft container containing:

80 drums of 180kg each net (14,400kg) Ethyl Acetate

Gross weight per drum – 197.50kg   Tare 17.5kg

TOTAL WEIGHT – 15,800KG   GROSS TARE – 1,400KG

MARKS: Mellpack
          Addis Ababa
          Ethiopia

Ethyl Acetate
U.N. No. 1956

Yours sincerely,

David Wilson
International Sales Manager
Bureau Veritas

RESPONDING TO ENQUIRIES AND ORDERS
Letter 50: Acknowledging an order – goods temporarily out of stock

This is a courteous, standard letter, notifying that an item on an order is out of stock. It doesn't have a personalised ring to it. The clue to this is that the title is not mentioned in the letter, only on the invoice. And no reference is made to the way the customer has actually paid – it says what happens depending on how he has paid.

A hint of personal attention comes through in the second paragraph, where a promise is made to be in contact if the order cannot be supplied within two weeks. Another nice touch is shown in giving a 'phone number to ring if there is a problem. This is on the letterhead anyway, but it makes the number easier to find and subtly reassures the customer.

Grange & Turner Ltd

Telephone (01993) 107888
Fax (01993) 107843

32 WESTBOURN ROAD, WITNEY, OXON OX6 7HY

Reg. No: England 13078453
VAT No: 75698764

---

15 St Patricks Road
Cottingham
Hull
HU5 3SR

12 August 2005

Dear Mr Black,

Your Order 134987
Thank you for your recent order. I am afraid that we have temporarily sold out of the title indicated on the invoice.

New stocks have already been ordered and we expect delivery shortly. Of course, I will contact you again if I cannot despatch your book within the next two weeks.

If you have paid in advance, your cheque will not be banked until we have despatched all the items on your order. If you have paid by credit card, we will only debit for those items you have received so far.

All our books are supplied under our usual ten-day examination offer. If you have any further questions, please do not hesitate to ring me on 01993 107888.

Please accept my apologies for this delay.

Yours sincerely,

Kevin Mason
General Manager

RESPONDING TO ENQUIRIES AND ORDERS
Letter 51: Telling a customer it's too late to amend an order

A customer has made a mistake with an order and the supplier is responding. The supplier gives the buyer an option to amend part of the order as he is only part way through the job.

The supplier's reply is courteous and to the point. He could have taken a tougher line saying 'you must accept the 150 ringbinders already made'. Instead he takes the softer approach of '...we will have to ask you...' as he knows the customer is in the wrong and there is no need to add insult to injury.

RPP Holdings Plc
35/38 New Road, Paignton, Devon TQ3 4UU
Tel: 01803 175653 Fax: 01803 187908
Reg. No: England 1976143

FAX MESSAGE

To: Tom Greate
         Wilson Smith Ltd

Fax No: 01777 121233

From: Bob Taylor   Date: 29 August 2005

Dear Tom,

Your Order No. 30596
I received your fax this morning, requesting that your order for 500 ringbinders with a 30mm diameter ring be amended to binders that take 350 leaves.

Unfortunately, your order has already been in production for two days and we have made up 150 ringbinders. As these have been tailored to your requirements with your company's logo, we will have to ask you to accept the 150 ringbinders already made.

Please let me know today if you want a further 500 ringbinders with a 35mm diameter ring made or just 350.

Yours sincerely,

Bob Taylor
Sales Manager

MAKING APOLOGIES
Letter 52: Apologising to a person receiving unwanted mail

Unwanted mail can be a major source of irritation – mainly to consumers. Businesses seem to accept more readily that it is part and parcel of their daily life. With most respectable companies, it should be possible to restrict the amount of direct mail you receive, simply by asking to be taken off their mailing lists.

This letter reassures the recipient that appropriate action is being taken. Note how it opens: thanking the customer for taking the trouble to write, a nice way of disarming a complainant.

The letter doesn't grovel but points out exactly what the person can expect to happen. It offers a course of action if things don't improve and reminds the consumer that it is in the company's interests, ultimately, to keep mailings down – something the person writing in would not think about automatically.

Grange & Turner Ltd

32 WESTBOURN ROAD, WITNEY, OXON OX6 7HY

Telephone (01993) 107888
Fax (01993) 107843

Reg. No: England 13078453
VAT No: 75698764

Mr P Brooks
33 Little Lane
East Bridgford
Nottingham
NG55 6YH

16 May 2005

Dear Mr Brooks,

Thank you for taking the trouble to write, asking for your name to be removed from our mailing list. From today, your name and address will be excluded from all mailing lists produced here.

I should warn you that most mailings are prepared a long way in advance and it is almost certain that some are yet to be posted. I can only apologise for the irritation these further mailings may cause, but please be assured that they will soon come to a stop.

However, if they cause you concern, and you would like me to carry out an additional check, simply return the unwanted letter using our FREEPOST address:

Jane Harvey
List Controller
Grange & Turner Ltd
FREEPOST
Witney
OX6 7HY

We are always keen to keep our mailing costs down, wherever possible, and to mail only those who wish to hear from us.

If you have any further questions, please do not hesitate to contact me.

Yours sincerely,

Jane Harvey
List Controller

MAKING APOLOGIES
Letter 53: Notifying a customer that corrective action has been taken

The customer writing in obviously appreciates the service being offered and the tone of the letter fits the degree of the complaint. If there is a hint of good news in the complainant's letter, it is well worth latching on to it, as here. It helps to remove some of the sting and put your company into a more positive light.

You still want to remedy the situation and, provided that you can take action or be seen to be taking action to satisfy the customer, you should not be troubled in the future.

Grange & Turner Ltd

32 WESTBOURN ROAD, WITNEY, OXON OX6 7HY

Telephone (01993) 107888
Fax (01993) 107843

Reg. No: England 13078453
VAT No: 75698764

Mr H Mason
15 Longfield Road
Boars Hill
Oxford
OX568JH

24 February 2005

Dear Mr Mason,

Thank you for your letter dated 17 February addressed to our Managing Director, which has been brought to my attention. It is very nice to hear that you appreciate receiving our promotional material from time to time.

However, I am very sorry that you have been inundated with mailings to your son at your address. This has happened because he requested us to send goods to your address as above; with hindsight, we should have made sure that our computer was 'flagged' no mailings on his name.

I would like to confirm that we have amended our records so that he will only receive his mailings at his Leighton Buzzard address and have arranged that only our literature is sent in future. You may receive unwanted mailings for about a month as there may be some in the pipeline but, after that period of time, they should stop.

Once again, please accept my apologies for the annoyance and inconvenience caused. If you have any more queries, please do not hesitate to contact me.

Yours sincerely,

Jane Harvey
List Controller

MAKING APOLOGIES
Letter 54: Replying to a complaint about poor service

The company complaining about the poor service here believes that the cleaning company has ignored its first letter, even though it seems that it has genuinely gone astray. This is unfortunate, because it means the writer will have to work doubly hard to convince the customer that the fault is completely innocent. This is successfully achieved here.

Being seen to do more than is strictly required is a useful tactic for handling complaints. Here, the cleaning company takes the precaution of allocating a new person to the job and offering a discount off the month's invoice.

Be modest also in the extent to which you claim to be compensating the other party. Note how the writer says '...and trust that this helps in compensating for your dissatisfaction'. She could have written '...and trust this compensates you for your dissatisfaction', which would appear slightly presumptuous and probably negate all the profuse apologies that have been made.

BAKER CLEANING SERVICES

29 Cunningham Street
London
N32 6JG
Telephone: (020) 7016 1350
Facsimile: (020) 7016 1351
Reg. No: England 118974165

Mrs E Bjornsen
General Manager
Hansoms Auctions
153 Simpson Street
London
WC3 4RT

11 July 2005

Dear Mrs Bjornsen,

Thank you for your letter of 5 July, expressing concern over the cleaning service that we provide for your company.

You say that you have written to us once already on this matter, but, having looked into this, we can find no record of ever having received your letter. We are not sure what happened here, but we very much regret that this has meant a continuation of your problem.

In your letter, you state that toilet areas are not adequately cleaned or disinfected and that the office area, although always vacuumed properly, is often not dusted or polished.

I have spoken to the four staff who clean your offices on a rota and I believe I have now isolated the problem. Although the cause seems to have arisen out of a temporary problem affecting one of our cleaners, I have taken the precaution of assigning a permanent replacement to your team and I have reminded all cleaners that only the highest standards are acceptable.

I very much regret the inconvenience and disappointment caused and hope that the measures taken will now restore the service we offer to its former high standard. As a token of our goodwill, I have arranged for a discount of 30 per cent off this month's invoice and trust that this helps in compensating for your dissatisfaction.

Once again, please accept our sincerest apologies.

Yours sincerely,

Jill Hooper
Account Manager

MAKING APOLOGIES
Letter 55: Apologising to a customer for a delay in supplying a product

When you are relying on a distributor or wholesaler for a product who in turn is relying on the main supplier overseas to supply an item, it is easy to find yourself the piggy in the middle between a customer and the people who can influence getting the product to you.

Obtaining reliable information about timescales or delivery through the chain of suppliers is often difficult. When this occurs, your main line of defence with the customer has to be that you are applying pressure as regularly as possible.

H J KINGSLEY (NORWICH) LTD
Kingsley House, Morris Street, Norwich NR6 7JM
Tel: (01603) 117097 Fax: (01603) 117099 Reg. No: England 12086215 VAT No: 8793519

Mr F Goodge
Goodge, Turner and Weatherall
12 Macers Row
Holt
Norfolk
NR16 5TR

11 February 2005

Dear Mr Goodge,

Axe Accounting Package

I am sorry that you have still not received this software package.

It is an American import which is distributed by a UK software house and there is a delay in getting stocks from the States. We are nagging the UK software house twice a week, who assure us that they are doing the same to their American colleagues.

I will keep you informed of progress.

Yours sincerely,

Anne Goode (Mrs)
Sales Assistant

MAKING APOLOGIES
Letter 56: Apologising for a missed appointment

The two people who were due to meet know each other well. Even though one of them has been inconvenienced, the tone is friendly, fitting their established relationship. Bob knows that Andrew Taylor is to be trusted and doesn't make a habit of missing appointments. If they had not known each other, a much more formal tone would be called for.

Even though the letter is friendly, note how the feeling is still sincere – Andrew empathises with Bob, saying: 'I know how frustrating it is to be left high and dry...'. A recompense is offered in the form of a lunch. Another highlighting device is used with the PS – here, Andrew wants to confirm that he really means June and has not made another mistake.

Taylor Taylor & Shaw

Benton House, Clifton, Bristol BS16 7LJ
Tel: (0117) 1089254   Fax: (0117) 1089211

Mr R Hodds
Director
RLO (of Bristol) Ltd
32 Gloucester Road
Clifton
Bristol
BS8 4UP

14 June 2005

Dear Bob,

I am very sorry that you were left waiting at your offices for the meeting that we had arranged last week.

I know how frustrating it is to be left high and dry and I take all the blame for getting it wrong. I wrote your appointment down for 13 July instead of 13 June.

To make amends, can I offer you lunch when we meet? How are you fixed for 17 June at 12 o'clock? I suggest we meet at my office, if that is convenient to you.

Yours sincerely,

Andrew W Taylor

PS: I really do mean June this time!

Partners: AW Taylor & GS Taylor

MAKING APOLOGIES
Letter 57: Making a gentle apology to an established customer

Here, there is not a serious complaint, although the customer has noticed that goods are taking longer to arrive. The fault lies outside the direct control of the supplying company although it is within its power to amend, as it is the courier whose service has deteriorated.

The tone is conciliatory, without treating the situation as a big problem.'We are, of course, concerned...' is another useful phrase, helping to create the impression that you empathise with the reader and recognise the problem.

 WILSON SMITH LTD
A wholly owned subsidiary of The Wilson Group PLC
16 Willow Walk, Retford, Nottingham NG6 8WS
Tel: (01777) 121211 Fax: (01777) 121233
Reg. No: England 1212298762

Mr J West
General Manager
Idenden Industries
Porter House
Hull
HU7 4RF

16 May 2005

Dear Jim,

Re: Delivery Times

Thank you for returning the delivery cards, showing how long it is taking for our goods to arrive with you.

Your observation that deliveries seem to be taking longer than a year ago is correct. On average it is taking one extra day for goods to arrive with you, although our overall turnaround time from receiving your order to goods leaving the warehouse has not changed.

The cause of this extra time seems to be the courier service we are currently using. We are, of course, concerned to offer you the best possible service, so for the next three months we shall be trying out an alternative service, to see if there is any improvement.

Please do continue to return the cards showing the date you receive the goods and please accept our sincere apologies for this slight deterioration in service.

Yours sincerely,

Peter Grey
General Manager

MAKING APOLOGIES
Letter 58: Explaining an apparent quality defect

A customer may specify that a product must meet certain criteria. Unfortunately, he may not appreciate that meeting those criteria could have a knock-on effect elsewhere. Here, the customer wants the inks to be tolerant of high temperatures and retain their glossy appearance. The key phrase here is '...I assure you this is perfectly normal and will not impede its function'. 'I trust everything is in order...' is a useful phrase to use when you are confident that what you are suggesting should satisfy the reader, but it still leaves the door open if he has any more queries.

 WILSON SMITH LTD

A wholly owned subsidiary of The Wilson Group PLC
16 Willow Walk, Retford, Nottingham NG6 8WS
Tel: (01777) 121211 Fax: (01777) 121233
Reg. No: England 1212298762

Mr Brian Adams
Production Director
FGH Products Ltd
Unit 8 Potters Lane Ind. Est.
Almondvale
Perth
PH1 2EL

29 September 2005

Dear Mr Adams,

Many thanks for the cheque for £394.00 received this morning, and I understand the reason for the delay in this payment.

I note that you were unhappy with the quality of some of the materials we sent and I would like to explain the situation. Your order specified that the product should be tolerant of high temperatures. The gloss version has a lower tolerance, which is why we supplied the matt to you. This is why the product may appear slightly rough, although I assure you this is perfectly normal and will not impede its function.

I trust everything is in order and I look forward to being able to provide further quotations for you in the future.

Yours sincerely,

Mike Rose
Sales Department

APOLOGIES WITH A HINT OF GROVELLING
Letter 59: Apologising for breaking a verbal assurance

Letters that explain the reason for a mistake can give the customer an impression that you are being very defensive in passing the buck on to someone else instead of accepting responsibility for your actions. This can reduce still further the customer's estimation of you, rather than restoring his faith in your ability to deliver the services. This letter tackles this issue nicely in the second paragraph, with the phrase 'If I could perhaps explain the circumstances, not as an excuse, but so you can see the exceptional....'

The sincerity of this letter is emphasised by the phrases 'I was most disturbed...'; 'I am deeply sorry...' and 'This unfortunate event....' And it is not just simple apologies the reader is being asked to accept but 'unreserved' apologies. The use of these emphatic words builds up a greater sense of remorse.

RPP Holdings Plc
35/38 New Road, Paignton, Devon TQ3 4UU
Tel: 01803 175653 Fax: 01803 187908
Reg. No: England 1976143

Mr P Piggott
Managing Director
TMP UK Ltd
Manor Park
Hitchin
Herts
HP7 9UM

22 April 2005

Dear Mr Piggott,

I was most disturbed to receive your letter of 20 April, informing me of your dissatisfaction with our performance. I am deeply sorry that we have let you and your client down. We take great care to ensure that our customers are satisfied, as this is essential to the continuation of our business.

If I could perhaps explain the circumstances, not as an excuse, but so you can see the exceptional and unexpected difficulties we faced. When I telephoned you on Tuesday, your order was on track to be supplied the following day. Soon after we spoke, I had to leave the factory for an unavoidable meeting. An hour later, the machine developed a fault which took four hours to rectify and this meant we were unable to complete your order. Because I was expected back the same day, it was left for me to telephone you to explain the situation. By bad luck, I was detained longer than expected and did not return to the factory the same day.

This unfortunate event has highlighted a gap in our procedures, which we are correcting. In future, in my absence, our Production Manager will notify you of any deviation from the agreed schedule.

Please accept our unreserved apologies. We shall, subject to documentary proof, of course, make good any losses that you incur as a result of our failure to meet your deadline.

Yours sincerely,

JH Hardy
Customer Services Manager

APOLOGIES WITH A HINT OF GROVELLING
Letter 60: Apologising to a customer for items that have not arrived

When a customer complains, it is not just the current order that you may lose. That customer could be worth a lot of money to you over time – accounting for thousands of pounds of revenue during the time he does business with you.

If mistakes do happen, your aim should be to mitigate the damage. Here, the supplier achieves this by reassuring the customer that it is a '...very rare occurrence...', supporting the claim with '...it happens about once a year....'

The customer is made to feel extra-special, with the remedy of having the item sent by special delivery, being referred to as a '...highly valued customer...' and being given a voucher for a discount off the next purchase – a cunning technique to tempt the customer back, which costs very little and boosts sales at the same time. Brilliant!

Grange & Turner Ltd

32 WESTBOURN ROAD, WITNEY, OXON OX6 7HY

Telephone (01993) 107888
Fax (01993) 107843

Reg. No: England 13078453
VAT No: 75698764

Mr W Holmes
154 High Road
Oakley
Oxford
OX7 8PL

21 June 2005

Dear Mr Holmes,

Re: The Power to Win

I was extremely concerned to hear that you have not received the above book, which should have been despatched to you a week ago.

I have made enquiries and have discovered that, in this instance, one of our internal procedural systems failed. This is a very rare occurrence (it happens about once a year, although we continue to try to eradicate such mistakes entirely).

I can only ask that you accept our most sincere apologies for this inconvenience. To make amends, I am sending you a copy of the above book by special delivery. In addition, as you are a highly valued customer, I am enclosing a £5 voucher, which can be redeemed against any future order.

I do hope that this will go some way to restoring your faith in us.

Yours sincerely,

Susan Taylor
Customer Service Manager

HANDLING AWKWARD CUSTOMERS
Letter 61: Handling a customer who is trying it on

Occasionally, you may come up against a situation where the facts just don't fit. You don't have the evidence to say: 'I don't believe you; you're lying', so how do you handle it? The simple business decision is to refuse to do business with the customer any more.

The supplier here produces the evidence that the goods are being delivered correctly and then in the third paragraph tells the customer that the supplier smells a rat with the phrases '...very odd indeed' and the fact that goods are '...apparently...' not being received safely. This gets as close to a specific challenge as you can afford.

The customer is the loser in the end, as he will now be blacklisted and unable to receive any more goods.

Grange & Turner Ltd

32 WESTBOURN ROAD, WITNEY, OXON OX6 7HY

Telephone (01993) 107888
Fax (01993) 107843

Reg. No: England 13078453
VAT No: 75698764

Mr T P Smith
124 Vale Road
Clifton
Bristol
BS5 7HY

25 July 2005

Dear Mr Smith,

Our Statement Dated 12 April 2005

We have supplied you with books on four separate occasions to the value of £75, for which we have asked for payment three times.

You are claiming that you have never received the items ordered and that they must have been lost in the post. Our carrier's records demonstrate that the goods were despatched and each time signed for by a D M Martin. You claim that no one of that name lives at your address and that the goods must have been incorrectly delivered.

We could understand if a parcel was incorrectly delivered on one occasion, but the fact that parcels have been delivered and accepted four times by the same person seems very odd indeed.

As our debt cannot be settled and goods supplied to this address are apparently not being received safely, we have no alternative but to cease fulfilling orders to you. We shall write off the amount of £75 on this occasion.

Yours sincerely,

T P O'Neil
Customer Accounts Manager

HANDLING AWKWARD CUSTOMERS
Letter 62: Handling a very rude customer

Some people's reaction to receiving an abusive letter is to bin the letter, because it obviously comes from a crank. But wait a minute. That person isn't reacting for no reason at all – he obviously feels very strongly about the issue. And, since he has cast aspersions on the reputation of your business, you should use the opportunity to set the record straight.

The first sentence tackles the abusiveness head-on. The phrase 'In spite of your rude tone I will respond...' is designed to make him feel that you almost decided not to write and that he should appreciate that you have taken the trouble.

Note how the tone of the reply is cold and unapologetic. It offers a frank explanation without saying either 'sorry' or 'please accept our apologies'.

PARKER
Glass Ltd
Unit 27 Willow Park
Christchurch, Dorset BH23 6MM
Tel: 01202 109111
Fax: 01202 109112

Reg. No: England 962578762
VAT No: 9120564

Mr S Wright
157 Colder Way
Basingstoke
Hants
BP6 5TG

12 December 2005

Dear Mr Wright,

It is not often I receive such an offensive letter. In spite of your rude tone I will respond to the issues you raised.

I understand that your letter is caused by your frustration at not being supplied immediately with the goods that you ordered. We take great pride in being able to supply all goods *held in stock* within 28 days at the latest. Our average turnaround time is, however, far shorter, at just nine working days. But there are occasions, such as this instance, when the demand for our goods is much greater than we anticipate. Normally we would simply reorder and aim to supply you within about two weeks. However, when the goods have to be imported from overseas, delays can be considerably longer. These are the circumstances that caused you such offence.

We are doing everything in our power to obtain the goods and supply them to you. I would like to reassure you that we shall not deduct the amount owed from your credit card until the day the goods are despatched to you. We always take complaints seriously and are ready to respond to all of them. I accept you feel strongly about this situation, but I would ask that any future correspondence between us is conducted in more appropriate language.

Yours sincerely,

Peter Jones
Managing Director

HANDLING AWKWARD CUSTOMERS
Letter 63: Denying liability following a complaint

Sometimes you may feel that a customer has completely ignored proper instructions. If you cave in to the complaint, you risk opening the flood gates to other unjustified complaints. A better course is to stand firm and politely point out that the product was not used for the purpose intended. After all, the product is being called into question and to offer any recompense may be interpreted as an admission that the product is at fault.

The evidence needs to be irrefutable, as here, when warnings are given in the instruction manual about which materials the drill is suitable for and which it is not. Note how the line of evidence is separated out from the rest of the text, since it is the crux of the argument. Emboldening it heightens the eye's attention to it. The door is shut firmly in the customer's face with the phrase '...I regret that we are unable to assist you further in this matter', a wonderfully polite and understated way of saying 'get lost' without causing offence.

IDENDEN INDUSTRIES
A division of Idenden Plc
Porter House, Hull HU7 4RF, England

Tel 01482 119087 Fax 01482 119088
Registered in England No: 1218943

Mr D Redwood
Cedar Cottage
Little Lane
Wass
York
YO9 6TG

3 February 2005

Dear Mr Redwood,

I have considered your letter of 21 January and your assertion that our K31 power drill does not fulfil the claims made for it.

In your letter you maintain that this drill was used by you as directed, in the construction of a new extension to your house, as a result of which the motor burnt out only a month after the expiry of the guarantee. A telephone call to you from one of our staff subsequently revealed that you used this drill with a large masonry bit, for drilling into concrete.

I feel that I should point out that our K31 model is an *excellent* drill for the purposes for which it is sold, that is, for light jobs around the home. This point is made quite clearly in the instruction manual which come with your drill, in particular at the bottom of section two: 'Suitable Material', where it states:

'This drill is not suitable for heavy-duty drilling in materials such as concrete.'

Much more suitable would be one of our K80 or K90 range, in that they have more robust motors as well as an impact facility, normally expected for drilling into materials such as concrete. The K31 boasts no such facility.

For these reasons I regret, therefore, that I cannot agree with your assertion.

Since your guarantee has expired, and since your drill has been used for purposes *specifically* stated as unsuitable, I regret that we are unable to assist you further in this matter.

Yours sincerely,

Frank Pillow
Customer Services Director

HANDLING AWKWARD CUSTOMERS
Letter 64: Denying a potential breach of contract

This is a tricky issue and one that would probably give the lawyers a field day. The legal issue is whether the prior contract set up with Mr Bone's predecessor overrides the contract which Mr Bone issued stating that 'time was of the essence'.

The legal issue aside, Michael Hardcastle clearly believes that he has a clear-cut case. The letter emphasises this belief, with phrases that are designed to knock his opponent off course: 'I would like to draw your attention to the agreement...' and '...we deny your claim...' are examples. The only attempt to mollify Mr Bone occurs at the end, with the assurance that the order will be given priority.

IDENDEN INDUSTRIES
A division of Idenden Plc
Porter House, Hull HU7 4RF, England

Tel 01482 119087 Fax 01482 119088
Registered in England No: 1218943

Jim Bone
Purchasing Manager
Wilson Smith Ltd
16 Willow Walk
Retford
Nottingham
NG6 8WS

11 February 2005

Dear Mr Bone,

I am in receipt of your letter of 9 February.

You are claiming that if we do not deliver your goods ordered by 14 February that we shall be in breach of contract and you will cancel your order.

I would like to draw your attention to the agreement I set up with your predecessor, Malcolm Bute (see his letter dated 21 June 2004), which specifies that we shall only be in breach of contract if the goods are not supplied due to circumstances within our control. The industrial action at the distribution depot is clearly outside our control and we deny your claim to have the right to cancel the order.

We are doing everything in our power to compel our distributors to resolve the dispute swiftly. I am hopeful that the mediation being attempted will result in a speedy conclusion. I will ensure that your order is given priority, so that it is delivered to you at the earliest opportunity.

Yours sincerely,

Michael Hardcastle
Sales Director

REFUSING CUSTOMERS
Letter 65: Advising a customer that new orders cannot be supplied

A situation in which orders are stopped because of non-payment is usually battled out between the two financial departments of the businesses. The sales and customer-services departments will become involved if there are orders pending.

Here, a friendly letter is sent mainly to inform the customer that payments are overdue. Both parties know it is not directly their responsibility but the appeal in the closing line: 'Is there anything you can do?' is designed to influence the customer into taking action. The sender emphasises her own efficiency (contrasted with the customer's inefficiency) by saying that the next orders are ready to be despatched. A good, friendly, influential letter.

B & R HENDERSONS LTD
Marlows Road, Aberdeen AB20 5GT
Tel: 01224 267855 Fax: 01224 267977
Reg. No: 16497811 VAT No: 7387945

Helen Mitchell
Sales Manager
Good & Peabody
34 Kiln Street
Aberdeen
Scotland
AB8 7HY

12 August 2005

Dear Helen,

Re: Order Numbers 112568 and 112572
I am afraid that our Financial Director has put these orders on hold, due to payment problems. He faxed your office last week regarding the two overdue payments but he has had no reply.

I have processed your orders, since I want them to be ready for despatch as soon as I am authorised to release them. However, this will not happen until the problem is resolved. Is there anything you can do?

I look forward to hearing from you.

Regards,

Tina Cox
Sales Manager

REFUSING CUSTOMERS
Letter 66: Refusing to accept that a carriage charge be deducted

This letter is firm but friendly in tone. The main paragraph takes a persuasive stance with the phrase '...the carriage charge is only a contribution towards the final cost of delivering the goods to you'. It is worth noting how the request to pay gradually builds up, rising to a crescendo in the final sentence. Criticism of the charge itself is deflected by an acknowledgement that it is only a contribution towards the cost. Next comes the point that the customer's prevarication over the delivery address contributed to the adjustment having to be made. The customer is subtly made to feel indebted to the supplier because '...we do everything we can to keep the charges...as competitive as possible...', which is designed to counteract the pain that is inflicted with the information that the supplier can't '...absorb the cost...'. Note how the formal request to pay comes right at the end of the letter, in a firm sentence with a diplomatic double negative: '...I do not consider it unreasonable...', a softer, less abrasive way of saying 'please pay'.

GKT Products Ltd, Unit 10, Castleway Lane, Alloway, Ayr, KA7 4BE
Telephone (01292) 177900 Fax (01292) 199855   Reg. No: 17964583 VAT No: 679845

Mr B Holmes
Marketing Manager
Beresford-Biggs Ltd
39 Cavalry Drive
Histon
Cambs
CB7 4FE

16 June 2005

Dear Bill,

Our Estimate No. 229674 and Our Invoice No. 113975
Thank you for your letter of 13 June, concerning the carriage charge on our invoice.

The document on which we gave you our price was clearly headed as an estimate, and not a quotation as you claim. This permits us to make any necessary adjustments. The adjustment of the carriage charge is only a contribution towards the final cost of delivering the goods to you. You may also recall that you were unable to provide us with details of where the goods were to be delivered, when you asked us to give you a price. While we do everything we can to keep the charges for our goods as competitive as possible, I regret that on this occasion we are unable to absorb the cost of delivery in our prices.

Given all these circumstances, I do not consider it unreasonable to ask you to pay the carriage charge and would appreciate it if you could settle the account by the end of this month.

Yours sincerely,

Tony Bright
Customer Services Manager

REFUSING CUSTOMERS
Letter 67: Negotiating an amendment to an order

Occasionally, a customer will want to change his order while it is being processed. If this involves additional cost, you should stand by the original order. 'I am afraid it has not been possible...' lets the customer down lightly. Your aim, though, should be to appear as helpful as possible. Note how the supplier explains that he can do the extra copies and gives a provisional delivery date.

RPP Holdings Plc
35/38 New Road, Paignton, Devon TQ3 4UU
Tel: 01803 175653 Fax: 01803 187908
Reg. No: England 1976143

Mr A D Nelson
Sales Manager
Healthaware Co Ltd
56 Barrow Street
St Albans
Herts
AL2 1LD

14 October 2005

Dear Mr Nelson,

Your Order No. 29785

Thank you for your fax, which I received this morning, asking if it was possible to increase your print order from 10,000 to 15,000 copies.

Your brochure went to press yesterday. I am afraid it has not been possible, therefore, for us to print an additional 5,000 copies within the existing run and give you the benefit of a lower price. We can still print the extra copies, although they will be at the slightly higher reprint price we gave you. We could deliver these by next Wednesday. Do you still want us to go ahead?

The main run, I am pleased to say, is going smoothly and we are on course to deliver it to you on Friday.

Yours sincerely,

George Stevens
Account Manager

REFUSING CUSTOMERS
Letter 68: Refusing a customer a refund – outside the time period

Some customers may try to abuse your terms and conditions. It can be tricky – do you risk losing a potential customer or allow yourself to be taken advantage of? The solution here is to take a firm line and point out politely how far your terms and conditions have been exceeded.

Note the technique designed to show how reasonable you are. The supplier achieves this by saying that he doesn't mind that one of his conditions has been exceeded; the real objection is to the condition in which the shirt has been returned.

H J KINGSLEY (NORWICH) LTD
Kingsley House, Morris Street, Norwich NR6 7JM
Tel: (01603) 117097 Fax: (01603) 117099 Reg. No: England 12086215 VAT No: 8793519

Mr Lester Patterson
30 Virgin Close
Doncaster
S Yorks
DN9 0DB

26 May 2005

Dear Mr Patterson,

I am writing concerning your request for a refund on the shirt which you purchased from us.

As you know, under our conditions of sale, we offer all our customers a ten-day, no-quibble, money-back guarantee, provided the goods are returned within this period in a saleable condition.

We despatched your parcel to you on 15 March. The parcel in which you returned the item to us was date stamped 16 May. Even allowing five days for our parcel to reach you, this means that you have had the goods in your possession for 56 days, some 41 days outside our guarantee period. While we would be willing to overlook this point, we were concerned to find that the shirt you returned had clearly been worn and was soiled to an extent that it cannot be offered for resale.

I very much regret, therefore, that we shall be unable to offer you a refund. I am returning the shirt to you under separate cover.

Yours sincerely,

P Phillips
Customer Services Manager

THANKING CUSTOMERS
Letter 69: Responding to a letter of appreciation

Customers' letters of thanks are some of the best (although often the rarest) letters to receive in business. When they do come, you should not ignore them. Instead, you should respond, reaffirming in the customer's mind that you are a good company to be doing business with.

The style of this letter is good because it takes a modest approach by saying '...we haven't done anything 'special'...'. The closing line has a nice ring to it, showing the real appreciation that is felt for the letter. The customer cannot fail to think this is a business worth dealing with.

Grange & Turner Ltd

32 WESTBOURN ROAD, WITNEY, OXON OX6 7HY

Telephone (01993) 107888
Fax (01993) 107843

Reg. No: England 13078453
VAT No: 75698764

Ms Olive Short
Purchasing Manager
Parker Bright Ltd
72 Dudley Road
Brighton
East Sussex
BR6 5RT

11 March 2005

Dear Ms Short,

Thank you for your letter of 7 March, which reached me today.

It was very kind of you to take the trouble to write to say how our service has helped you. As I am sure you are aware, it is always very uplifting to be thanked – and I find letters of thanks when we haven't done anything 'special', just gone about providing our normal service, the most pleasant of all.

How do we seem to match your needs?

Firstly, there is quite a lot of choice. Approximately eight new products are introduced each month, roughly one hundred different products in the course of a year. So there is a good chance of meeting the need of the moment of each individual person.

But secondly, and much more importantly, it is the market that ultimately selects the products. It is the products that sell well (and are not returned under our guarantee) that stay in the leaflets. In fact, they have been voted for by other customers. The needs of one customer are often very like the needs of another.

So, we don't need a mole in your business – we just have to watch what everyone else wants! Of course, we make the initial choice, but even this is based on years of experience of what it is that makes a bestselling product that everybody wants to buy.

Once again, thank you very much indeed for taking the trouble to write to me.

Yours sincerely,

Herbert Short
Manager

THANKING CUSTOMERS
Letter 70: Thank-you letter for hospitality

When writing letters of thanks, it is always nice not only to thank the person you are writing to, but also to ask for your thanks to be passed on to other people you met.

Saying something appreciative which engenders a positive feeling, for example, how your expectations were exceeded, is another useful tip for earning credit with the customer. This is done here with the declaration that the company is ahead of the game in fields other than 'systems'.

Charles Cunningham Ltd

29 Baker Street, LONDON N34 6GH, England
Tel: (020) 7015 1290 Fax: (020) 7015 1271
Reg. No: England 1104398135 VAT No: 82108643

Ms Debra Clifton
Vice President
Winger & Ewing Inc.
7853 Wateridge Drive
Pleasanton
CA 95488
USA

24 May 2005

Dear Deb,

Having arrived safely back in the UK and having adjusted to the time difference, the size of the place and the fact that coffee is served at the end of meals, I am now in a position to write to you concerning our visit to your offices.

Firstly, I would like to say thank you, to you and all your colleagues for the wonderful hospitality and the time you were willing to devote to our visit. We would be grateful if you would thank your colleagues on our behalf.

We were very impressed with the obvious professionalism that runs throughout your organisation. Having been told that you were 'the number one for systems', not only was this confirmed, but our impression is that you are excellent at all the other aspects as well.

All this leaves to say is thank you once again for your hospitality; I hope we will have the opportunity to respond in a similar fashion if you, or any of your colleagues, visit the UK.

With kind regards,

D Dean
Director

THANKING CUSTOMERS
Letter 71: Thanking a satisfied customer

This letter shows how, even though the sender, Thomas Griffiths, doesn't know Mr Drake, a friendly, informal tone can be struck. It is even better, because the customer, who had vowed (in an earlier letter) never to have anything more to do with the business after a hiccup in the customer-service system, was won back by a highly personalised letter explaining what went wrong.

Asking the reader to imagine how encouraging it is to receive this type of letter has the effect of pulling the customer closer – getting him to empathise with your situation – and builds the common bond that you have.

The enthusiasm shines through in the use of adjectives designed to emphasise the genuine feeling of pleasure: '...your extremely pleasant letter...'; '...very considerably'; '...even greater pleasure...', which all add up to a great sense of warmth.

Grange & Turner Ltd

32 WESTBOURN ROAD, WITNEY, OXON OX6 7HY

Telephone (01993) 107888
Fax (01993) 107843

Reg. No: England 13078453
VAT No: 75698764

Mr D Drake
24 Berry Green
Wellingborough
Northants
NN43 5MN

12 August 2005

Dear Mr Drake,

Thank you very much indeed for your extremely pleasant letter, which arrived this morning. It brightened my day very considerably.

I do not know whether you can imagine how very encouraging it is in a mail-order company to get letters of appreciation (most people are moved to write only to complain!). And, of course, there is even greater pleasure in restoring a damaged relationship with a long-standing customer.

Thank you very much indeed for taking the trouble to write to reassure me. Please do let me know if anything goes wrong again.

Yours sincerely,

Thomas Griffiths
Director

THANKING CUSTOMERS
Letter 72: Thanking a good client, slightly cheekily

If you decide to write an informal, jovial letter, make sure it doesn't overstep the mark. The person receiving this letter would need to be on very good terms with the sender.

By playing on the list of excuses that could have been made, there is a danger that the tone could be misconstrued and interpreted as being heavily sarcastic. The letter redeems itself, though, with the genuine note of thanks at the end.

Note how, even though the main paragraph has been written as a list, it is left as a piece of consecutive prose, which reflects how it would have been spoken. The numbers are there to emphasise, rather than separate, the text.

Fenner & Sons

16 George Street, Woodbridge,
Suffolk IP3 7KL
Tel: (01394) 198423
Fax: (01394) 198444
Registered in England: 91221299
VAT No: 919129075 80

Mr Bob Holmes
Senior Buyer
H J Kingsley (Norwich) Ltd
Kingsley House
Morris Street
Norwich
NR6 7JM

13 September 2005

Dear Bob,

Just a note to say thank you for the cheque.

And how wonderfully refreshing, to receive a cheque the day after being told it is being sent!

Thank you for not: 1) passing the cheque on to a colleague on holiday for counter-signature, 2) despatching it to your Kings Lynn accounting centre for final approval and speedy processing, 3) including it in the next cheque run, 4) endeavouring to ensure it receives priority attention even though (a) Tuesday is too late in the week to be included in this week's cheque run, and (b) payments due after the 5th cannot normally be actioned in the same month.

In other words, hearty thanks.

Kind regards,

John Smith
Accounts Manager

THANKING CUSTOMERS
Letter 73: Thanking a business associate for a referral

If you end up getting business (or even the prospect of business) from a recommendation, it is not only courteous but also sound business sense to thank the person who recommended you. If you don't thank him, why should he bother to do it again? People like to feel appreciated and useful; it will make your associate more inclined to recommend you again in future. Ignoring the person who made the recommendation looks as if you are taking him for granted. Alternatively, he may think that you didn't like the potential client and next time an opportunity comes along he will send it to a competitor!

RPP Holdings Plc
35/38 New Road, Paignton, Devon TQ3 4UU
Tel: 01803 175653 Fax: 01803 187908
Reg. No: England 1976143

Mr David Cross
Sales Director
P P Plus Ltd
Grove Industrial Estate
Warwick
CV7 1PL

18 February 2005

Dear David,

I am writing to thank you for recommending me to Peter Norman at DAS UK. Your kindness is very much appreciated.

If I remember rightly, you did, in fact, recommend me to this firm when they had offices in Kingston, although at the time nothing came of the enquiry.

We have put a price to them on a job of printing four-colour process posters and, if anything comes of it, I will be in touch with you.

I hope that you are keeping well and busy; things are still very quiet here. We keep getting a lot of enquiries but many fall by the wayside when followed up. Anyway, we have survived two major recessions so we must be doing something right, and things are bound to pick up eventually.

I remember the last time I spoke to you that things were quiet at your end also; I hope things are going better for you now.

Thank you once again for your kindness.

Yours sincerely,

Richard Price
Director

KEEPING CUSTOMERS INFORMED
Letter 74: Appointment of a new General Manager

If there is a gap between appointments, customers or suppliers may feel that their interests are not being looked after or they may notice a slip in service caused by the changeover. To prevent this happening, it is worth announcing details of the new appointment and the date when the new person is due to join, in a personal letter. Emphasising how much experience he has gives confidence in the competence of the person. Offering a back-up or intermediate contact is also a good idea, in case an urgent matter arises before the appointee arrives.

Thomas King & Palmer Ltd
serving the world

24 Fuller Road, Welling,
Kent DA16 7JP
Tel: (01322) 100132
Fax: (01322) 100178

Reg. No: England 1212298762
VAT No: 92905643

Mr D Jenkins
Director
Chester Wood Ltd
35 Grand Hill Road
Waverton
Chester
CH6 5FG

30 August 2005

Dear Mr Jenkins,

New General Manager

We are pleased to announce the appointment of Gerald Best as General Manager from 5 September 2005. His appointment follows the retirement, due to ill health, of Tony March, in August.

Gerald comes to us with considerable experience of marketing and he will be contacting all of our clients as soon as he arrives, to introduce himself and to deal with any queries which may arise.

We are happy to assure all of our clients of the same, continuing, high-quality service for which we are proud to enjoy such a good reputation.

Should you, however, have any urgent enquiries, please do not hesitate to contact me personally.

Yours sincerely,

Brian Moore
Director

KEEPING CUSTOMERS INFORMED

Letter 75: Personal announcement to a customer about your new position

This is one of those 'just keeping in touch' letters that is not absolutely necessary but is often welcomed by the recipient.

It can be quite a shock to 'phone a company, only to be told that the person you wish to speak to has left. Letters like this also benefit customers and suppliers, because they are kept informed about who to contact. If a new contact-name is not given, the customer may feel that your company isn't concerned to communicate with him, so why should he keep doing business with you, even though such claims may be totally unjustified?

If a lot of the goodwill in the relationship is tied up in the personal nature of the contact, it is worth bringing into the letter a comment expressing your confidence in the continuing relationship after you have left.

Wright & Simpson

157 Colder Way
Basingstoke
Hants RG21 5TG
Tel: (01256) 125907
Fax: (01256) 190986

Mr Robin Gillett
Marketing Director
Taylor Jones Ltd
23 Green St
Liverpool
L17 6HY

28 July 2005

Dear Robin,

Just a quick note to let you know that I have successfully completed my assignment at Wright & Simpson and will be taking up my new position as Director of International Business with Jackson Powell on 10 August.

I believe that Wright & Simpson has once again regained its position as one of the leading training consultancies and I am pleased to have been associated with this success.

It is also my pleasure to advise you that the General Manager's position will be filled in-house by Graham Fox; and he will be assisted by John Birch and Sheila Cox, who will be responsible for enquiries and order-processing respectively.

It has been a pleasure working with you and I am confident you will continue to enjoy a long and successful association with Wright & Simpson.

Best regards,

Stuart Davis
Consultant

Partners: EG Wright MA & FA Simpson

KEEPING CUSTOMERS INFORMED
Letter 76: Reawakening a business relationship

You may run into an old acquaintance with whom you used to do business. You would like to reawaken that business relationship. This letter attempts to bridge the gap, with a copy of the latest catalogue.

Note how the writer draws the reader's attention to the content of the catalogue, not just the fact that there is a catalogue. This device tries to tempt the reader to turn the page – and to stop her from putting the catalogue to one side.

H J KINGSLEY (NORWICH) LTD
Kingsley House, Morris Street, Norwich NR6 7JM
Tel: (01603) 117097 Fax: (01603) 117099 Reg. No: England 12086215 VAT No: 8793519

Ms Gail Wilson
Marketing Manager
Bridgewater Bright Ltd
76 Chalmers Way
Andover
Hants
SP4 7JK

28 September 2005

Dear Gail,

In conversation with your colleague Mary yesterday, it emerged that you have not had up-to-date information from us recently on our range of products. So I am putting that right immediately.

As promised, I am enclosing our newly revised catalogue, which brings you right up to date with our new products and innovations.

At the front of the catalogue are the most recent acquisitions, with a breakdown of their key features. The bestsellers follow and I am certain these will be familiar to you. At the back, we have more specialist topics, some of which are esoteric enough for the most confirmed devotees. I hope these will be of interest to you.

If you would like further information, please ring us on (01603) 117097 or fax us on (01603) 117099.

Best wishes,

Nina Davis
Marketing Manager

KEEPING CUSTOMERS INFORMED
Letter 77: Surveying customer attitudes

Gaining feedback from customers is essential. How else are you going to improve your service? Feedback from questionnaires can also provide some wonderful surprises – have you ever thought about using the favourable feedback as testimonials on future promotions? There is no more powerful seller of a product or service than a satisfied customer.

One difficulty with customer-attitude surveys is the comparatively low response they generate. A small, low-cost gift acts as an incentive and may increase the number of responses that you receive.

Grange & Turner Ltd

32 WESTBOURN ROAD, WITNEY, OXON OX6 7HY

Telephone (01993) 107888
Fax (01993) 107843

Reg. No: England 13078453
VAT No: 75698764

Mr F V Bland
Director
Taylor, Taylor & Hall
25 Glebe Lane
Darlington
Co Durham
DL6 5TG

16 June 2005

Dear Mr Bland,

As a company committed to providing a quality service, we like to keep in regular touch with your needs and your views of the products we produce and promote.

To maintain our high standard of quality products and service to you, I would be very grateful if you could complete the enclosed questionnaire.

In appreciation of your time, I shall be delighted to send you one of our superb quality Parker Pens on receipt of your completed questionnaire.

I look forward to receiving your reply and hope that we continue to be helpful to you in the future.

Yours sincerely,

Mrs A Frank
Marketing Director

KEEPING CUSTOMERS INFORMED

Letter 78: Using a customer-service exercise to revive a lapsed customer

If you find customers buying once from you but not again, it can be worthwhile conducting a customer-service exercise to find out why they are not coming back to you. This letter dresses the investigation up to make it look like an after-sales service questionnaire. If you are asking for a large chunk of time, it may be worth sending a personalised letter in advance, explaining what you want to do and why.

Note how the letter empathises with the customer: 'I appreciate this is a busy time for you...' and rather than asking her to 'phone you, announces that you will be in touch in a day or two. If you do say this, make sure not to leave it too long, so that the customer doesn't forget your letter.

H J KINGSLEY (NORWICH) LTD
Kingsley House, Morris Street, Norwich NR6 7JM
Tel: (01603) 117097 Fax: (01603) 117099 Reg. No: England 12086215 VAT No: 8793519

Ms Ruth Hope
Senior Buyer
Frank Fuller Ltd
34 Crester Street
Windrush
Oxon
OX7 9JU

3 October 2005

Dear Ruth,

I hope the last order we supplied to you was satisfactory and met your expectations.

We are currently looking at ways of improving our product range and services to our customers. I appreciate this is a busy time for you, but I wonder if you would be prepared to spend half an hour discussing the service that you have received from us; what your expectations are about the products we supply; how those expectations have been met or exceeded and where you feel there is room for improvement. I would like to cover everything from initial supply of the order to the after-sales service that you have received.

I hope you are willing to help us in this matter. If I may, I will telephone you in a day or so to fix up a convenient date for us to meet.

Yours sincerely,

Nina Davis
Marketing Manager

CHAPTER 3

Sales and marketing management

What you'll find in this chapter

✔ Sales letters that sell
✔ Requesting an agency
✔ Managing an agent's performance and conduct
✔ Handling queries about an agent's commission
✔ Notifying agents of changes
✔ Managing public relations
✔ Dealing with advertising agencies

Writing a really good sales letter that persuades customers to buy your product is one of the toughest assignments. You need to have an ear, not only for your product or service, but also for what makes your customers place their orders. Letters associated with other forms of selling are also depicted (e.g. through agencies and distributors), as well as responses to the media for information and dealings with advertising agencies.

Letters that sell

Eleven letters that are designed to sell a product or service are given here (letters 79–89). Each one takes a slightly different standpoint and picks a different approach for getting through to the customer. You have to accept that you won't get through to everyone; it's all a question of which one produces the biggest response.

Letters to agents and distributors

Handling agents is a skill of its own and operating at a distance raises the importance of letters and faxes in maintaining the lines of communications. As letters 90–105 show, many different types have to be written to agents, from simple responses to motivational letters, reprimands and dismissals, each one requiring a different tone.

Advertising agencies

When dealing with advertising agencies, a tough line is needed to make sure they stick to your instructions and don't try to get off the hook when matters don't go to plan. The secret to making sure everything goes smoothly is having instructions firmly in writing.

SALES LETTERS THAT SELL
Letter 79: Inviting the customer to visualise

'Just imagine...' is a useful tactic which can be used to plant the reader into imaginary situations as here: 'Wouldn't you love to be a fly on the wall of your competitors...'.

Note how the letter reserves underlining for the financial benefits of the service. The eye is drawn to this part of the letter first and, with the interest aroused, you are encouraged to read the complete letter.

Brendall Thomas Consultancy
Bringing Business to Business

65 Brentwood Road
Sheffield
South Yorkshire
S18 2JP
Tel: (0114) 200132
Fax: (0114) 200178

Reg. No: England 1298762122
VAT No: 56439290

16 May 2005

Dear Business Manager,

Wouldn't you love to be a fly on the wall of your competitors, finding out how they operate?

Just imagine finding out what the secrets of their success are – how they manage to do things faster and smarter. But why turn to your competitors? There are simply dozens of organisations with whom you don't compete who are willing to share their secrets with you. Secrets which could, quite literally, <u>save you thousands of pounds</u>. How?

They have discovered, through sheer hard work and experimentation, different and better ways of operating. Ways that they can pass on to you and which will have tangible results for your business. And why should they be interested in sharing their secrets with you? Because you will also have different ways of operating which will be of interest to them. It all works on the time-honoured principle of 'if you scratch my back, I'll scratch yours'.

This system, which you may know as 'benchmarking', has worked for literally hundreds of companies worldwide. At the Brendall Thomas Consultancy, we have the contacts and experience to match your business up with another like-minded firm. Step by step, we guide you through a systematic benchmarking programme that is specifically designed to deliver tangible results. Bottom-line results which will far exceed the cost to your business of implementing the programme. <u>One company found that by restructuring its despatch services it was able to save over £10,000 per annum.</u>

To find out how our benchmarking programme will improve your bottom line, call me now on (0114) 200132.

Yours faithfully,

Simon Framlington
Brendall Thomas Consultancy

PS: Remember, our results are guaranteed!

SALES LETTERS THAT SELL
Letter 80: Using the lure of large potential gains

Using the lure of what might have been 'if only' is a handy way of attracting interest, especially where the gain is spectacular. Here, it is used as an attention grabber, even though the letter goes on to mention a much more modest performance.

Tying up with another organisation to create a 'special offer' is another trick to catch people's interest. Note how the telephone number is referred to in the text, to make it easier for people to contact the writer, and how the PS urges you to call him now, even if you may only be interested later. This aims to catch a wider audience than might otherwise be reached.

RPP Holdings Plc
35/38 New Road, Paignton, Devon TQ3 4UU
Tel: 01803 175653 Fax: 01803 187908
Reg. No: England 1976143

Mr J Cox
56 Brighton Road
Reading
Berkshire
RG2 6GF

16 June 2005

Dear Investor,

If you had invested £2,000 in Yossiver shares in January, today they would be worth £9,500. However, an investment of £2,000 in Yossiver warrants in the same period would have been worth over £98,000 – a rise in excess of 4,800%!

Warrants are one of the most exciting investment opportunities available. But be warned. They are not for the faint-hearted. Without professional guidance, it is very easy to go astray. While we can guarantee that you will have an exciting time seeing some really spectacular gains, at the same time, we recommend that you hold a mixed portfolio to cushion the downside. However, our performance to date is excellent, with an average per annum return for our clients of 35%.

Now you, too, can enjoy these returns at special preferential rates to readers of Investment Today. For a limited period, if you have £5,000 or more to invest, you can take advantage of our private client expertise, for a fixed fee of £100 and 1% of the cost of transactions to buy warrants and 2% of the cost of selling transactions.

For this special rate we will:

- structure a balanced portfolio to suit your needs;
- provide expert guidance on the performance of warrants;
- advise on new exciting opportunities;
- handle all the documentation on your behalf.

Whether you are a seasoned investor or would just like to dip your toe into the market for the first time, call me now on 01803 175653 for a confidential discussion about how we can open up these opportunities to you.

Yours faithfully,

Tony Granger
Marketing Manager

PS: Call me now, even if you may not be interested until later.

SALES LETTERS THAT SELL
Letter 81: Using a force-free trial to increase response

This is a useful sales technique when you are trying to sell something which the customer cannot see. People are naturally reluctant to subscribe to a service unseen. Getting the product in front of the potential customer increases confidence and the propensity to buy.

Incentives are also used to increase the desire for the product. Note also the tone used in this letter – it is very confident, which, combined with its enthusiasm for the product, should engender customer-confidence in the product.

SIMPSON & MARTIN

39 TOP STREET
STOKE-ON-TRENT
ST2 3DR, UNITED KINGDOM
Tel: (01782) 156232 Fax: (01782) 120899

Reg. No: England 96223978 VAT No: 91210674

22 November 2005

Dear Business Manager,

The best way to tell you about **Business Now** is to show it to you. So here, with my compliments, is an issue for you to see.

Business Now is packed with practical advice for busy managers. It's brief, succinct and to the point. It delivers tried and tested techniques and shortcuts *that work*. To save you time, money and hassle again and again.

It's published every fortnight; sifting and distilling the latest ideas from the ever-growing mountain of management publications and seminars available. Covering just about every aspect of your work as a manager of time, people and resources.

There's no waffle ... no padding ... no advertisements.

Just practical, valuable tips and tactics that you can lift right off the page and put to work in your job. And it's delivered direct to your desk every two weeks, 24 issues a year.

Take a look yourself – I'm sure you'll find some ideas in this issue that you can use at once.

What's more, join now and we will send you **absolutely FREE (a saving of £19.95), Dirty Negotiating Tactics and Their Solutions**, one of the most popular reports ever produced, which exposes 39 underhand tactics that suppliers may try to use against you while negotiating. We expose every one – and show you how to counter them.

I've also enclosed a copy of the latest Business Now index – listing hundreds of different topics Business Now has tackled over the last six months. I'm certain you'll find it packed with articles that will interest you.

To get your own, regular issue of Business Now, simply fax back the yellow order form enclosed on 01782 120899. I look forward to welcoming you as a subscriber.

Yours faithfully,

Andrew Clifford
Marketing Manager

PS: Reply before 30 November and we'll also send you a superb compact calculator in addition to your Special Bonus Report worth £19.95. So hurry – fax me now!

SALES LETTERS THAT SELL
Letter 82: Using curiosity to arouse interest

If you make people curiosity, they will want to know more. This sales letter is unusual in that the nature of the business is kept secret. To find out more, you have to buy the book. There is a money-back guarantee, so customers will have nothing to lose.

It also uses the technique of painting an attractive image that assumes you have already put the plan into action and reaped the results – which is often the hardest part of all – yet it makes it sound so easy – you don't need much money or time.

Note how it also succeeds in overcoming many objections and suspicions that people may harbour: 'If it is so great, why give the secret away?'.

Grange & Turner Ltd
32 WESTBOURN ROAD, WITNEY, OXON OX6 7HY

Telephone (01993) 107888
Fax (01993) 107843
Reg. No: England 13078453
VAT No: 75698764

Mr A C R Lloyd
3 Black Horse Lane
Kings Heath
Birmingham
B14 5TG

14 February 2005

Dear Mr Lloyd,

Would you like to earn over £15,000 by working in your spare time from home? Or much more if you work longer? This plan shows you precisely how to do it.

The only premises you need – your home. The only start-up money – £500. The only time you need (once the business is set up and running) is around two hours a day telling others what to do.

Is this just an unproven idea? No! This plan gives you full details of a specific business. It tells you how to set it up. Where to buy your supplies. Who to go to for help. It names names. It shows you how to find others to do the selling required for you – and why you should not do it yourself. It shows you why no experience is necessary – indeed, previous experience has been found to be a real disadvantage.

And above all, it works! There are already people up and down the country making money from this type of business. For example, there is an ex-sales manager for a car manufacturer. He started this business ten years ago when the author introduced him to the idea. He has been making good money ever since.

So why haven't I told you what this business is about? The answer is that it needs a full description before you can fairly judge. Since I heard about this business and read the book I have told many friends about it. As soon as I outline the business they automatically bring all their preconceived notions to bear. They at once think of other businesses which at first sight appear very similar – businesses which are not outstandingly profitable and which really do need great expertise.

It is not until I have had the chance to describe the whole plan in detail that these initial negatives are cleared away. Then it becomes clear just how great an opportunity for money-making it is. And that no experience at all is a positive advantage – because there is no tendency to tinker with the system to make 'improvements'.

If it is so great, why give the secret away? Well, this is the sort of business which could be set up anywhere. There is room for thousands up and down the country – so the author loses nothing by offering his secret.

Sounds too good to be true? Judge for yourself, it is on ten days' free approval. So you can delve into the programme as soon as you receive it and weigh it up for yourself. When you have read this book from cover to cover you too will be convinced that the plan does work.

Yours sincerely,

J P Parsons
Marketing Director

PS: Do you want to get rich? Are you prepared to take risks?

SALES LETTERS THAT SELL
Letter 83: Seeking new business with a personalised letter

If you offer a product to someone with whom you have had no personal dealings before, you have, at first, nothing in common. You are often left searching around for points of mutual interest.

The pain of searching for that common ground can be reduced if you are able to demonstrate a mutual acquaintance. It does, at least, give you a topic of conversation to build upon, and is considerably easier than appearing to be just another salesperson on the make. If you can get referrals like this, seize them.

IDENDEN INDUSTRIES
A division of Idenden Plc
Porter House, Hull HU7 4RF, England

Tel 01482 119087 Fax 01482 119088
Registered in England No: 1218943

Mr A Begoyu
Managing Director
News Today – Teban Kian Pte Ltd
BLK 31 Heng Gardens Road,
Tampines Industrial Park
5100 Kuala Lumpur
Malaysia

16 February 2005

Dear Mr Begoyu,

I have been advised by John Williams of Newspaper Supplies Limited that you may be interested in web offset news black.

We have in the past supplied New Independent as well as many other newspapers in Malaysia and, therefore, we feel fully confident that our product will be suitable for your requirements. I believe that we can offer competitive prices at £1.10 per kg C & F for 11,000kg and approximately £1.06 per kg for 15,000kg. If you find this of interest, please advise and we will send to you the necessary proforma invoices.

I enclose our brochure, outlining some of the major products which we are able to supply. You may also be interested to learn that we have recently obtained the Agency for Malaysia from the company who have taken over from Hill & Webb, to manufacture gravure ink. If, therefore, you require any prices for cigarette carton inks which were previously supplied by Hill & Webb, we will be happy to quote for these.

I look forward to hearing from you with regard to any of our printing products.

Yours sincerely,

Richard Russell
International Sales Director

SALES LETTERS THAT SELL
Letter 84: Outlining services on offer

This is a good letter to write when making an approach to a company out of the blue.

It doesn't pressurise the customer at all. It sets out the services on offer clearly and concisely and uses the company brochure that had been left earlier as an excuse for following up the enquiry.

It also highlights the benefits that many businesses may not automatically think about: that wasted space may be costing them more than they think.

GKT Products Ltd, Unit 10, Castleway Lane, Alloway, Ayr, KA7 4BE
Telephone (01292) 177900 Fax (01292) 199855   Reg. No: 17964583 VAT No: 679845

Mrs N Hall
Purchasing Manager
Johnson & Cole Ltd
226 Mill Road
Hawick
Roxboroughshire
TD9 8UK

16 April 2005

Dear Mrs Hall,

On a recent visit to your company, I left for your attention our company brochure, and this letter is to outline our service, which may be of interest to you.

GKT Products Ltd specialise in the design, supply and installation of commercial and industrial partitioning, suspended ceilings, raised-access flooring and mezzanine storage platforms. We also supply and install all types of shelving and racking, as authorised distributors for the major manufacturers. We can, therefore, offer a complete and comprehensive service should you be considering, now, or in the future, developing your existing facility.

Many companies have benefited from our expertise in assisting with redesign of office and factory space, and making the best use of wasted space, which is, invariably, costing money.

We fully understand that, in the current economic climate, expenditure on these items may not be a priority, but, with the benefit of professional advice, it is possible to make savings by careful planning and design. As licensed credit brokers, we can also offer a full leasing service on our products. By taking advantage of this, you can spread payment over varying terms to suit your budget; cash-flow is protected by not having to pay fully upon completion of the work, and leasing is subject to 100% tax relief.

If you are interested in our services, for current or future purposes, please do not hesitate to contact us. We will provide, absolutely free of charge and without obligation, detailed costings and designs to assist you in your future planning.

If, for some reason, you did not receive our brochure, please let me know and one will be sent to you without delay. I look forward to hearing from you.

Yours sincerely,

Garry Stream
Sales Manager

SALES LETTERS THAT SELL
Letter 85: Using a testimonial to gain interest

A letter that aims to sell the benefits of an organisation is not easy to make original. There are so many sales letters landing on people's desks that the potential buyer can quickly become immune to the messages being sent. Or he may feel that what is being said is just sales talk from the company, which may stop him responding.

This letter takes a different tack. Demonstrating that you have a host of satisfied customers proves more than simply saying 'our product is the best'. It is sufficient to make the reader sit up and think about what you are saying. At the very least, it gives him someone to contact to get a reference from. If you do use this approach, make sure you obtain the permission of the people mentioned in the letter.

16 George Street, Woodbridge,
Suffolk IP3 7KL
Tel: (01394) 198423
Fax: (01394) 198444
Registered in England: 91221299
VAT No. 919129075 80

Fenner & Sons

Mr J Jenkins
Training Manager
A M Clifton Ltd
18 Coltsfield
Royston
Herts
SG8 9LK

16 May 2005

Dear Mr Jenkins,

Who are Fenner & Sons and why are we writing to you?

Fenner & Sons is a team of professional trainers, dedicated to helping management teams operate more effectively through tailor-made courses that enhance and perfect personal skills. Our courses really can help you:

- deliver professional presentations every time;
- negotiate to win;
- gain an extra ten hours a week.

But you don't have to take our word for it. Ask Janice Mitchell at BT, Kay Lewis at Smiths Accountants, John Allen at Anglian Water, Marcia Cavendish at Campbell and Young and Tim Free at Johnsons.

They all come to us regularly because we give them exactly what they ask for. Tailor-made training that develops the personal skills of their management teams – helping them to achieve what they want in their businesses.

Ask them about our understanding of these skills; our attention to detail; how we get the best out of you and, most importantly, the results in enhanced team performance. Janice Mitchell will be able to tell you how she saved BT thousands of pounds by using just one of the negotiating tactics she learned in the day.

And don't forget to ask them about the cost – I am sure you will then be convinced that our courses offer the most cost-effective way of training teams. If you are not entirely satisfied that the course was value for money, we will even give you your money back. So what have you got to lose? Don't delay. For a confidential, no-commitment chat, call me now on 01394 198423.

Yours sincerely,

Roger Harvey

PS: Don't forget our money-back guarantee. No other training company is willing to go this far to guarantee your satisfaction!

SALES LETTERS THAT SELL
Letter 86: Selling on enthusiasm, immediacy and personal attention

This letter uses the sense that you are being let in on a secret here, something that is new and incredible. This sense of curiosity is built up by 'Just a quick note to let you know...'. Having it come from an enthusiastic devotee of the product, rather than the publisher, gives the endorsement greater weight and credibility in the eyes of the reader. Note how this personal enthusiasm is sustained in phrases such as '...that make the guide, for me, utterly irresistible'.

There is also a nice grouping of words that add power and persuasion in phrases like: '...quickly and confidently check and challenge...'. The persuasive manner is sustained to the end with the urgent 'Do have a look at it...'. A subtle touch is deployed in the PS: calling the brochure a 'working draft' adds to the sense of immediacy and urgency, by implying that the writer couldn't wait to let you know about the new book.

SIMPSON & MARTIN

39 TOP STREET
STOKE-ON-TRENT
ST2 3DR, UNITED KINGDOM
Tel: (01782) 156232 Fax: (01782) 120899
Reg. No: England 96223978 VAT No: 91210674

1 July 2005

Dear Business Manager,

The Insider Guide to Bank Lending

Just a quick note to let you know that 'The Insider Guide to Bank Lending' has just arrived from the printers and it is so extraordinarily revealing that I felt I must personally urge you to take a look at it.

I wouldn't expect you or any senior manager to discuss your company's finances with people outside the organisation – but I defy anyone to look through 'The Insider Guide to Bank Lending' and still be confident that he is getting the best deal from his bank. It reveals things non-bankers simply don't know about banks. It is bound to confirm some suspicions you have and it will blow away some seriously wrong assumptions.

But, critically, you can now see where and how you can negotiate down the costs, fees and charges we had all been encouraged to believe were written in stone.

It really is the most extraordinarily revealing guide to the way banks and bankers make lending decisions for business. I find the implications for the shift in negotiating power from the banks back to the customer very heartening indeed. For under £200, this heavyweight guide has the potential to save many businesses thousands. I am convinced it will be able to do the same for your business.

Incidentally, it also has over 400 pages of interest-rate tables and explanatory notes that make the guide, for me, utterly irresistible. The way the bank arrives at its figures has always been a frustrating mystery. Its numbers never seemed quite to tally with mine. There is only so much time and energy you can give when the individual instances are not that large. But they do mount up.

The interest-rate tables explain exactly what is going on and, for the first time, you can now quickly and confidently check and challenge the bank's figures. You might also discover some instances where you just could be better off on a different type of loan.

I have enclosed a copy of the brochure we are preparing for 'The Insider Guide to Bank Lending'. Do have a look at it – I am sure you will see why I am so enthusiastic about this book and why I felt it was important to write to you immediately about it.

Yours faithfully,

Andrew Clifford
Marketing Manager

PS: Although the enclosed brochure is still our working draft, please feel free to use it to order your copy.

SALES LETTERS THAT SELL
Letter 87: Telling a story to grab attention

Capturing attention is one of the main ingredients of success with sales letters. Everyone likes a story – particularly one that arouses your curiosity and makes you want to read on. It is, therefore, a style that fits naturally with letters that sell.

Here, a semi-tragic story is used to arouse emotional feelings in the reader that will make him respond with a donation to the charity. The appealing to emotion is sustained with phrases like: '...go a little way to help...'; '...find the heart to help...' and 'It's not a lot to ask'.

Save the Kids in Rio Mission
114 St Vincents Street, LONDON N3 9GH England
Tel: (020) 7115 1280 Fax: (020) 7115 1811
Registered Charity No: 4577606

Mr J Garfield
Hill Rise
High Street
Milton Keynes
MK12 7HY

15 April 2005

Dear Mr Garfield,

Three years ago Pablo, a nine-year-old child, was left on the streets of Rio to die. He was turned out by his parents, who were too poor to look after him. For over a year, he managed to eke out a living by begging on the streets. But it was no life - every day was a nightmare of survival - just to get enough to eat. With nowhere to live and nowhere to sleep it could hardly get worse. Except for Pablo it did.

One day, Pablo found himself 'in the way' of a group of other boys, scarcely older than himself, who decided that he was 'on their patch'. A fight ensued in which Pablo received several stab wounds from a six-inch blade and was left to die in a gutter. Pablo had done no wrong. He had committed no crime. His only fault was to be in the wrong place at the wrong time. Luckily for Pablo, a helper from the Save the Kids in Rio Mission was walking along the street seconds after the attack happened. Without this miracle of timing, Pablo would now be dead.

Today, thanks to the Save the Kids in Rio Mission, Pablo has recovered from his wounds. And although his life is still no bed of roses, he does at least receive enough to eat, he has a place to sleep safely and he has started to learn to read and write.

The sad fact is that every year hundreds of kids like Pablo are needlessly dying on the streets of Rio. But the good news is that the Save the Kids in Rio Mission are doing just that – saving them. We can't cure the problem, but we can go a little way to help and that is what we are asking you to do. Not to cure the problem, but to go just a little way to help the hundreds of kids like Pablo that we manage to save each year.

I hope that you will be able to find the heart to help Pablo – £15 will provide Pablo and others like him with enough food for two months. It's not a lot to ask. Of course, if you would like to sponsor a child under the Save the Kids in Rio scheme, then we can send you a full information pack, telling you how you can save a life. Just tick the box on the enclosed reply-paid envelope and send it back to us.

Yours sincerely,

H A Hart
Appeals Manager

PS: Remember, £15 is all it takes to feed Pablo for two months.

SALES LETTERS THAT SELL
Letter 88: Encouraging a customer to renew a subscription

If customers are subscribing to a service, at some point they may actively have to renew their subscriptions.

Never take it for granted that they will continue. Instead, treat a renewal letter as an opportunity to remind them of the benefits they are receiving from their subscription and to sell the idea to them again. If they are undecided whether to renew, it could be enough to tip the balance in your favour.

Here, incentives of lower subscriptions and the chance to win a free safari are used to sustain subscribers' interests.

Wildlife Today
11 Courtney Way, Evesham, Worcestershire WR11 3RF
Registered in England No: 39789622 VAT No: 911674210

Mr M Little
1 Chelmwood Road
Lincoln
LN6 7JU

7 May 2005

Dear Mr Little,

Your subscription to Wildlife Today will be expiring within the next three months.

I am sure that you wish to avoid the irritation of an interrupted delivery and the inconvenience of missed issues. To help us avoid this, please return the attached Renewal Invoice, together with your cheque or credit card authorisation, as soon as possible.

This may seem excessively early to remind you, but it helps us to keep your issues flowing. The sooner we receive your renewal, the sooner you can rest assured your magazines will keep coming.

Remember, subscribing for three years will save you a staggering 50% off the cover price, 45% off two years and 40% for one year. Now, isn't that unbeatable value?

You can also have the chance to win a free safari to Kenya. To take advantage of this opportunity, all you need to do is to complete the enclosed questionnaire, which is designed to tell us what you think about Wildlife Today, and return it with your renewal payment advice.

Yours sincerely,

D A Cross
Editor

PS: Don't forget to enclose the customer questionnaire with your payment advice. Without it you will not be eligible for our free prize draw to win a safari to Kenya.

SALES LETTERS THAT SELL
Letter 89: Following up a meeting to solicit new business

Meetings present good opportunities to develop contacts and demonstrate the services that you can offer. Their difficulty is that they tend to be ephemeral and quickly forgotten.

Follow up with a letter, though, and you are doubling your impact on the person you met, giving a more lasting way of remembering you. It also demonstrates your professionalism and interest in him.

You won't get results from this type of letter all the time, but, from the ones that you do, it could well have been the follow-up letter that made all the difference.

 Kelso Limited
16 Abbots Road, Luton, Bedfordshire MK44 7YT
Tel: (01234) 136953 Fax: (01234) 136422
Registered in England No: 9126719 VAT No: 91523489 76

Mr T Collins
J T Cunningham & Co
74 Bridgend
Maidstone
Kent

17 April 2005

Dear Tony,

It was a pleasure to meet you yesterday, especially as our only previous contact was a dim and distant conversation by 'phone.

I confirm that we would be delighted to help with your computing needs, when the time is right for you. As promised, I enclose a summary of the computing services we can offer, which have been created and driven entirely by the needs of our customers.

The situation you described and your experiences with mainframe computing have a familiar ring. Your ideas on the PC approach would be well worth pursuing and I am certain we would be able to give you access to your data in the way you want, on either an interim or a long-term basis.

As I mentioned, William Smith is our computer specialist and he would be very happy to look at the situation with you in due course, to see what might be done.

In the meantime, if you have any queries, please give me a ring.

Best wishes,

Colin Frost
Sales Manager

REQUESTING AN AGENCY
Letter 90: Declining a distributor's offer

The company here could have decided to play one company off against the other, to negotiate the best deal for itself. It has, though, developed considerable goodwill and trust with Morplan, whom it finds satisfactory. It is therefore unwilling to jeopardise that relationship and decides to decline the other offer. Note how it makes a positive suggestion with the line 'I am sure Morplan would be pleased to supply you with stocks'.

IDENDEN INDUSTRIES
A division of Idenden Plc
Porter House, Hull HU7 4RF, England

Tel 01482 119087 Fax 01482 119088
Registered in England No: 1218943

Tony Fuller
Marketing Manager
BSG Ltd
19 West Walk
Wallsend
Tyne & Wear
NE28 7DF

16 March 2005

Dear Tony,

Thank you for your letter dated 10 March, regarding Idenden Seal distribution for Europe.

Currently, Morplan are distributing this product for us in Europe and we are presently discussing a sole agency deal with them. In the circumstances, I must turn down your request. If you consider the opportunity for the Idenden Seal in Europe is important to you, I am sure Morplan would be pleased to supply you with stocks.

Thank you for your interest in our range of products.

Yours sincerely,

Peter Collins
Marketing Director

REQUESTING AN AGENCY
Letter 91: Asking for an agency

Obtaining representation of a company's products is a highly competitive business. It is a relatively easy field to enter so there can be many players in a market. The one factor that people will be looking out for, though, is performance. If you can demonstrate your advantage and success, you should at least get the opportunity to make a presentation to a business.

This letter uses a combination of gentle flattery: 'I am very impressed by their versatility...' and a clear demonstration of results: 'In the last three years we have increased the value of our sales in Europe by over 150%'. The overall tone is one of crisp professionalism and would certainly help to open many doors.

Thomas King
& Palmer Ltd
serving the world

24 Fuller Road, Welling,
Kent DA16 7JP
Tel: (01322) 100132
Fax: (01322) 100178

Reg. No: England 1212298762
VAT No: 92905643

Mr P George
Marketing Manager
Norton & Brand Ltd
Hall Farm Ind. Est.
Wallington
Surrey
SM6 7HJ

16 July 2005

Dear Mr George,

I recently saw details of your company's range of conference, presentation and planning products. I am very impressed by their versatility, design and practicality.

We act as European agents for a select number of companies that produce presentation equipment. Instead of selling through stationers and office suppliers, we sell products direct to the end user. Our customers are large and medium-sized companies throughout mainland Europe. In the last three years we have increased the value of our sales in Europe by over 150%.

Over 1,000 major European companies do business with us every year and our team of representatives visits each of them regularly. The secret to our rapid increase in sales is that we offer a faster supply and more personal service than our competitors. This simple formula, combined with the professionalism of our representatives, has made us the leading agent in the mainland European market.

I would like to discuss acting for you in this market and hope you can agree to an early meeting. I can be contacted on 01322 100132.

I look forward to hearing from you.

Yours sincerely,

Helen Bye
European Sales Manager

REQUESTING AN AGENCY
Letter 92: Accepting an agency – outlining the terms

It is important that you engage in a formal agreement with an agent or distributor. This letter precedes the agreement and outlines the terms and procedures governing the agency.

It serves the purpose of pre-empting awkward issues that may have been overlooked or misunderstood in the course of discussions and which still need to be ironed out.

The layout is clear and numbering paragraphs gives the recipient a reference point, if he needs to refer to it in a reply.

IDENDEN INDUSTRIES
A division of Idenden Plc
Porter House, Hull HU7 4RF, England

Tel 01482 119087 Fax 01482 119088
Registered in England No: 1218943

Herr Gunter Mann
Stepham Meins and Co
Burgstr 18
D-87600 Kaufbeuren
Germany

7 January 2005

Dear Gunter,

Agency – North Western Europe

I am pleased to confirm your appointment as agent for north-western Europe. A formal contract will be drawn up this week, but I would like to clarify the main points that we agreed.

1. **Period of appointment.** Your appointment will be for an initial trial period of four months. At the end of the trial period, we shall review the performance of the agency. Thereafter, if either party wishes to terminate the agency, three months' notice must be given in writing to the other side, subject to issues regarding the solvency of either party, which will be specified in the formal agreement.

2. **Territory.** The territory of your agency will be north-western Europe. This will include, specifically, the countries of: Belgium, Netherlands, Luxembourg, Germany and Switzerland. We will not appoint any other agents to these countries during the term of our agreement.

3. **Targets.** You will achieve a minimum sales target within the first year of £500,000 of business. If this target is not met, we reserve the right to terminate the agency. The target will be reviewed on 1 January each year. If a new target is not agreed by either party, the new target that will apply will be the current target plus five per cent.

4. **Commission.** You will be paid by commission only and receive ten per cent of the invoiced value of the goods sold by your agency. All credit notes issued in respect of invoices will be deducted from the invoiced value, for the purposes of calculating the commission. With the following exceptions, all costs and expenses will be borne by your agency:
   - Travel to and from the United Kingdom at the company's request.
   - Accommodation expenses for overnight stays in the United Kingdom required by the company.

REQUESTING AN AGENCY
Letter 92: Accepting an agency – outlining the terms (continued)

5. Procedure and payment. We will send you a copy of all purchase orders received and invoices issued for sales made in your territory. At the end of each month, you will send us a statement of the commission which is owing on sales made within the calendar month, quoting the correct invoice number, invoice total and commission claimed. We will pay your statement within ten days of its receipt.

6. Representation. All representations that you make to customers will be within the guidelines laid down in our conditions of sale. You will not have any right to negotiate terms outside our normal, standard terms without the written permission of the Sales Manager. You will not have the right to enter into any contract in our name. All contracts with customers will be between the company and the customer. You will not, during the period of this agency, represent any of our competitors or any product which competes with the sales of our products.

7. Law. Our agreement will be made under English law.

This covers the main points of our agreement. A detailed contract will be drawn up within the week, but if you have any queries or concerns about any of the items confirmed, please let me know as soon as possible.

Yours sincerely,

Bill Tanner
European Marketing Director

REQUESTING AN AGENCY
Letter 93: Declining an agency but offering distribution

The supplying company for whom Mr Smith is planning to act wants to try to persuade him not to take up an agency status (supplying orders and earning commission), but to become a distributor, who would take stock on a consignment basis to sell.

Note how the supplying company tries to persuade Mr Smith to accept this offer. It is phrased initially as a gentle suggestion: 'I wonder if you might be interested in becoming...'. The proposal is supported by a reasonable and logical argument: 'It seems that if you are already handling the distribution for Hermann's, our product range would complement it well'.

The supplier then appears to deal with one of the main objections that Mr Smith might raise: 'We would be prepared to supply the range to you on consignment...'. The reader is gently persuaded to consider the offer.

RPP Holdings Plc
35/38 New Road, Paignton, Devon TQ3 4UU
Tel: 01803 175653 Fax: 01803 187908
Reg. No: England 1976143

Mr T G Smith
22 Rue De La Cambre
B2100 Brussels
Belgium

26 June 2005

Dear Mr Smith,

Further to my letter of 13 June and our telephone conversation about you becoming a European agent for RPP, I have the following suggestion to make.

We have discussed this in some detail and, while we are keen to create new opportunities for our products in international markets, we have decided that we do not have the resources to give our customers a level of service that they need and expect. The delays which would inevitably occur in supplying individual customers on the continent from the UK, combined with the additional costs of delivering single orders, does not make it feasible for us to contemplate a commission-only agency.

I wonder if you might be interested in becoming a distributor for us instead? It seems that if you are already handling the distribution for Hermann's, our product range would complement it well. We would be prepared to supply the range to you on consignment, rather than asking you to purchase the goods on your account, which would reduce the risk for you.

Please let me know if this arrangement is of interest to you and perhaps we can then meet to discuss the details further.

Yours sincerely,

P F Davis
Director

MANAGING AN AGENT'S PERFORMANCE AND CONDUCT
Letter 94: Thanking an agent for obtaining some business

This is a straightforward thank-you letter for some business that has been obtained. These kinds of letters help to build goodwill amongst business colleagues and encourage further deals. It costs nothing to say 'Thank you for your time and effort on our behalf' and 'Thank you again for your assistance...'. It can be worth more than the ten per cent commission that has been paid here.

GKT Products Ltd, Unit 10, Castleway Lane, Alloway, Ayr, KA7 4BE
Telephone (01292) 177900 Fax (01292) 199855   Reg. No: 17964583 VAT No: 679845

Ms Claire Norman
Tuttle & Parkin Ltd
29 High Road West
Stranraer
DG9 7TG

13 December 2005

Dear Claire,

It was a pleasure to meet with you at Falkirk Fashions just prior to Christmas and we are pleased to advise you that Mr Fitzsimmons has ordered one of the bottom-seal units – unfortunately, we missed out on two units. However, it is good to get one. Thank you for your time and effort on our behalf.

We hope to deliver the unit during the first week of February and, we hope, those of Mr Fitzsimmons colleagues in the clothing industry who use sellotape to close bags might also be interested, if Mr Fitzsimmons' bottom-seal unit proves to be a success.

As mentioned to you prior to our visit, we will reserve you a commission of ten per cent against this sale.

Thank you again for your assistance and all good wishes for a successful 2006.

Yours sincerely,

Paul Fisher
Marketing Manager

MANAGING AN AGENT'S PERFORMANCE AND CONDUCT
Letter 95: Motivating an agent with an extra discount for higher sales

Increasing the capacity of agents to earn more is a big motivating factor for them. Recognition plays a part too, and this letter combines both elements.

The agent of the year award provides recognition, but recognition is given in the letter as well: 'I am confident it is going to give us our best year ever. Your role in this is, of course, pivotal. In recognition of this...'. The prospect of a hefty bonus if a target is met gives the monetary incentive to perform.

Fenner & Sons

16 George Street, Woodbridge,
Suffolk IP3 7KL
Tel: (01394) 198423
Fax: (01394) 198444
Registered in England: 91221299
VAT No: 919129075 80

Craig Scott
P C Wright Ltd
4 Nightingale Way
Skipton
North Yorkshire

19 December 2005

Dear Craig,

Congratulations. You came very close to achieving our agent of the year award for an outstanding performance but John Wills in the south-west pipped you to the post. I wish you every success in achieving this accolade next year.

In the last 12 months, you have achieved 1,200 unit sales with a total value of £600,000. As the latest edition of our catalogue shows, we have an excellent range of new products for this forthcoming year. I am confident it is going to give us our best year ever. Your role in this is, of course, pivotal. In recognition of this, I would like to readjust our terms with you. You are currently receiving a flat eight per cent commission on all sales achieved in your territory. I would like to maintain that flat rate with you, but if you achieve £750,000 sales value or more within the 12 months commencing 1 January, we shall award you a bonus of two per cent on the value of all sales achieved within the year. The bonus shall be payable one month after the end of the calendar year. However, if the value of sales does not reach £750,000, the bonus will not be payable.

I hope you have a very successful and prosperous New Year.

Yours sincerely,

Mark Turner
Sales Director

MANAGING AN AGENT'S PERFORMANCE AND CONDUCT
Letter 96: Complaining to an agent who is acting beyond his powers

If the mark has been overstepped, a severe rap on the knuckles is called for, to bring an agent back into line.

Note how the severity of the tone develops over successive phrases: 'Our agreement expressly forbids you...'; 'You have not had the authority...'; '...your failure to notify us...'; '...caused us considerable embarrassment...'; '...nearly jeopardised our relations....' And rises to a crescendo in the final paragraph: 'Your conduct in this matter has been extremely disappointing...'; '...you must, in future, adhere strictly...' and '...we shall have no option but to terminate....'

The letter conveys the depth of the writer's feelings but, despite its sternness, retains a calm tone.

IDENDEN INDUSTRIES
A division of Idenden Plc
Porter House, Hull HU7 4RF, England

Tel 01482 119087 Fax 01482 119088
Registered in England No: 1218943

Pierre Balan
Director General
Roodebeek Associates
Ev Swedenlann 7
B-2100 Brussels
Belgium

11 November 2005

Dear Pierre,

Re: Hermann's of Hannover
We have been contacted by Hermann's of Hannover with regard to the discount given on their latest invoice. This was for a batch of items which you had sold to them on your last visit. Their complaint is that they have not received the special discount which was promised when you sold the goods to them. They have supported their claim with a copy of a fax from you, which confirms your agreement to increase the discount to them by ten per cent. This is enclosed.

Our agreement expressly forbids you to negotiate discount terms unless they have been otherwise agreed in writing between us, prior to discussing them with the customer. You have not had the authority to grant an extra discount and, furthermore, your failure to notify us of your agreement has caused us considerable embarrassment with what is one of our most important European customers. It also nearly jeopardised our relations with them, since they were expecting to receive this additional discount not only on this order, but also on all future orders as well. Fortunately, they have been understanding on the issue and, while we have agreed to the extra discount on this invoice, our terms will revert to the original discount agreed on all future business placed by them.

Your conduct in this matter has been extremely disappointing and if we are to continue with your agency, you must, in future, adhere strictly to the letter of our agreement. We are prepared to give you another chance, but if there is another serious breach, we shall have no option but to terminate the agreement.

Yours sincerely,

Bill Tanner
European Marketing Director

MANAGING AN AGENT'S PERFORMANCE AND CONDUCT
Letter 97: Reprimanding an agent who is working for a competitor

This letter is threatening strong action to be taken unless the agent ceases to act for a competitor.

The company would be within its rights to terminate the agreement immediately. However, it is prepared to give the agent a second chance because of the '...exemplary performance...' which he has shown.

Note the opening, which doesn't declare how the news reached him (something that the agent will be curious to know) but just states, quite simply: 'It has come to my attention....'

IDENDEN INDUSTRIES
A division of Idenden Plc
Porter House, Hull HU7 4RF, England

Tel 01482 119087 Fax 01482 119088
Registered in England No: 1218943

Pierre Balan
Director General
Roodebeek Associates
Ev Swedenlann 7
B-2100 Brussels
Belgium

11 November 2005

Dear Pierre,

Re: Hugh Murphy Limited

It has come to my attention that you are acting as an agent for one of our competitors, Hugh Murphy Limited.

As you know, the terms of our agreement expressly forbid you either to act for any of our competitors or to promote or sell any product or item which may be construed by us as competing with our products. Although we have every right to cancel your agreement, because of your exemplary performance to date, we are prepared to give you a second chance. I would, though, like your written assurance that you will not in future act for this or any other competitor of ours. If you are in any doubt about whether a company is a competitor or not, would you please discuss the matter with me personally.

If you feel that you are unable to generate sufficient business from our range of products or to give the assurance requested, then we shall have no option but to cancel our agreement and look for an alternative agent.

I look forward to hearing from you.

Yours sincerely,

Bill Tanner
European Marketing Director

MANAGING AN AGENT'S PERFORMANCE AND CONDUCT
Letter 98: Explaining why agency powers have been exceeded

When such a stern reprimand has been received and the accusations are completely erroneous, the denial must be equally strong to carry sufficient weight. This is achieved with a series of firm phrases: 'I was very disturbed...'; '...I wish to deny in the strongest terms possible...'; 'I am well aware of the restrictions to which I am bound...' and '...would not dream of stepping beyond the powers...'.

Roodebeek
Associates

Roodebeek Associates
Ev Swedenlann 7
B-2100 Brussels
Belgium
Tel: 2 7567001
Fax: 2 7569400

Bill Tanner
European Marketing Director
Idenden Industries
Porter House
Hull
HU7 4RF
England

24 November 2005

Dear Bill,

Re: Hermann's of Hannover
I was very disturbed to receive your letter concerning the Hermann's account.

Firstly, I wish to deny in the strongest terms possible that I ever consented to giving them an additional ten per cent discount. It is true that their previous buyer, who was there for only two months, had requested more discount from me, but I refused to budge on the issue, referring him to yourself.

The fax which you copied to me is a forgery. I have never written such a letter. I am well aware of the restrictions to which I am bound in my agreement with you and would not dream of stepping beyond the powers which you have granted to me. If you compare the signature with my own, I think you will realise how different the two are. The typeface is also not one which I use in my correspondence.

I understand the buyer with whom I dealt was subsequently sacked for theft and incompetence just two months after he had been appointed to the position. I can only imagine that it was this buyer who perpetrated this deception out of spite and that fax has lain dormant in the file, before being discovered by the new buyer.

I will aim to arrange a meeting next week with their new buyer to discuss this matter, which is as disturbing to me as it is to you.

Yours sincerely,

Pierre Balan
Director General

MANAGING AN AGENT'S PERFORMANCE AND CONDUCT
Letter 99: Dismissing an agent for working for a competitor

Dismissing an agent who has breached a contract requires a little thought. You need to make sure that you are acting completely within your rights, in case the agent decides to bring an action for damages against you.

This letter records the story word for word, making sure that the steps that have been taken can be defended, even if the agent decided to bring legal action. Note how the letter mentions the meeting at which he was '...unable to give us a satisfactory reason...' why he had been working for a competitor. The fact there has been '...previous misconduct...' will also support the claim.

This letter should deter the agent from bringing an action against the company for wrongful dismissal (if he was considering it) as well as act as a record of what happened.

IDENDEN INDUSTRIES
A division of Idenden Plc
Porter House, Hull HU7 4RF, England

Tel 01482 119087 Fax 01482 119088
Registered in England No: 1218943

Pierre Balan
Director General
Roodebeek Associates
Ev Swedenlann 7
B-2100 Brussels
Belgium

20 December 2005

Dear Pierre,

Re: Johnson Murray Ltd

It has been brought to my attention that once again you are acting for a competitor of ours, in direct contravention of our agreement.

At our meeting today, you were unable to give us a satisfactory reason why you have been acting for Johnson Murray Ltd at the same time as for ourselves. I would also like to remind you that, on 12 November, you admitted to having worked for Hugh Murphy Ltd at the same time as for us. In your letter of 13 November, you gave us your written assurances that you would not act for any competitor, under any circumstances, while you were acting as our agent.

In view of your previous misconduct, and clause 6b of our agreement, which forbids you to act for any of our competitors, I regard this as a serious breach of our contract and have no alternative but to cancel our agreement with immediate effect.

Yours sincerely,

Bill Tanner
European Marketing Director

HANDLING QUERIES ABOUT AN AGENT'S COMMISSION
Letter 100: Recommending that prices be reduced

You should always remember that agents have a lot more to offer than simply to generate sales. Being on the ground gives them a unique perspective on the market. They are far closer to customers than anyone in a head office and will be able to judge more easily how they are reacting to the products on offer.

Here, the agent is giving some feedback about prices, based on the experience of three months in the market with the company's product. He is trying to persuade the reader that a different pricing regime needs to be considered for the mainland European market.

The company has to decide which part of the market it wants to be in and if it should alter prices accordingly.

Roodebeek
Associates

Roodebeek Associates
Ev Swedenlann 7
B-2100 Brussels
Belgium
Tel: 2 7567001
Fax: 2 7569400

Bill Tanner
European Marketing Director
Idenden Industries
Porter House
Hull
HU7 4RF
England

12 June 2005

Dear Bill,

Re: Prices in Europe

Thanks for sending through the latest price changes.

Now that we have been running your agency in Europe for three months, I wanted to discuss some difficulties that our team are experiencing in some local markets. Unfortunately, we have discovered more resistance than we initially anticipated to stocking your range of gift products. The main objection we are finding is that your prices are too high and uncompetitive compared with the alternative ranges that are available. Frankly, we are losing out on bulk orders, which I know we could secure if only we were able to price according to local market needs. I am confident that if your European prices were reduced by 15 per cent we could achieve 30 per cent more sales.

Could we discuss this when I come over to the UK next week?

Yours sincerely,

Pierre Balan
Director General

HANDLING QUERIES ABOUT AN AGENT'S COMMISSION
Letter 101: Responding to a request for lower prices

The company responds with a reaffirmation of the market that it is trying to reach. The tone of the letter is questioning, particularly the penultimate paragraph, which picks out a number of issues that need to be talked through. Asking a series of questions like this is a good tactic to use if you want to stall or slow down the progress of a project.

IDENDEN INDUSTRIES
A division of Idenden Plc
Porter House, Hull HU7 4RF, England

Tel 01482 119087 Fax 01482 119088
Registered in England No: 1218943

Pierre Balan
Director General
Roodebeek Associates
Ev Swedenlann 7
B-2100 Brussels
Belgium

19 June 2005

Dear Pierre,

Re: Prices in Europe
Many thanks for your letter of 12 June about the prices of our products in Europe.

As I am sure you are aware, the costs of servicing European orders are substantially more compared with UK orders and I am reluctant to take any action that is going to erode our margins. Before we make any decision about establishing a local European price, I would like my reservations to be satisfied.

As you know, we never anticipated taking a share of the mass market in Europe for giftware. Our strategy with the product has always been to focus on the quality end of the market. I wonder if your team is attempting to take it into outlets for which it was never really intended? I think we need to review urgently the way the product is being sold.

Could you also be specific about the competition we are up against? I think we need real examples to analyse the position. Can you supply brochures of the competition's products? Although you are confident about increasing sales by 30 per cent with a 15 per cent drop in prices, what about the higher level of returns that we would have to accept? Have you costed this into your assessment?

I agree we should discuss this when you come over next week and I will put it at the top of our agenda.

Yours sincerely,

Bill Tanner
European Marketing Director

HANDLING QUERIES ABOUT AN AGENT'S COMMISSION
Letter 102: Asking for more commission

Putting in a claim for a higher payment or commission always requires careful thought. It will inevitably be met by a wall of resistance from the other side, as no one wishes to have his margins affected.

Note the arguments that the company has to consider. The agency has obtained a strong sales growth for the company. It has cost the agent a lot to achieve those sales – costs that the agency, not the company, has borne. What the agency is banking on, to make its negotiations succeed, is the success that it has enjoyed in obtaining a strong sales growth. It therefore does not seem unreasonable to request an increase in commission '...by a modest five per cent...', which the agent understates by calling it a '...small contribution towards our continued mutual success...'.

Hart & Tucker Ltd
19 Green Street, Maidstone, Kent ME41 1TJ
Telephone: (01622) 109109
Facsimile: (01622) 108106
Reg. No: England 96223978 VAT No: 91210674

Brian Henderson
Marketing Director
B & R Hendersons Ltd
Marlows Road
Aberdeen
AB20 5GT

30 June 2005

Dear Brian,

We have been reviewing our commission structure and, in particular, the relationship between the cost of making sales to the amount we receive from you.

Since we took over this agency five years ago, sales of your products in our territory have risen from £250,000 to £650,000 a year. In that time, the activities that we have been compelled to make to obtain the increase have risen out of all proportion. We now hold the view that unless we are able to agree an increase in commission (only by a modest five per cent), we shall not be able to sustain the growth rates that have been achieved formerly.

I hope that you are able to agree to this small contribution towards our continued mutual success, and look forward to receiving your reply.

Yours sincerely,

Barry Hall
Marketing Manager

HANDLING QUERIES ABOUT AN AGENT'S COMMISSION
Letter 103: Negotiating a request for more commission

If the company refuses to increase the agent's commission, it will demoralise them. The agency is clearly successful and this success increases its negotiating power. If the company accepts the agency's demand, its margins will be affected.

Instead, the company finds a lateral solution. It cleverly latches on to the point made by the agency when it said '...we shall not be able to sustain the growth rates that have been achieved formerly'. The company's counter-proposal, therefore, links an increase in performance to an increase in commission in that the increase will have to '...be earned through additional sales'. This way, no one is the loser and everyone has the potential to earn more.

B & R HENDERSONS LTD
Marlows Road, Aberdeen AB20 5GT
Tel: 01224 267855 Fax: 01224 267977
Reg. No: 16497811 VAT No: 7387945

Barry Hall
Marketing Manager
Hart & Tucker Ltd
19 Green Street
Maidstone
Kent
ME41 1TJ

15 July 2005

Dear Barry,

Thank you for your letter of 30 June, requesting an increase in your commission from ten per cent this year to 15 per cent next year on all the sales you make.

While I wish that we could say a straight 'yes', we could not accept a reduction in our margins without any guarantee of a return. Any increase that we give in commission will have to be earned through additional sales. As an incentive, if you achieve £750,000 sales value or more within the next 12 months, we are prepared to award you a bonus of two per cent on the value of all sales achieved within the year. The bonus would be payable one month after the end of the calendar year, but would be subject to the threshold of £750,000 being achieved within the year.

I hope this proposal might be of interest to you and look forward to hearing from you.

Yours sincerely,

Brian Henderson
Marketing Director

NOTIFYING AGENTS OF CHANGES
Letter 104: Notifying an agent of revised prices

Selling a price increase to agents can be as difficult as selling a price increase to customers. Anything that gets in the way of maximising sales will find resistance.

Here, the company tries to counter any resistance to a price increase by emphasising that it is concerned to offer '...affordable products with a perceived higher added-value...' coupled with the news that they have '...striven to keep the price increases to an absolute inflation-only minimum...'.

Expressions of confidence that '...the market for them will not be adversely affected' with the reminder that they can '...negotiate special discounts...' should help to offset any concern the agents may feel.

B & R HENDERSONS LTD

Marlows Road, Aberdeen AB20 5GT
Tel: 01224 267855 Fax: 01224 267977
Reg. No: 16497811 VAT No: 7387945

Barry Hall
Marketing Manager
Hart & Tucker Ltd
19 Green Street
Maidstone
Kent
ME41 1TJ

20 August 2005

Dear Barry,

Re: Price Review

We have reviewed the price changes to our products for the next 12 months. Enclosed with this letter is a copy of the price list, with the revisions which will take effect from 1 September.

When making our review, we looked critically at our competitors' prices in the market as well as our own pricing strategy. I am delighted to say that our strategy of providing a superb range of affordable products with a perceived higher added-value than our competitors remains unchanged. We have striven to keep the price increases to an absolute inflation-only minimum, although a few of the products which are not so price-sensitive are increasing by around ten per cent. These are the premier brands in their field and we are confident the market for them will not be adversely affected.

We would obviously be interested in any feedback on these price changes that you receive from customers. And, don't forget, you are welcome to negotiate special discounts within the company's guidelines.

Yours sincerely,

Brian Henderson
Marketing Director

NOTIFYING AGENTS OF CHANGES
Letter 105: Notifying a distributor about a need for a surcharge

Agents and distributors can take a lot of managing. If you can avoid it, try not to spring nasty surprises on them – give them ample warning about changes to prices or commission.

Issuing an advance warning gives the agent the chance to get used to the idea before it is implemented. It will be a lot easier for him to swallow and will be less likely to cause bad feeling, in what is often a delicate relationship that relies on goodwill from both sides.

Here, the company is issuing a warning that a surcharge may become necessary. The circumstances are outside the company's control as it is due to exchange-rate fluctuations. Setting a clear timetable for action puts everyone clearly in the picture and will be a lot easier for the distributor to accept than if it was suddenly sprung upon him.

IDENDEN INDUSTRIES
A division of Idenden Plc
Porter House, Hull HU7 4RF, England

Tel 01482 119087 Fax 01482 119088
Registered in England No: 1218943

Mr D Basantani
Director
Teban Kian Pte Ltd
Blk 31 Heng Gardens Road
Tampines Industrial Park
5100 Kuala Lumpur
Malaysia

1 October 2005

Dear Mr Basantani,

Notice of Proposed Surcharge

As you are no doubt aware, recent events in the financial market have put intense pressure on sterling, which has lost considerable ground against most major currencies. The majority of products we sell are paid for in Euros, and the effect on our transactions has been considerable.

We recognise that turbulent exchange-rate fluctuations could mean that the current situation improves, and, therefore, we will refrain from implementing a surcharge immediately.

If, however, the situation does not improve by the end of October, we will be forced to implement a surcharge on all orders received after 30 October 2005.

I sincerely hope we shall not have to resort to this action, but trust you appreciate its necessity should the situation not improve.

Yours sincerely,

John Black
International Marketing Manager

MANAGING PUBLIC RELATIONS
Letter 106: Friendly letter to the media about the loss of a key person

This letter appears to adopt an open attitude towards the newspaper. It admits that a person is leaving the company and accepts that there were differences about the future direction of the business.

But it successfully covers up any notion that the parting is not amicable on both sides, by expressing sorrow at losing the person and confirming that his departure is '...entirely voluntary'. It also uses the opportunity to give an optimistic impression about the company's future, for which there are '...new and exciting opportunities...', without giving anything tangible away.

Thomas King & Palmer Ltd

serving the world

24 Fuller Road, Welling,
Kent DA16 7JP
Tel: (01322) 100132
Fax: (01322) 100178

Reg. No: England 1212298762
VAT No.: 92905643

The Editor
Attica Magazine
27 Mason Street
London
N1P 4KK

13 March 2005

Dear Sir/Madam,

Thank you for your request for a comment on the departure of our Managing Director, John Roberts.

We are all very sorry to be losing John so unexpectedly, especially as he has committed such a large part of his career to us. I would like to make clear that, although we had our differences on the future direction of the business, John's decision to leave was entirely voluntary. He has made a brilliant contribution to the business both here and internationally and he has a superb record of achievement, which I am confident will stand him in good stead for the future.

However, I believe the change will be mutually beneficial. It is true that the company is experiencing upheaval as it responds to the challenges we face in our industry, but we have a major investment programme under way and we are creating new and exciting opportunities, which will reap rewards for us in the future. In addition, we have recently reorganised our management structure to allow our operating executives a greater degree of autonomy.

I will be taking over John's duties for the foreseeable future, until a successor is appointed.

Yours faithfully,

Peter Abraham
Chairman

DEALING WITH ADVERTISING AGENCIES
Letter 107: Confirming an advertisement to an agency

When dealing with an advertising agency that is in turn placing an advertisement on your behalf in a magazine, there is scope for mistakes to occur as messages get passed down the chain of command. If the company is not careful, the agency may blame mistakes on the magazine, while the magazine blames the agency for not giving proper instructions.

Spelling out the terms in a tough manner, when placing the business through the agency, will prevent a lot of arguments later on.

BELLS OF BASILDON

Bells of Basildon Ltd, Unit 12, Way Park, Basildon SS12 6DE
Tel: 01268 109 9954 Fax: 01268 109 5576 Reg. No: England 13078453 VAT No: 75698764

Peter White
PIR Media Direct
38 St Marys Street
London
E9 5TG

17 June 2005

Dear Peter,

This is to confirm the details and the key terms of the offer we have accepted for advertising space.

Medium: **IT Magazine**
Issue date: **2 July 2005**
Copy date: **27 June 2005**
Gross cost: **£2,400**
Media discount: **15 per cent**
Space and agreed position: **Full-Page, Right-Hand, Front-Half**
Key Code: **UH9**

1. Position.
The position is an integral part of this deal. No deviation is acceptable, except where this has been specifically agreed in writing by us before the copy date. Otherwise, if a change in position becomes inevitable, the advertisement MUST NOT BE RUN. Where an advertisement is run in the wrong position, any payment will be entirely at our discretion, and will normally be in the range of ten per cent to 50 per cent of the above price, depending on the degree of variation from the agreed position.

2. Payment.
Payment falls due on the 28th of the month following insertion. Payment on any advertisement under dispute will be withheld until a satisfactory outcome has been negotiated by your agency with the media owner.

Yours sincerely,

Rita Smith
Marketing Production Manager

DEALING WITH ADVERTISING AGENCIES
Letter 108: Note to an agency about the incorrect position of an advertisement

The position of an advertisement in a magazine can affect the response that is received. The position was crucial to the company placing it and an express part of the agreement.

This letter is a firm and abrupt rebuttal to the agency, spelling out that the agreed rate will not be paid. It is written with the negotiating strength of the agreed terms and conditions. Note the forceful tone that several of the phrases give: '...on the strict understanding...'; '...we are exercising our right not to pay...'; '...we will not pay any more...' and 'I hope this makes our position clear'.

BELLS OF BASILDON

Bells of Basildon Ltd, Unit 12, Way Park, Basildon SS12 6DE
Tel: 01268 109 9954 Fax: 01268 109 5576 Reg. No: England 13078453 VAT No: 75698764

Peter White
PIR Media Direct
38 St Marys Street
London
E9 5TG

6 July 2005

Dear Peter,

IT Magazine advertisement

As you know, the advertisement which went in 'IT' magazine on the 2 July issue was placed on the strict understanding that it would appear on a Right-Hand, Front-Half position. This position is crucial to us if the response that we predict is not to be depressed.

The advertisement we placed appeared on page 53, a left-hand page which is three-quarters of the way through the magazine. Under the terms on which our order was placed, we are exercising our right not to pay the agreed rate. In the circumstances, we will not pay any more than 30 per cent of the agreed price for the advertisement.

I hope this makes our position clear. On this understanding, please negotiate a revised rate with the magazine.

Yours sincerely,

Rita Smith
Marketing Production Manager

DEALING WITH ADVERTISING AGENCIES
Letter 109: Refusing one offer to advertise and accepting another

Getting hold of distress space (low-cost advertising space which a magazine is desperate to fill) can be a very cost-effective way of advertising.

You have to be prepared to be flexible about when your advertisement appears, though, and to have artwork for your advertisements ready to meet tight deadlines. Nevertheless, substantial discounts can be achieved and you will often be helping out a publication which has had another advertiser cancel at the last minute and suddenly has a blank space to fill.

BELLS OF BASILDON

Bells of Basildon Ltd, Unit 12, Way Park, Basildon SS12 6DE
Tel: 01268 109 9954 Fax: 01268 109 5576 Reg. No: England 13078453 VAT No: 75698764

Peter White
PIR Media Direct
38 St Marys Street
London
E9 5TG

17 August 2005

Dear Peter,

Thanks for looking into the possibility of arranging last-minute advertising deals in World magazine and Attica.

It is disappointing that Attica don't go in for distress space, but thanks for trying. The rate of £4,995 is just too much for us to be able to justify, bearing in mind the response that we have obtained from our entry last year.

World magazine's rate of £4,500 is better and we just about broke even on the last advertisement we ran with them. I am willing to give the 28 October issue another try, provided we can obtain a front-half position that faces editorial for this same rate. We will get copy organised by the deadline of 21 October.

Yours sincerely,

Paula Little
Advertising Manager

DEALING WITH ADVERTISING AGENCIES
Letter 110: Making a very low offer to advertise

If an advertising salesperson contacts you, it can be worth making a ridiculously low offer to see what happens. You have to be prepared to lose the space, but it will certainly test how desperate the publication is to obtain some cash. Sometimes your offer will be accepted, making you the winner.

Note the style of the letter, which is designed to catch the advertiser off guard: 'I have to be completely honest and say that there is no way we can pay your rate-card price...'. The argument that '...we have almost exhausted our advertising budget...' tantalisingly suggests that there is some money available, which any company offering advertising is likely to chase. Laying your cards on the table about the amount available to spend is sufficient bait to tempt those who are interested.

BELLS OF BASILDON

Bells of Basildon Ltd, Unit 12, Way Park, Basildon SS12 6DE
Tel: 01268 109 9954 Fax: 01268 109 5576 Reg. No: England 13078453 VAT No: 75698764

Mr R Turner
Readers' Journal
Napier Close
London
N76 5TG

14 October 2005

Dear Roger,

Advertising in Readers' Journal

Thank you for contacting me about the availability of advertising space in your journal.

I have to be completely honest and say that there is no way we can pay your rate-card price of £2,500. All our off-the-page advertising has to be justified by the number of responses that we are able to generate, and our past experience of your journal is that the responses are not as high as from other media. Coupled with the fact that we have almost exhausted our advertising budget for this year, my instinctive reaction is to say 'no'.

However, we do have just £250 available, which we are willing to spend. If this is of interest, let me know.

Yours sincerely,

Paula Little
Advertising Manager

CHAPTER 4

Debt collection and credit control

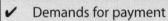

What you'll find in this chapter

✔ Demands for payment
✔ Stronger demands for payment
✔ Final demands for payment
✔ Granting credit
✔ Refusing credit
✔ Handling queries and disputes
✔ Responding to requests for payment
✔ Involving the lawyers

Chasing for payment can be a soul-destroying activity, as customers either try to wriggle out of paying at all, or test your patience by seeing how long they can go without having to pay up. Many of the letters in this chapter are proven winners at getting recalcitrant customers to dig deep into their pockets and pay their dues. So, you can be confident about using them, knowing that they have been genuinely tried and tested.

Choosing the right tone

Hitting the right note, first time, in a letter demanding payment, is not always easy. To help you choose, the collection letters have been divided broadly into three areas, as the Contents show: straightforward first-time demands for payment (letters 111–114), stronger demands (letters 115–118) and final demands that choose sterner phrases (letters 119–122).

Incentives and deterrents

If you want to try to avoid sending a letter chasing payment, the section on granting credit (letters 123–126) shows how to open a new account, notify a new account of their terms of trading, offer an incentive for prompt payment and announce a credit surcharge.

Queries and disputes

Sorting these out need not always be a headache. Letters 131–133 show how to handle them successfully.

Handling a demand for payment

If you find yourself on the receiving end of a demand for payment, letters 134 and 135 show how to keep the pack at bay for a little longer.

DEMANDS FOR PAYMENT
Letter 111: Gently reminding a customer about payment not received

The tone of this collection letter is neutral. It is a simple enquiry, taking a non-confrontational standpoint.

Enquiring if there is a problem with the order is a subtle attempt to flush out any reasons for non-payment. Accounts departments are often the last to hear about any reasons why an invoice has not been paid. Note the fairly emphatic last sentence, not just asking when the invoice will be paid but for '...immediate settlement'.

RPP Holdings Plc
35/38 New Road, Paignton, Devon TQ3 4UU
Tel: 01803 175653 Fax: 01803 187908
Reg. No: England 1976143

FAX MESSAGE TO: Janet Turner

FAX NO: 01559 887766

FROM: Sue Frost – Accounts   DATE: 17 May 2005

OUR INVOICE NO. 115689 DATED 11 FEBRUARY 2005
Our Invoice No. 115689 dated 11 February 2005, which refers to your Order No. AL2158, should have been paid at the very latest by the end of April.

To date, we have not received your payment. I wonder if there has been a problem with this order of which we are not aware?

If not, please arrange immediate settlement.

Many thanks,

Sue Frost

THIS MESSAGE CONSISTS OF ONE PAGE. PLEASE LET ME KNOW BY 'PHONE OR FAX IMMEDIATELY IF ANY PAGE IS ILLEGIBLE.

DEMANDS FOR PAYMENT
Letter 112: Requesting confirmation of when items will be paid for

This is an initial letter chasing payment. Its sole purpose is to exact confirmation of when payments will be forthcoming. Note how the tone is completely neutral and unhostile. Laying out the outstanding items in a table, giving relevant dates, invoice references, details of what was purchased and the value of each invoice, will help prevent the company from claiming that it can't find the information.

RPP Holdings Plc
35/38 New Road, Paignton, Devon TQ3 4UU
Tel: 01803 175653 Fax: 01803 187908
Reg. No: England 1976143

Fax Message to:	Maurice Brown
	Manilla Stationery Ltd
Fax Number:	020 7189 2008
From:	Tom Richards, Financial Director
Date:	29 July 2005

Listed below are open items on your account that I believe are past their due date for payment. Please confirm when each will be paid.

Manilla Stationery Ltd – Sales Account History

Tp	Date	Ref	Details	Amount
SI	03.03.05	20331	M/R continuous computer paper	£214.73
SI	10.03.05	20334	DL envelopes non-window S/S	£522.00
SI	03.04.05	20354	M/R continuous computer paper	£864.23
SI	21.04.05	20362	A4 Photocopier paper	£442.00

Total due:	**£2,042.96**

Regards,

Tom Richards
Finance Director

THIS MESSAGE CONSISTS OF ONE PAGE. PLEASE LET US KNOW BY 'PHONE OR FAX IMMEDIATELY IF ANY PAGE IS ILLEGIBLE.

DEMANDS FOR PAYMENT
Letter 113: Reminding a customer about credit terms and requesting payment

With new trading partners, you can never tell what the payment record is going to be like. This one adopts a rather prickly tone. The line at the end of the first paragraph: '...I look after the money at Simpson & Martin' is designed to emphasise that this is not a standard chasing letter, but it is about a more serious issue. The prickly feeling is enhanced in the second paragraph, with the metaphor: '...this thorny issue of payment....'

The organised way in which the Finance Director knows exactly which payments are meant to be made at what time contrasts with the chaotic payment received, suggesting that the customer's is not in order. The goal here is to make it quite clear to the trading partner that you are aware of what is going on and so encourage him into a more timely payment pattern, before alternative action becomes imperative.

SIMPSON
& MARTIN

39 TOP STREET
STOKE-ON-TRENT
ST2 3DR, UNITED KINGDOM
Tel: (01782) 156232 Fax: (01782) 120899
Reg. No: England 96223978 VAT No: 91210674

Mr Frank Little
Finance Director
P G Black Ltd
Turner Way
Denton
Peterborough
PE6 8HJ

26 May 2005

Dear Mr Little,

Thank you for the business which you have brought to us; we've invoiced you almost £10,786.56 since the beginning of our financial year (August). We haven't met, but I look after the money at Simpson & Martin.

It's always pleasing to see new business – but even more pleasing to be paid for that business. And it is this thorny issue of payment that causes me to write to you.

Four orders have been accepted on 'Mailing Date plus 60 days' credit and subsequent orders have been accepted on 'Mailing Date plus 30 days' credit. This means that we expect to receive payment within, respectively, 60 and 30 days of the mailing date. But this has, so far, not happened.

We expected to receive a payment at the end of March for your orders 115684 and 115712 (see attached account history). And we expected two further payments to follow.

We did finally receive a payment on 12 May. But we have had no advice from your accounts to say which invoices are being paid or what the gross amount transmitted was, and the amount received does not tally with any combination of outstanding invoices.

In the interim, more invoices have fallen due for payment. Please confirm to me that these will be paid promptly and that future business will be conducted as expected.

I look forward to hearing from you.

Yours sincerely,

William Patterson
Finance Director

DEMANDS FOR PAYMENT
Letter 114: Chasing up a commission payment

New arrangements that require a special payment – for example, a commission as in this case – can be easy to forget, particularly if it is due only once a year. A reminder is almost certainly necessary.

Where the amount owing is a percentage of a larger sum, don't forget to list each contract, calculate the total, and show how the percentage was arrived at. If the company here had simply issued an invoice for £9,699.72, there would have been no way of telling how that sum had accrued.

Tyler & Piper Associates

76 Whites Lane, Stevenage, Herts SG1 8JP, England
Tel: (01438) 186465 Fax: (01438) 164323

Mr P Street
International Sales Manager
Hughes & Hickle Ltd
5 Bedford Way
Milton Keynes
MK55 6JJ

23 September 2005

Dear Mr Street,

Commission Invoice No. 119747
I would like to remind you of our Export Consultation Agreement and draw your attention to the clients below who placed orders in 2004. A ten per cent commission is now outstanding.

Holz Engineering (Germany)	£32,047.05
Pierres (France)	£21,106.17
Jolon Export/Import Co. (Burma)	£43,844.00
TOTAL	£96,997.22
Total Commission due @ 10%	£ 9,699.72

We are, therefore, looking forward to the receipt of your cheque for the above sum by return.

Yours sincerely,

John Dunn
Financial Manager

Partners: DA Tyler BA & SR Piper MA

STRONGER DEMANDS FOR PAYMENT
Letter 115: Notifying that an account is overdue and requesting payment

This chaser is a fairly pleasant example of a final demand. Referring to the series of chasing faxes and telephone call acts as a reminder of how much effort you have exerted, without response.

Note how the amount outstanding and account number are outside the main body of the text, the implication being that everyone knows what is outstanding.

Giving the bank details again will pre-empt any excuses that this information is missing. The phrase at the end of the fax '...in view of the one-sided nature of our correspondence...' adds a touch of mordant wit that should increase the embarrassment of the recipient as well as slightly drawing the sting of the serious threat to begin legal action against him.

Thomas King & Palmer Ltd
serving the world

24 Fuller Road, Welling, Kent DA16 7JP
Tel: (01322) 100132
Fax: (01322) 100178

Reg. No: England 1212298762
VAT No: 92905643

Facsimile Cover Sheet

To:	Peter Johnson
Company:	Peter Johnson Inc.
Phone:	00 1 505 171 623
Fax:	00 1 505 171 698

From:	James Steven
Company:	Thomas King & Palmer
Phone:	01322 100132
Fax:	01322 100178

| Date: | 7 November 2005 |
| No. of Pages: | 1 |

Please let us know by 'phone or fax immediately if any page is missing or has been garbled in transmission.

Amount outstanding: £2,658.89   **Account number: PL98358**

I have now sent you a number of fax messages and spoken personally to you on the telephone (on 3 October).

My most recent fax was sent on 25 October. I am disappointed to have had no response to it.

Please will you arrange immediate payment of the amount due to our bankers:

RSH Bank,
Main Street, Welling (Sort Code 10-12-13)
For account of: Thomas King & Palmer, Account No. 3
Account number: 26479310

If we have not received payment within seven days, then, in view of the one-sided nature of our correspondence, I can see no option but to seek the assistance of attorneys to resolve the situation.

Yours sincerely,

James Steven
Financial Manager

STRONGER DEMANDS FOR PAYMENT
Letter 116: Requesting payment within seven days

This letter strikes a polite tone, although it contains a veiled threat. The seriousness is conveyed by stating that the letter has been sent by recorded delivery (to nullify any excuse that it was not received and must have been 'lost in the post').

Signing the letter 'Legal Department' (even though the signatory may not be a lawyer) is designed to apply further pressure.

It is clear that legal action will be taken, but note how this is not made explicit, only implied in the euphemism '...passed into other hands...'. Another effective phrase that can be applied in similar letters is '...render this action unnecessary...'.

Charles Cunningham Ltd

29 Baker Street, LONDON N34 6GH, England
Tel: (020) 7015 1290 Fax: (020) 7015 1271
Reg. No: England 1104398135 VAT No: 82108643

By Recorded Delivery

Hugh Buggs
Financial Director
Edwards & Davis Ltd
Western House, Bridge Street
Preston
Lancs
PR5 3FD

19 May 2005

Dear Mr Buggs,

I am surprised to have received no reply to our previous letter, asking for immediate settlement of the attached statement, which is long overdue.

Unfortunately, I cannot allow this account to remain unpaid any longer, and I regret that the matter will be passed into other hands in seven days.

I am still hopeful that you will render this action unnecessary by sending your remittance in full to arrive here within seven days.

Yours sincerely,

Keith Vail
Legal Department

STRONGER DEMANDS FOR PAYMENT
Letter 117: Requesting more timely payment

Quoting the words of the debtor back at him is a valuable technique for inducing payment. The person is made to feel that he is not to be trusted, having broken his promises.

Note some of the emphatic phrases that intensify the meaning behind a sentence: 'I must say...'; 'I do not see why...'; '...have still to hear...'; 'I would like, at the very least...'. All these strengthen the thrust of the letter.

Wright & Simpson

157 Colder Way
Basingstoke
Hants RG21 5TG
Tel: (01256) 125907
Fax: (01256) 190986

Eric Barker
Director
Charles Cunningham Ltd
29 Baker Street
London
N34 6GH

9 March 2005

Dear Mr Barker,

Thank you for your fax regarding payment for your orders.

Our bank details are:

National Westminster Bank
Acc No: 46789124   Sort Code: 00 12 34

I must say that I regard your statement that we should 'expect payment in approximately two weeks' as extremely disappointing.

Outstanding Amount: £768.54   Invoice Nos: 316789 and 316790

The above invoices are dated 24 January and on our 30-day terms were due for payment by 23 February. As these payments are already overdue, I do not see why we should tolerate a further two weeks' delay; we have still to hear when one of the invoices might be paid at all.

I would like, at the very least, a firm commitment for the latest date we can expect payment – preferably well within the two weeks.

I look forward to hearing from you.

Yours sincerely,

Mary Taylor
Customer Account Manager

PS: We supplied our bank details as you requested in January 'in order that payment for the above invoices could be made as soon as possible'.

Partners: EG Wright MA & FA Simpson

STRONGER DEMANDS FOR PAYMENT
Letter 118: Appealing to a customer's sense of fair play to obtain payment

Threats are omitted from this letter but the message is just as potent. The customer's sense of fair play and common courtesy is called into question, by the perfectly reasonable request that 'we are only trying to talk to you'.

The last sentence should strike a chord – the implication being that a failure to pay will mean your services being withdrawn. The 'wall of silence' idea is echoed in the request for a 'communicative' business relationship in the final sentence.

H J KINGSLEY (NORWICH) LTD
Kingsley House, Morris Street, Norwich NR6 7JM
Tel: (01603) 117097 Fax: (01603) 117099 Reg. No: England 12086215 VAT No: 8793519

FAX MESSAGE TO: Jim Clements; Copy to Accounts Dept

FAX NO: 01654 789654

FROM: Tim Good, Finance Director   DATE: 6 July 2005

THIS MESSAGE CONSISTS OF ONE PAGE. PLEASE LET ME KNOW BY 'PHONE OR FAX IMMEDIATELY IF ANY PAGE IS ILLEGIBLE.

Our Invoice No. SP56732
In April this year you ordered a shrink-wrapping machine from us: Order No. 115682, placed by Jim Clements.

Payment on our invoice (No. SP56732, copy follows) for this order was due 30 days from invoice date – i.e. 31 May 2005.

I have sent faxes to both yourself and your accounts department asking for confirmation that the invoice has been received and that it will be paid. It is now several months overdue.

To date I have had no reply.

We supply to valued customers in good faith and on the understanding that what we supply will be paid for. It is somewhat disconcerting when we endeavour to communicate with a customer regarding payment and are met with a wall of silence.

Please arrange for immediate payment direct to our bankers:
RSH Bank Plc – England
Sort Code: 00 12 34
Account Name: H J Kingsley (Norwich) Ltd
Account No: 978164978

I look forward to receiving confirmation of payment and to a long, fruitful and communicative business relationship.

Yours sincerely,

Tim Good
Finance Director

FINAL DEMANDS FOR PAYMENT
Letter 119: Notifying that an account is seriously overdue

This is a stern but, on the whole, polite letter. It gives the recipient an opportunity to give a reason why payment is being withheld. It is interesting because the other hands into which this case will be put, if payment is not received, are 'collection agents', which somehow has a slightly more sinister tone than lawyers. It conjures up images of the men in dark coats being sent round to sort things out. Another interesting feature is the closing line. This phrase '...please disregard this letter' is usually found in correspondence with consumers (rather than other businesses), but it is useful if you don't want to appear more heavy-handed than is absolutely necessary.

B & R HENDERSONS LTD
Marlows Road, Aberdeen AB20 5GT
Tel: 01224 267855 Fax: 01224 267977
Reg. No: 16497811 VAT No: 7387945

Mr A Scott
General Manager
Scott Bros
Morton House
Station Road
Glasgow
G6 7HY

13 September 2005

Dear Mr Scott,

Account No: 527BSGPR
Post Date: 10 July 2005
Outstanding Amount: £21.86

Your account with us is now SERIOUSLY OVERDUE. Should you have any justification for withholding payment, we would be obliged to hear from you concerning the problem.

However, if we do not hear from you by return or receive payment for the above account within the next seven days, you will leave us no alternative but to instruct our Collection Agents to take sufficient action to secure the amount outstanding.

We would very much regret having to take this decision and suggest that you immediately make the necessary arrangement for payment.

If you have sent your remittance in the last few days, please disregard this letter.

Yours sincerely,

Jane Fuller
Credit Controller

FINAL DEMANDS FOR PAYMENT
Letter 120: Requesting payment from a company which seems to be going under

'We've been rumbled' would be the response of the recipient of this letter (if the business was in genuine trouble). If the suspicion of insolvency is unfounded, on the other hand, it should provoke a firm rebuttal – no genuine business likes to get this kind of reputation because it is going to dent its credit rating severely.

An interesting point worth noting is the use of a specific time and day for payment to be received. If the writer had put '...received payment by Tuesday 22 November...', the creditor would not be able to take action until first thing Wednesday. Putting a specific time limit means that appropriate action can be taken at one minute past noon on the Tuesday. A small point, but one worth remembering if you are very anxious to get your money back. Setting a time limit also makes you sound more determined – as if your lawyers are lined up, ready and waiting to be sent in.

Charles Cunningham Ltd

29 Baker Street, LONDON N34 6GH, England
Tel: (020) 7015 1290 Fax: (020) 7015 1271
Reg. No: England 1104398135 VAT No: 82108643

Mr E Wright
Senior Partner
Wright & Simpson
157 Colder Way
Basingstoke
Hants
RG21 5TG

11 November 2005

Dear Mr Wright,

Our Undisputed Invoice No. 005694

Your account has been passed to me for attention because we are receiving from your business the classic signals of one about to go under. Apparently, our 'phone messages are not responded to and the only member of your staff we can speak to is a temp, who is unable to provide any answers.

I sincerely hope that this is not the case, and that there is some misunderstanding which can be easily explained.

But we are owed £3,652.00 for our undisputed Invoice No. 005694, relating to your Order No. BNN5643. And payment was due at the end of September.

To avoid any further misunderstanding, please forward your payment by return.

Please treat this as a formal and final request. If we have not received payment by noon on Tuesday 22 November, legal proceedings will commence without further notice to you.

Yours sincerely,

Keith Vail
Legal Department

FINAL DEMANDS FOR PAYMENT
Letter 121: Asking for payment in full – keeping up the pressure

Some customers may try to buy time to pay off their debts. They may have genuine difficulties that can be solved in time and a more conciliatory approach may be appropriate.

But if they have not provided you with a satisfactory reason for the delay and you suspect that they are simply playing for time, this type of letter may be necessary. It contains some good phrases: 'We appreciate this act of good faith...' and '...regrettably, this amount does not clear your account...'.

RPP Holdings Plc
35/38 New Road, Paignton, Devon TQ3 4UU
Tel: 01803 175653 Fax: 01803 187908
Reg. No: England 1976143

Mrs Jane Markham
Finance Director
Grange & Turner Ltd
32 Westbourn Road
Witney
Oxon
OX6 7HY

28 February 2005

Dear Mrs Markham,

Re: Outstanding Account
Thank you for your cheque for £1,500 in partial settlement of your account.

We appreciate this act of good faith, but, regrettably, this amount does not clear your account and leaves £1,297.98 still outstanding on invoices that are now 76 days overdue for payment.

We shall give you seven days from the date of this letter to settle your account. If we have not received payment in full by that date, we shall instigate court proceedings to recover the sum.

Yours sincerely,

Tom Richards
Finance Director

FINAL DEMANDS FOR PAYMENT
Letter 122: Announcing court proceedings in seven days

If you send this type of letter, you must be certain about carrying out your threat. Some unscrupulous companies may decide to call your bluff and test your threat before deciding to settle.

This letter has got past the threatening stage. Its power lies in the double implication that not only will you take him to court to recover the sum, but also you are considering winding up his company.

GKT Products Ltd, Unit 10, Castleway Lane, Alloway, Ayr, KA7 4BE
Telephone (01292) 177900 Fax (01292) 199855 Reg. No: 17964583 VAT No: 679845

Mr T Freeborn
Managing Director
F & G (Packaging) Ltd
12 The Industrial Park
Morley Road
Dartford
Kent
DA1 2TH

11 November 2005

Dear Mr Freeborn,

Account No: 2698745
Amount Due: £4,896.89

This account has now been passed into legal hands. We will issue court proceedings against you seven days from the date of this letter, unless before then we receive a cheque for this sum.

There will be no further warning. The proceedings will include additional claims for legal costs and statutory interest resulting from your prior failure to pay. Upon judgment we will forthwith execute against you.

If we are not placed in full funds within the above time limit, we reserve the right alternatively, where grounds exist, to instruct our solicitors to issue the relevant petition under the Insolvency Act 1986.

We look forward to your immediate remittance.

Yours sincerely,

For & on behalf of
GKT Products Ltd
Legal Department

GRANTING CREDIT
Letter 123: Opening an account for a customer

This letter starts an account on a firm, business-like basis. Four key points are worth noting and including in similar letters: an opportunity for the account holder to correct any errors in the address details; his attention drawn to the terms and conditions of sale and his point of contact in the sales department named. The most important piece of information, the credit limit and terms, is given prominence in the heart of the letter. Note that the word 'concurrent' is used here to prevent the other party from running up invoices that exceed £1,500 until he has paid the amount due within the 30-day period.

H J KINGSLEY (NORWICH) LTD

Kingsley House, Morris Street, Norwich NR6 7JM

Tel: (01603) 117097 Fax: (01603) 117099 Reg. No: England 12086215 VAT No: 8793519

Mr L Evans
Purchasing Manager
Parker Glass Ltd
Unit 27 Willow Park
Christchurch
Dorset
BH23 6MM

27 April 2005

Dear Mr Evans,

Thank you for your application for a credit account. We have pleasure informing you that your account is now open; your account number is 013649780.

Please check the above address details and inform us of any amendments.

A credit limit of £1,500 has been fixed to your account, concurrent to our 30 days' net credit terms. Subject to your payments reaching us on the said date and your adherence to our terms, we will review your credit status on application.

If you have any queries regarding our conditions of sale, they can be found on the reverse of most of our documentation. Additionally, our accounts department will be more than pleased to advise you.

Your Area Sales Manager, Mr Thomas Carter, has been informed that your account is now open.

Yours sincerely,

Rose Adams
Accounts Administrator

GRANTING CREDIT
Letter 124: Notifying a new trading account

When a new account is opened, the terms of trading should have been agreed in advance.

Before accepting an order on a credit basis, the company should take up trade references and conduct a credit check to ensure that there is a good prospect of receiving payment. The company should then confirm that a credit account has been opened, as in the letter here.

This is a good opportunity to inform the customer about individual operating procedures, which will lead to a harmonious business relationship and reduce the chance of nasty surprises being sprung.

B & R HENDERSONS LTD
Marlows Road, Aberdeen AB20 5GT
Tel: 01224 267855 Fax: 01224 267977
Reg. No: 16497811 VAT No: 7387945

Helen Mitchell
Sales Manager
Good & Peabody
34 Kiln Street
Aberdeen
Scotland
AB8 7HY

12 August 2005

Dear Ms Mitchell,

Thank you for returning our credit application form.

I have pleasure in informing you that a credit-trading account has been opened for you with a limit of £3,000 as requested. For your information, here are a few important points concerning our operating procedures:

1. Office hours are 8.30am to 5.30pm inclusive, Monday to Friday.

2. Orders are dispatched by carrier on a three-working-day service. This means that for orders received by, for example, 12 noon on Monday, delivery will be on Thursday.

   2.1 Next-day delivery is available, at an extra cost.

3. A detailed, but unpriced, delivery note is included in each consignment.

4. Invoices are posted at the time of dispatch and often arrive ahead of the goods.

5. Your sales contact is either Sue Spreadborough or Richard Selby, but, for your convenience, all of our staff can accept telephone orders.

6. The threshold for carriage-paid orders is £500, although we have no minimum order quantity. A carriage charge will be levied for small orders.

Please do not hesitate to contact me, should you require further information.

Yours sincerely,

Peter Lee
General Manager

GRANTING CREDIT
Letter 125: Notifying a buyer about a discount for prompt payment

This request adopts a formal tone but is nonetheless quite friendly. On most occasions it would be unusual to enclose a letter with a statement. If you are suggesting a special arrangement or this is a new benefit which you are introducing for the first time, it is worth enclosing a letter drawing it to the customer's attention.

IDENDEN INDUSTRIES
A division of Idenden Plc
Porter House, Hull HU7 4RF, England

Tel 01482 119087 Fax 01482 119088
Registered in England No: 1218943

Michael North
Sales Director
Beta Engineering Co
Silver Street
Foxhill
Swindon
SN3 7NM

30 May 2005

Dear Mr North,

Please find enclosed our statement as at 29 July for £2,903.86.

We have pleasure in offering a prompt payment discount with this invoice of £87.12. To claim it, our account must be credited with the full amount of £2,816.74 within seven working days of the date of this invoice, otherwise I regret we must ask you to pay £2,903.86.

We look forward to receiving your payment.

Yours sincerely,

John Goodge
Finance Director

GRANTING CREDIT
Letter 126: Announcing a credit surcharge on all accounts

This type of letter is likely to raise a few hackles and may prove controversial with some of your better-established customers. Attempting to change general terms and conditions once trading has begun is bound to produce some resistance. When the terms affect the amount that (potentially) has to be paid, it is likely to produce some waves. You must be prepared to lose some customers who prefer to obtain their supplies elsewhere.

The advantage of this term is that those who do pay on time should not really have any reason to object, since it is not directed at them, while if they are likely to be affected you should be questioning whether to do business with them anyway.

Note the need to obtain the written agreement of your customers to introduce the term.

IDENDEN INDUSTRIES
A division of Idenden Plc
Porter House, Hull HU7 4RF, England

Tel 01482 119087 Fax 01482 119088
Registered in England No: 1218943

Mr B Holmes
Marketing Manager
Beresford-Biggs Ltd
39 Cavalry Drive
Histon
Cambs
CB7 4FE

15 July 2005

Dear Mr Holmes,

Credit Surcharge

As I am sure you are aware, the current economic climate is pressurising supplier and customer alike. The continued high cost of credit now means that we are obliged to insist upon prompt payment of our sales invoices, within the agreed terms of 30 days net.

A five per cent credit surcharge will apply to all sales invoices from 3 August.

A value of an equal amount will be allowed as a prompt payment discount, provided that full payment is received within 30 days of the date of the invoice.

This will be rigorously applied, as we can no longer fund the extended credit that a small percentage of our customers is abusing.

You have placed an order for wing nuts with us; before we process this further, I am obliged to seek your written agreement to our terms of trading.

Please sign this amendment to our terms of trading and return it without delay.

Yours sincerely,

John Goodge
Finance Director

I agree to the application of a credit surcharge of five per cent on all my invoices and I agree that, in the event of my payment exceeding the 30 days limit, I shall not deduct the surcharge but accept it as a valid invoice item and remit the debt in full.

Signed B Holmes.............................

For Beresford-Biggs Ltd   Date:

REFUSING CREDIT
Letter 127: Sending a proforma invoice

If you sell low-cost items that would take a lot of administrative time in credit control, it is probably not worth giving credit on the items unless your customers are regular buyers. Here, the product costs only £32.90. If the debtor decided to delay payment, any profit on the sale would soon be swallowed up in having to send collection letters. With the certainty of payment in advance, you can be confident that your profit remains intact.

H J KINGSLEY (NORWICH) LTD
Kingsley House, Morris Street, Norwich NR6 7JM
Tel: (01603) 117097 Fax: (01603) 117099 Reg. No: England 12086215 VAT No: 8793519

Mr G Johnson
General Manager
Taylor & Ball
25 South Lane
Norwich
NR4 5EK

16 June 2005

Dear Mr Johnson,

Your Order No. FG6799
Thank you for the above order.

We enclose our Proforma Invoice No. SD2495 for £32.90.

When we receive your remittance, the goods will be despatched to you the same day.

Yours sincerely,

Barry Fuller
General Manager

REFUSING CREDIT
Letter 128: Sending a proforma invoice, due to a poor record of payment

Occasionally, a customer may get into cash-flow difficulties and notch up a record of poor payment. Even though the cash-flow problems may be temporary, it is prudent to consider withdrawing the credit terms that the customer was previously permitted.

Note in this letter how the supplier makes it explicit when the goods will be despatched, not simply when the cheque has been received but when it has cleared through the account.

The final sentence should help to take some of the sting out of the mistrust that is conveyed – although the customer has only himself to blame.

 WILSON SMITH LTD

A wholly owned subsidiary of The Wilson Group PLC
16 Willow Walk, Retford, Nottingham NG6 8WS
Tel: (01777) 121211 Fax: (01777) 121233
Reg. No: England 1212298762

Mr Brian Adams
Production Director
FGH Products Ltd
Unit 8 Potters Lane Ind. Est.
Almondvale
Perth
PH1 2EL

29 September 2005

Dear Mr Adams,

Re: Your Order No. TE3156
Thank you for the above order.

Your previous payment record precludes us from offering you our normal credit terms. We therefore enclose our Proforma Invoice No. BN8164 for £456.76.

If you would like to send us a bank draft for the amount or arrange a credit transfer to our account, we shall gladly supply you with the items ordered by return.

Alternatively, we can accept a cheque, although the goods will not be despatched until the amount has cleared through our account.

We regret having to impose these stringent terms on you and hope that we may soon be able to resume a normal trading relationship.

Yours sincerely,

Jim Tay
Finance Director

REFUSING CREDIT
Letter 129: Complaining about credit terms not being adhered to

The tone of this letter is stern, with an undercurrent of irritation. The customer is playing the old game of ignoring agreed terms and paying when he feels like it. Listing the sequence of events (showing yourself as being completely reasonable and the customer's accounts department as completely unreasonable) gives greater weight to your actions when you announce that credit is being withdrawn.

Note how the supplier defines the credit terms of '...30 days...'. This is important, because some companies mean literally 30 days from the date of the invoice, while others mean (as here) at the end of the month following that in which the invoice is issued. Another effective technique is use of the rhetorical question in the penultimate paragraph: 'I wonder when it would have been?', which underlines your lack of trust in the customer.

Grange & Turner Ltd

32 WESTBOURN ROAD, WITNEY, OXON OX6 7HY

Telephone (01993) 107888
Fax (01993) 107843

Reg. No: England 13078453
VAT No: 75698764

Mr A Scott
General Manager
Scott Bros
Morton House
Station Road
Glasgow
G6 7HY

13 September 2005

Dear Mr Scott,

I am writing to you because I want you to know of our experience when attempting to be paid on agreed terms by your company.

Names are rented by your company from our mailing lists department. Terms agreed, and signed by your company secretary, are '30 days', i.e. payment is due at the end of the month following that in which the invoice is issued.

Yet repeatedly we are told by your accounts department that the terms are 60 days. Colleagues have 'phoned and spoken to the people who place the orders with us and carefully reminded them of the agreed terms. And yet nothing changes.

On 18 April, I 'phoned to request payment for a February invoice. I was told 'we pay on 60 days'. That day I wrote to Helen Winters, who had placed the order.

Today, having had no reply, I 'phoned her – to be told that she has left. And when I spoke to the accounts person, I was told that 'a cheque will be put in the post today'.

Despite all those previous conversations, 78 days from the date of our invoice, on agreed terms of 30 days, your cheque has not even been mailed. I wonder when it would have been?

Given this experience I am sure that you will understand when I say that I can no longer make credit facilities available to your company. Any future orders will have to be paid for in advance.

Yours sincerely,

Jane Markham
Finance Director

REFUSING CREDIT
Letter 130: Writing off a debt and refusing to supply a company

This is a variation of a letter asking a customer not to come back, ever.

The phrase '...it will give us great pleasure...' sounds as if it is preceding a compliment so it is a shock for the reader when the compliment turns into a pointed insult. Its meaning is clear and uncompromising and no one receiving such a letter will be in any doubt about the intention.

RPP Holdings Plc
35/38 New Road, Paignton, Devon TQ3 4UU
Tel: 01803 175653 Fax: 01803 187908
Reg. No: England 1976143

Attn. Brian O'Neil
Taylor & Shaw Ltd
Grafton Way
Exeter
Devon
EX44 7MB

27 January 2005

Dear Sir,

We note that you have failed to respond to our previous demands to settle the debt of £34.80 that you owe this company.

Should you ever wish to receive items from this company in the future, it will give us great pleasure to refuse you.

Yours faithfully,

Tom Richards
Finance Director

HANDLING QUERIES AND DISPUTES
Letter 131: Enclosing a copy of an invoice requested

If you are asked for details about an invoice, try to give as much information as possible: not only the invoice number, but also the customer's purchase order number, its date and, if possible, the name of the person who placed the order.

Thomas King & Palmer Ltd
serving the world

24 Fuller Road, Welling,
Kent DA16 7JP
Tel: (01322) 100132
Fax: (01322) 100178

Reg. No: England 1212298762
VAT No: 92905643

Frank O'Neil
Marketing Manager
Benton Copleys
Roundtree House
Kennet
Newmarket
CB8 7LP

24 June 2005

Dear Frank,

Thank you for your fax dated 20 June.

I enclose a copy of our Invoice No. 85930 as requested. These items were ordered against your Purchase Order No. 45844, dated 2 May and signed by Hazel Partridge.

I hope this clears up the matter, but if you do have any other queries, please do not hesitate to contact me.

Yours sincerely,

Bill Vail
Accounts Manager

HANDLING QUERIES AND DISPUTES
Letter 132: Rejecting an invitation to 'contra' invoices

Setting your debts to a business against theirs to you is another trick accounts departments like to play.

The difficulty with this arrangement (as highlighted here) is that, unless the trades are simultaneous and the payment terms identical, it means that one side inevitably obtains more credit than the other. No wonder someone is going to cry 'foul'.

Highlighting how many days it has taken for payments to arrive (or not to arrive) is another smart technique to use. The precision accentuates the point and creates a stronger impact than simply saying that payment is 'overdue'.

SIMPSON & MARTIN

39 TOP STREET
STOKE-ON-TRENT
ST2 3DR, UNITED KINGDOM
Tel: (01782) 156232 Fax: (01782) 120899
Reg. No: England 96223978 VAT No: 91210674

FAX MESSAGE TO: Brian Johnson
ALF Services Limited
Maid House, West Road, Reading
Fax No: 01753 956717

From: William Patterson   Date: 3 October 2005

Re: Overdue Invoices

I was astonished when I telephoned your accounts department this morning to enquire when our July invoices would be paid, to be invited to accept setting them against your invoices to us not yet due. I thought that it was only fair that you were put in the picture.

I have sent the following message to Tracey Macer, who requested this:

'Here is a copy of our Order No.101687, which resulted in your invoice D4/09210 and credit D40931. You will see that the terms agreed with Brian Johnson included payment '30 days from mailing date'.'

The relevant mailing date was 15 September 2005. Payment is not yet due.

The payment which I am requesting from ALF is for invoices dated 11 July 2005. According to the terms signed by ALF (copy follows), payment was due 30 days later. Today, 82 days later, we have not been paid.

You have asked me to accept setting Simpson & Martin's debt to ALF against ALF's debt to Simpson & Martin. This I cannot accept. ALF's debt is very much overdue, while Simpson & Martin's is not yet due.

I reserve the right to treat agreed credit terms in the same way ALF treats them.

I would be grateful if you would arrange immediate payment of your overdue account with us.

ALF's history of payment is not brilliant. In the last year it has taken more than 100 days for us to be paid for some invoices.

Regards,

William Patterson
Finance Director

HANDLING QUERIES AND DISPUTES
Letter 133: Informing a customer that a statement has already been paid

Occasionally, you may find that statements are accidentally duplicated. (It can be surprising how many companies who receive a duplicate invoice actually pay it as well!) This letter should sort matters out.

Note the way this letter closes. This is a useful phrase that can be applied in any situation where you want to signal that you don't expect to hear from the supplier's accounts department again.

IDENDEN INDUSTRIES
A division of Idenden Plc
Porter House, Hull HU7 4RF, England

Tel 01482 119087 Fax 01482 119088
Registered in England No: 1218943

Jim Little
Marketing Director
York Plastics
54 East Street
York
YO9 8BM

22 February 2005

Dear Jim,

We have recently received the enclosed statement from you.

We are at a loss to know why this should have been re-issued, as the sum in question was paid directly to your bankers from our bank on 18 February 2005. I enclose a copy of the advice from our bank.

I hope this matter can now be considered closed.

Yours sincerely,

John Goodge
Finance Director

RESPONDING TO REQUESTS FOR PAYMENT
Letter 134: Advising that immediate payment is on its way

If you find yourself on the receiving end of an irate creditor on the warpath for his money, this letter should help to appease him.

Note how the 'reasons' are very conveniently side-stepped, with an all-embracing phrase (which could be used on a multitude of occasions) that explains that they are '...both tedious and convoluted'. A super phrase that says absolutely nothing, but will leave the other side with the impression of a good story left untold.

The last sentence should help to restore the creditor's faith in you; implying the invoice could '...slip through the net...' makes it sound like a one-off mishap.

Taylor Taylor & Shaw
Benton House, Clifton, Bristol BS16 7LJ
Tel: (0117) 1089254   Fax: (0117) 1089211

FAX MESSAGE

To: Sally White

Fax No: 020 8756 9841

From: Peter Pope   Date: 23 June 2005

THIS MESSAGE CONSISTS OF ONE PAGE. PLEASE LET ME KNOW BY 'PHONE OR FAX IMMEDIATELY IF ANY PAGE IS ILLEGIBLE.

Dear Ms White,

Re: Your Fax of 7 June 2005
Firstly, apologies for the delay in replying to your fax, which was caused by the absence of Michael Taylor and myself on business travel overseas.

Your Invoice No. CP25648 will be settled in full on Monday, when we should have received a corresponding cheque from Ferdinand Ramos of Marco Leathers Inc., which has been couriered to us from their offices in the Philippines today.

The reasons for the delay are both tedious and convoluted. Suffice it to say, your cheque will be despatched by special delivery on Monday, with a copy sent to you by fax to confirm despatch.

Should any future invoices 'slip through the net', please do not hesitate to bring it to my personal attention and I will attempt to resolve the problem immediately.

Regards,

P Pope
Financial Manager

Partners: AW Taylor & GS Taylor

RESPONDING TO REQUESTS FOR PAYMENT
Letter 135: Advising an international customer that payment is on its way

This is a pleasant, disarming letter. It sounds completely genuine. Saying you are '...extremely embarrassed...' should put the other side off their guard. Blaming your accounts department is OK (provided you won't get into their bad books).'I hope we haven't done our reputation too much harm' demonstrates your concern and how much you empathise with your supplier's plight.

 RPP Holdings Plc
35/38 New Road, Paignton, Devon TQ3 4UU
Tel: 01803 175653 Fax: 01803 187908
Reg. No: England 1976143

FAX MESSAGE TO: Mr M Wong, Finance Director

FAX No: (852) 2189 3698

FROM: T Richards, Finance Director   DATE: 4 October 2005

THIS MESSAGE CONSISTS OF ONE PAGE. PLEASE LET ME KNOW BY 'PHONE OR FAX IMMEDIATELY IF ANY PAGE IS ILLEGIBLE.

RE: YOUR INVOICE NO. 118597 DATED 8 AUGUST 2005

MESSAGE: I have today sent by international courier a cheque in the amount of £1,070, in full settlement of the above invoice.

I am extremely embarrassed over the long delay as a result, I am afraid, of our accounting department not being as familiar as I am (and as they should be) with currencies other than the US Dollar.

Please accept my assurances that we will do everything to ensure that this kind of delay is not repeated in future. I hope that we haven't done our reputation too much harm.

Regards,

Tom Richards
Finance Director

INVOLVING THE LAWYERS
Letter 136: Asking for a quotation from solicitors

If you think you may need to use the services of your lawyer, it is best to ask in advance what sort of bill you are likely to incur in recovering the debt. This will probably influence your decision about whether to take legal action or how far down the road to go.

The lawyers may be a bit cagey on costs, because a lot will depend on the time needed. If they sound unwilling to give you an indication, ask what their hourly charging rate is. Having an idea in advance, and warning lawyers of impending action, will save you time if you need to instruct them quickly.

H J KINGSLEY (NORWICH) LTD
Kingsley House, Morris Street, Norwich NR6 7JM
Tel: (01603) 117097 Fax: (01603) 117099 Reg. No: England 12086215 VAT No: 8793519

Mr J H Jones
Jones, Turner & Hills Partners
34 Frost Avenue
Norwich
NR3 7TF

23 June 2005

Dear Mr Jones,

Re: JW Mann (Packagers) Ltd

We have an outstanding debt of £12,501.90 with JW Mann (Packagers) Ltd. We have sent them a final demand for payment, but I have heard on the grapevine that they are experiencing some severe cash-flow difficulties and I am not hopeful that we shall receive payment within seven days.

If we do not receive payment in that time, I would like to instruct your firm to issue proceedings against JW Mann. Before we do, though, I would appreciate an estimate of the foreseeable costs (including your disbursements) that we are likely to incur, assuming our claim is undisputed.

If you are unable to give us an estimate, please give us details of the hourly charging rate of your firm and, from your experience, a rough approximation of the number of hours that a case of this nature might take.

I am confident that our case is very strong and that no credible defence will be made to our claim.

Yours sincerely,

Tim Good
Finance Director

CHAPTER 5

Employing people

What you'll find in this chapter
✔ Interviews and offers
✔ References
✔ Resignations
✔ Terminating contracts
✔ Warnings and dismissal
✔ General announcements and notices
✔ Notices to individual employees
✔ Maternity and other leave
✔ Motivating staff
✔ Offering congratulations
✔ Health and safety
✔ Holiday policy
✔ Offering sincere condolences

A scan of the letters contained in this chapter shows the diversity of employee-related subjects that demand correspondence. Some of them are fairly straightforward, such as asking a candidate to attend an interview. Others, such as contracts, warnings and dismissal, and maternity letters, require more consideration to make sure the correct legal regulations are being adhered to satisfactorily. All of them need to be carefully drafted if they are not to be misinterpreted by the recipient. Some of the highlights are examined here.

References

Giving references can be awkward, because of the need to give a fair and honest reply which does not conceal relevant information. A failure to do this could expose you to a claim from either the prospective employer or the employee. Letters 145 and 146 show how to give a qualified reference.

Giving warnings

Letters 149–151 cover the tricky issue of giving appropriate warnings to an employee about his conduct, from first written warning through to dismissal.

Dismissal

Great care needs to be taken before dismissing someone without giving them a warning. Letter 152 shows how to handle it for a case of gross misconduct. Remember, this letter may be used in evidence against you in an industrial tribunal.

Congratulations

Offering appropriate congratulations can sometimes be as awkward as writing a letter of condolence. Letters 166–168 show how you can write a sincere and well-phrased letter.

Condolences

For many people, a letter of condolence is one of the most difficult ones to write. But, at some time or other, most managers will have to face writing one. Letters 173–174 show how it can be done.

INTERVIEWS AND OFFERS
Letter 137: Asking a candidate to attend an interview

This approach strikes a fairly formal tone. Note how it sets a time and date for a candidate and asks her to confirm whether this is convenient. If you want to influence the schedule of interviews, use this letter. Most candidates will be inclined to agree to the time that suits you.

Fenner & Sons

16 George Street, Woodbridge,
Suffolk IP3 7KL
Tel: (01394) 198423
Fax: (01394) 198444
Registered in England: 91221299
VAT No: 919129075 80

Mrs F Godfrey
Woodland Green
Framlingham
Woodbridge
Suffolk
IP13 9PL

23 June 2005

Dear Mrs Godfrey,

Thank you for your application of 24 June for the post of Office Manager.

I would like to discuss the position in more detail with you and would be grateful if you could attend an interview at this office on Thursday 30 June at 10am.

Please confirm whether this time is convenient for you.

Yours sincerely,

Brian Goodge
Personnel Manager

INTERVIEWS AND OFFERS
Letter 138: Confirming an interview appointment

It is a good practice to confirm all meetings in writing. It can be easy to mishear a time or date over the 'phone, or to be distracted soon after a 'phone call is finished and forget to make a note of it in a diary.

You don't need to write a long letter – a brief note containing the date, time and place will suffice. It is simple, but it can save a lot of time and embarrassment later.

 Kelso Limited
16 Abbots Road, Luton, Bedfordshire MK44 7YT
Tel: (01234) 136953 Fax: (01234) 136422
Registered in England No: 9126719 VAT No: 91523489 76

Barry Hall
27 Steeple Drive
Hitchin
Herts
SG4 5HJ

21 January 2005

Dear Mr Hall,

This is to confirm our meeting at Abbots Road, Luton at 1.00pm on 25 January 2005.

We look forward to seeing you then.

Yours sincerely,

Faith Turner
Personnel Manager

INTERVIEWS AND OFFERS
Letter 139: Acknowledging a job application

Before inviting a shortlist of candidates to interview, you may want to give yourself time to consider all the applications. Candidates will be expecting to hear from you soon.

This letter helps to confirm that the application has been safely received and takes some of the anxiety out of the waiting. It doesn't raise any hopes that the applicant will be called for interview, nor does it dash them – it sits on the fence, leaving you with both options open.

SIMPSON & MARTIN

39 TOP STREET
STOKE-ON-TRENT
ST2 3DR, UNITED KINGDOM
Tel: (01782) 156232 Fax: (01782) 120899
Reg. No: England 96223978 VAT No: 91210674

Miss T Hussey
16 Clover Terrace
Werrington
Stoke-on-Trent
ST9 0PL

3 January 2005

Dear Miss Hussey,

Thank you for your completed application form for the position of Word Processor Operator.

I am now considering all applications and will be in touch with you again within the next few days.

Yours sincerely,

Elizabeth Bent
Personnel Officer

INTERVIEWS AND OFFERS
Letter 140: Rejecting a speculative job application

Letters sending in speculative applications deserve, at the very least, this kind of reply. It doesn't need to be long, but it puts the recipient clearly in the picture – even if the phrase '...we shall keep your letter on file...', followed by the promise to renew contact if circumstances change, is a promise that is rarely kept. Nevertheless, it shows willing but also demonstrates to the reader that he must look elsewhere for employment. Not bothering to respond to a speculative application shows a complete lack of courtesy and regard for the applicant.

Grange & Turner Ltd

32 WESTBOURN ROAD, WITNEY, OXON OX6 7HY

Telephone (01993) 107888
Fax (01993) 107843

Reg. No: England 13078453
VAT No: 75698764

Mr S K Robinson
43 Knights Drive
Kenilworth
Warwickshire
CV10 4ZN

13 June 2005

Dear Mr Robinson,

Thank you for your letter of 3 June enquiring if we have any vacancies for a personal assistant.

Unfortunately, all our situations are filled at present. However, we shall keep your letter on file and, should circumstances change, we shall contact you.

Yours sincerely,

Yvonne Mitchelle
Personnel Department

INTERVIEWS AND OFFERS
Letter 141: Rejecting a candidate after an interview

This letter is a straightforward, formal rejection letter. Note how the letter doesn't give an explicit reason why the candidate has not been successful but just implies that though the applicant was a good candidate, there were others even better qualified.

The phrase 'I regret that we have decided not to take your application further on this occasion' is a little oblique, although its meaning is clear. When rejecting a candidate, make sure that your choice of words leaves the reader clear about where he stands. Try to avoid vague phrases that may be open to different interpretations.

H J KINGSLEY (NORWICH) LTD
Kingsley House, Morris Street, Norwich NR6 7JM
Tel: (01603) 117097 Fax: (01603) 117099 Reg. No: England 12086215 VAT No: 8793519

Mr M Booth
18 Woodgate St
East Dereham
NR19 6JH

22 January 2005

Dear Mr Booth,

Thank you for attending the interview last week for the post of Office Manager.

The standard of applicants has been very high and, after careful consideration, I regret that we have decided not to take your application further on this occasion.

However, I would like to take this opportunity to thank you for the interest you have shown in our company and to wish you every success in the future.

Yours sincerely,

P J Cross
Personnel Manager

INTERVIEWS AND OFFERS
Letter 142: Rejecting a candidate who came very close to being appointed

If you have a very good candidate who you have to turn down, it may not be appropriate to write the applicant one of your standard letters of rejection.

This letter is a much friendlier way of turning the applicant down and shows at the same time that you know she came very close to the mark. Note how the letter makes it clear to the candidate that she has not been successful, to avoid any ambiguity.

If the person was particularly outstanding, she may be someone that you want to consider for the future, so offering to keep her name on file gives her some hope that the application was not in vain and, at the same time, lets her down more lightly.

H J KINGSLEY (NORWICH) LTD
Kingsley House, Morris Street, Norwich NR6 7JM
Tel: (01603) 117097 Fax: (01603) 117099 Reg. No: England 12086215 VAT No: 8793519

Mrs E Robinson
Downhill Cottage
Hingham
Norwich
Norfolk
NR9 4FG

23 January 2005

Dear Mrs Robinson,

Thank you for attending the interview last week for the post of Office Manager.

The standard of applicants has been very high and, after careful consideration, I regret that you have not been successful on this occasion. It is unfortunate that we could not appoint two people to this position, as your experience matches the requirements very closely. In view of this, I would like to keep your name on file and, should a similar position occur in the future, would be pleased to consider you again, should you also be interested.

In the meantime, thank you for the interest you have shown in our company and I would like to wish you personally every success in your future.

Yours sincerely,

P J Cross
Personnel Manager

INTERVIEWS AND OFFERS
Letter 143: Making an offer of employment

Offers of employment may vary from those that are highly detailed contracts, to those that contain the minimum of legally required information. A letter that contains all the details of a contract could appear intimidating to some employees and may even deter some candidates at the last minute. This letter allows the writer to adopt a friendlier but no-less-professional approach.

The points that need to be stated in a contract are: the position, the date of joining, the name of your employer, the salary, how frequently the salary is paid, when it will be reviewed, the normal hours of work, amount of holiday, rights to sick pay, pension arrangements, the period of notice that is required on either side and to whom the post reports.

You will want the employee to confirm his appointment in writing with you. Note how a duplicate copy is enclosed for the employee to sign and return, saving him the trouble of having to sit down and compose a letter.

H J KINGSLEY (NORWICH) LTD
Kingsley House, Morris Street, Norwich NR6 7JM
Tel: (01603) 117097 Fax: (01603) 117099 Reg. No: England 12086215 VAT No: 8793519

Mr John Price
45 Beeches Road
Thorpe St Andrew
Norwich
NR7 0LK

9 February 2005

Dear John,

Following our conversation this morning, I am delighted to confirm our offer of the job of Office Manager, with effect from Monday 28 February 2005.

I confirm that your annual salary will be £16,000, which will be paid monthly in arrears. Your salary will be reviewed after six months, in August. Thereafter, it will normally be reviewed annually in April.

The post reports to John Hibbert, our Managing Director. Our normal terms of employment will apply, as outlined on the attached sheet. We do operate a sick-pay scheme and although we do not have a company pension scheme, we give every help to anyone wishing to set up a personal scheme.

Your normal hours each week will be 9.00am to 5.00pm, Monday to Friday, with an hour's break for lunch.

You will be entitled to 20 days' holiday per year in addition to statutory holidays and the three days between Christmas and New Year. One month's notice is required on either side, and the first three months are viewed as a mutual trial period.

Your employer, for contractual purposes, is H J Kingsley (Norwich) Ltd.

Please sign the attached copy in acceptance of this offer.

Yours sincerely,

P J Cross
Personnel Manager

I accept the above offer of employment as set out in the above letter.

Signed .... Date ....

REFERENCES
Letter 144: Asking for a reference

When employing new staff, it is prudent to ask for a reference from their previous employer. This not only helps to verify that the candidate has worked where he says he did, but it also gives you an opportunity to find out more about him.

The questions asked here should enable you to find out how well he worked for and was judged by his previous employer.

Asking for two references from different people means you have a chance to spot any inconsistent replies, which could signal a need for further questions or enquiries.

Charles Cunningham Ltd
29 Baker Street, LONDON N34 6GH England
Tel: (020) 7015 1290 Fax: (020) 7015 1271
Reg. No: England 1104398135 VAT No: 82108643

Mr Peter Holmes
Personnel Manager
Thomas King & Palmer
24 Fuller Road
Welling
Kent
DA16 7JP

3 March 2005

Dear Mr Holmes,

We have received an application from John Hibbert for the position of Office Manager.

I would be grateful if you could answer the questions below concerning John Hibbert's employment with you.

1. What date did he join and leave your company?
2. What job(s) did he perform at your company?
3. How would you rate his timekeeping?
4. How much time in a year did he take off for sickness?
5. How many people was he supervising in his job with you?
6. Has any disciplinary action had to be taken against him, however minor?
7. Would you say he is a conscientious worker?
8. How would you rate his experience to perform the job for which he has applied?
9. Are there any reasons that you are aware of why we should not employ him?
10. What was his reason for leaving your company?

Thank you for your help with this matter.

Yours sincerely,

Sarah Milnes
Personnel Manager

REFERENCES
Letter 145: Replying to a request for a reference

If you are asked to give a reference, it must be given honestly and fairly.

When giving a reference, you are in a position of privilege that entitles you to say exactly what you think about a person, even if it might, in other circumstances, be defamatory. However, you must not say anything about the person maliciously, otherwise the position of privilege may be lost and you could face a claim from the employee.

Similarly, a failure to answer a question truthfully may expose you to a claim from the employer. This sense of having to walk a fine line often leads to referees giving fairly anodyne, non-judgemental references. It would, therefore, be a mistake to treat the answers to a reference as telling all there is to know about an employee. Nevertheless, it does give a worthwhile snapshot view and acts as a useful check.

Thomas King & Palmer Ltd
serving the world

24 Fuller Road, Welling,
Kent DA16 7JP
Tel: (01322) 100132
Fax: (01322) 100178

Reg. No: England 1212298762
VAT No: 92905643

Sarah Milnes
Personnel Manager
Charles Cunningham Ltd
29 Baker Street
London
N34 6GH

8 March 2005

Dear Ms Milnes,

Thank you for your request for a reference for John Hibbert.

I can confirm that John held the position of Office Assistant with us from June 2002 to April 2004. In April, he was appointed Office Manager and he stayed with us until December of the same year.

John's timekeeping was excellent and, although he had the occasional day off sick in a year, the amount was no more than one would expect. Most of the occasions were caused by seasonal bouts of 'flu.

In his post of Office Assistant, no one reported to John. However, in his role of Office Manager, he was responsible for managing a team of six personal assistants.

No disciplinary action has ever been taken against John and he is a very conscientious worker.

I am not aware of all the responsibilities that you are expecting him to perform, but, provided that they are broadly similar to those areas in which he has experience, I would say that he was well qualified to perform those tasks.

John told us he wished to leave because he was keen to work in a larger organisation, where there were greater opportunities for advancement and to learn more skills than we were realistically able to offer him.

I hope this gives you all the information you require, but if you do have any queries, please do not hesitate to contact me.

Yours sincerely,

Peter Holmes
Personnel Manager

REFERENCES
Letter 146: Giving a qualified reference

If there has been an incident (a disciplinary offence, for example) that is asked about, you should not ignore it in a reference. Note how the letter seeks to put the offence into its true context – it was a one-off and his performance apart from that one time has been exemplary.

Don't be afraid to state exactly how you interpret a particular question. Here, the former employer is unaware of all the responsibilities expected of the candidate in his new job, so note how the question is thrown back with the phrase '...provided appropriate training is made available to him...', which cleverly leaves the new employer with the responsibility for making the judgement.

Thomas King & Palmer Ltd
serving the world

24 Fuller Road, Welling,
Kent DA16 7JP
Tel: (01322) 100132
Fax: (01322) 100178

Reg. No: England 1212298762
VAT No: 92905643

Sarah Milnes
Personnel Manager
Charles Cunningham Ltd
29 Baker Street
London
N34 6GH

8 March 2005

Dear Ms Milnes,

Thank you for your letter requesting a reference for John Hibbert.

I can confirm that John held the position of Office Assistant with us for just over three years, from June 2001 to Jan 2005.

John's timekeeping was excellent and although he had the occasional day off sick in a year, the amount was no more than one would expect. Most of the occasions were caused by seasonal bouts of 'flu.

Although John is a conscientious worker, he was disciplined on one occasion for taking an additional day's holiday over and above his normal entitlement. This incident was very much an exception and I have never had cause to complain about any other matter.

I am not aware of all the responsibilities that you are expecting him to perform, but, provided appropriate training is made available to him, I would say that John is now ready to build upon his current experience and take on more responsibility in his new appointment.

He has a very affable personality and the ability to work well in a team environment, especially where it is essential to get on with a number of different types of people. I have every confidence he will make a valuable contribution to your business and am therefore pleased to be able to support his application.

Yours sincerely,

Peter Holmes
Personnel Manager

RESIGNATIONS
Letter 147: Resigning from a job

A letter of resignation should be succinct and to the point. It is useful to specify the date that you intend to leave on to avoid any misunderstanding later.

The second paragraph is not obligatory but helps set a friendly tone for the departure. It is always worth leaving on good terms. You never know when you may come into contact with the people for whom you work again, perhaps in other companies that you move to in the future.

23 Gladstone Walk
Chepstow
Gwent
NP6 6LP

Mr G Moore
Managing Director
G B Grey Ltd
Church St
Newport
Gwent
NP9 7JW

19 May 2005

Dear Mr Moore,

It is with regret that I tender my resignation as Assistant Export Manager. This follows my appointment as Export Manager with Abeltech. As I am required under my contract to give one month's notice, I understand my last day of employment will be 19 June 2005.

May I take this opportunity to thank you for all the invaluable help, advice and encouragement that you have given me during my three years with G B Grey. I have thoroughly enjoyed my time here, but I feel the moment is now right for me to take up new responsibilities and challenges.

Yours sincerely,

Peter King

TERMINATING CONTRACTS
Letter 148: Terminating a consultant's contract, due to a disability

The person here is not an employee as such but was working on a freelance basis for the company. The letter adopts a suitably concerned tone for the business relationship.

Although the recipient knows that he can no longer perform his contractual duties, the writer is keen to soften the impact of the termination of the agreement, by ending on an optimistic note which willingly offers the prospect of renewing the contract. Note how the writer doesn't commit himself as such, but instead offers to 'review' the contract.

GKT Products Ltd, Unit 10, Castleway Lane, Alloway, Ayr, KA7 4BE
Telephone (01292) 177900 Fax (01292) 199855 Reg. No: 17964583 VAT No: 679845

Mr Richard Green
Barton Close
Alloway
Ayr
KA7 4GB

16 April 2005

Dear Mr Green,

Many thanks for your telephone call concerning your disability. I am very sorry to hear about this and trust that something can be done to alleviate the pain and discomfort.

In the circumstances it would appear that you can no longer carry out your contract work for us as an Engineer and Consultant. I therefore regret that we must terminate our agreement, with immediate effect.

Perhaps you could keep in touch with me? If your health situation improves, let me know and we shall be pleased to review your contract.

Yours sincerely,

Mark Winters
Contracts Manager

WARNINGS AND DISMISSAL
Letter 149: First written warning to an employee (for breaching the safety code)

This letter has a formal air to it. It is designed to confirm what has already been discussed at a previous meeting. It is also written to prevent any disagreement at a later stage about what action has or has not been taken.

It demonstrates that the company has done all it can to explain the importance of adhering to the safety regulations, should this be necessary at a future health and safety or industrial tribunal.

An interesting point to note is the way the letter seeks to win the employee back on to the side of the company by explaining that the code is not operated '...for the benefit of the company but for the benefit of all our employees', and '...one employee's breach of the code may endanger another employee's life...'.

IDENDEN INDUSTRIES
A division of Idenden Plc
Porter House, Hull HU7 4RF, England

Tel 01482 119087 Fax 01482 119088
Registered in England No: 1218943

Mr Jack Turner
Welding Engineer

12 July 2005

Dear Mr Turner

Re: YOUR BREACH OF THE COMPANY'S SAFETY CODE

I confirm the points we discussed at our meeting on 12 July, concerning your negligence in adhering to the strict safety code we operate. The complaint was that on 12 July you did not wear a hard safety hat in the construction zone of the factory for a period of one hour, despite the fact that your manager had reprimanded you for not doing so a week earlier.

As we agreed, you must at all times adhere to the safety code of the company. I am reissuing a copy of the code to you and am asking your manager to go through it with you again, so you are quite clear about what is expected of you. If you are unclear about anything, however trivial it may seem, do not hesitate to ask. The safety code of the company is not operated for the benefit of the company but for the benefit of all our employees. You must understand that one employee's breach of the code may endanger another employee's life and it is for this reason that we enforce the policy strictly.

This is your first warning of a company rules violation. Future violations may lead to further disciplinary action being taken. You may appeal against this decision and if you wish to exercise this right, please notify me within seven working days.

Finally, please sign the enclosed copy of this letter to confirm that you have received this letter and another copy of the safety code and return the letter to me for my files.

Yours sincerely,

John Cooper
Director of Personnel

WARNINGS AND DISMISSAL

Letter 150: Final written warning to an employee (for breaching the safety code)

The final letter is much colder in its approach. It makes it clear to the employee what the consequences will be of failing to adhere to the safety standard. There is no attempt to persuade the employee to co-operate for his own and others' sake.

Note how the letter refers to specific dates, confirming the history in case the matter should come to a tribunal.

IDENDEN INDUSTRIES
A division of Idenden Plc
Porter House, Hull HU7 4RF, England

Tel 01482 119087 Fax 01482 119088
Registered in England No: 1218943

Mr Jack Turner
Welding Engineer

15 September 2005

Dear Mr Turner

Re: YOUR BREACH OF THE COMPANY'S SAFETY CODE

On 12 July, you breached the safety code by failing to wear a hard hat. On 15 September you were again discovered to have breached the code by not wearing the hard hat provided for you to use in the construction area of the factory.

It was made clear to you at the meeting on 12 July and in the letter to you of the same day that we expected you to follow the safety code strictly at all times. You have failed to do this.

For your own safety and for the safety of the others you must follow strictly all aspects of the safety code, especially wearing a hard hat in the zones required.

There has not been a satisfactory improvement in your conduct since your last warnings. Accordingly, any continued violations of company policy or failure to conduct yourself according to the rules of the company shall result in further disciplinary action being taken, which may result in you being dismissed.

We remind you that you have the right of appeal against this warning according to the Terms and Conditions of Employment as supplied to you and if you wish to exercise this right, please notify me in writing within seven working days.

Please contact me if you have any questions.

Yours sincerely,

John Cooper
Director of Personnel

WARNINGS AND DISMISSAL
Letter 151: Dismissing an employee (for breaching the safety code)

The letter confirming dismissal sets out the events in a clear, factual way. It highlights the dates, to reinforce that the company has carried out its duties to the letter. It makes it clear that the company has given the employee the opportunity to improve his conduct, in case this should be used as a defence at an industrial tribunal.

IDENDEN INDUSTRIES
A division of Idenden Plc
Porter House, Hull HU7 4RF, England

Tel 01482 119087 Fax 01482 119088
Registered in England No: 1218943

Mr Jack Turner
Welding Engineer

29 October 2005

Dear Mr Turner

Re: YOUR BREACH OF THE COMPANY'S SAFETY CODE

I refer to our meeting on 27 October when we discussed the matter of how you were, for a third time, discovered not wearing a hard hat in the construction zone of the factory.

On 12 July and 15 September it was made clear to you that failure to wear a hard hat in a safety zone amounted to a breach of the company's safety code.

You were given a warning on 15 September that if you failed again to adhere to the company's safety code, you would be dismissed.

You have been given the opportunity to improve your conduct but have repeatedly ignored these warnings given to you. In the circumstances we have no option but to dismiss you with effect from 1 November. You will receive one month's pay in lieu of notice.

You are entitled to appeal against the company's decision to dismiss you and if you wish to exercise this right, please notify me in writing within seven days.

Yours sincerely,

John Cooper
Director of Personnel

WARNINGS AND DISMISSAL
Letter 152: Summary dismissal

A summary dismissal can be difficult to defend at an industrial tribunal and a decision to dismiss instantly should not be taken lightly. If you do decide to dismiss, you must demonstrate that you have given the employee every opportunity to explain his conduct. A failure to do this may lead to a claim for unfair dismissal.

Grange & Turner Ltd

43!X FTUCP VSO!SP BE-!X JJOFZ-!P YPO!P Y7!8I Z

Telephone (01993) 107888
Fax (01993) 107843

Reg. No: England 13078453
VAT No: 75698764

Mr John Black
34 Green St
Cheltenham
Gloucestershire
GL51 7HY

13 June 2005

Dear Mr Black,

I refer to our meeting on 12 June.

I regret to inform you that we are terminating your employment with immediate effect. This decision is based on an incident reported to me on 10 June by your supervisor, Paul Smith, and on the explanation given at the disciplinary meeting. The report recommended your dismissal because of your repeated intoxication during working hours.

As you are aware, the first reported incident of your intoxication on the job was on 21 May. That report was placed on your personnel file, and you were informed at that time that another incident would result in a disciplinary action or possible dismissal.

This second incident of intoxication adversely affected the operational efficiency and effectiveness of your department and threatened the safety of other employees and this amounts to an act of gross misconduct.

You are entitled to appeal against the company's decision to dismiss you and if you wish to exercise this right, please notify me in writing within seven days.

Yours sincerely,

John Tome
Personnel Director

GENERAL ANNOUNCEMENTS AND NOTICES
Letter 153: Announcing a bonus

With good news for employees, you want to try to capitalise on it as much as possible and show how much you appreciate everyone's efforts in achieving these results.

The phrases '...thank you personally for all your hard work...' and 'Thank you once again for your contribution...' help get that message across in a more individual-sounding and less corporate way.

Note how the letter looks forward to the future, laying out a vision of a better bonus in the following year, which helps to motivate the staff and give them something to work towards.

Charles Cunningham Ltd

29 Baker Street, LONDON N34 6GH, England
Tel: (020) 7015 1290 Fax: (020) 7015 1271
Reg. No: England 1104398135 VAT No: 82108643

Mr Michael Tooke
UK Sales Manager

31 March 2005

Dear Michael,

Profit Sharing Scheme, Financial Year 2004/5

I am delighted to report that we have had an excellent year and I would like to take this opportunity to thank you personally for all your hard work that you have put in over the last 12 months. The launch of the new range of products has helped to contribute to the growth of the company, and we anticipate this growth increasing during the forthcoming year as newer products become available.

Our turnover is up ten per cent at £2,960,613 and profit before tax is up 12 per cent on last year at £298,415. Under the terms of our profit-sharing scheme, five per cent of the profits are eligible to be distributed amongst all the staff in proportion to each person's salary. I am therefore pleased to announce that £497 has been added to your salary this month.

Thank you once again for your contribution to the company this year. We have already got off to a tremendous start and I hope to be able to announce an even larger profit figure for next year, which, of course, will translate into a larger profit-share payment for you.

Yours sincerely,

Derek Law
Managing Director

GENERAL ANNOUNCEMENTS AND NOTICES
Letter 154: Advising employees of an intention to relocate

This is one of those letters that needs to be written to keep employees informed of a changing situation. You could announce this at a meeting or in a memo, but, occasionally, a letter may be appropriate. The aim must be to put people in the picture and stop any rumours that might be circulating. Employees often expect instant answers, which cannot always be given.

Here, the management go as far as they can to alleviate the concerns that employees may have about relocating, by explaining that they are trying to achieve a location within easy reach of the city.

SIMPSON & MARTIN

39 TOP STREET
STOKE-ON-TRENT
ST2 3DR, UNITED KINGDOM
Tel: (01782) 156232 Fax: (01782) 120899
Reg. No: England 96223978 VAT No: 91210674

Debra King
Sales Office

7 August 2005

Dear Debra,

Proposed Office Move

As you know, we have been working under cramped and sometimes difficult conditions, caused by the growth of our business. For several weeks we have been searching for new premises, but, so far, nothing suitable has turned up and we have now retained an agency to look for an appropriate location.

Our first choice is to keep the business within the city centre, but we are also looking at any location up to 25 miles outside the city boundary. One strict criterion is that any location outside the city centre must be on a suitable public transport route, to enable those of you who live within the city to travel with the minimum inconvenience.

This is as far as we have got in choosing a new location, but I will keep you informed, as and when developments occur.

Yours sincerely,

Francis Vince
Managing Director

GENERAL ANNOUNCEMENTS AND NOTICES
Letter 155: Notifying staff about the resignation of an employee

When people leave, it is nice to announce the departure to keep everyone informed. Again, a short note saying when the person is leaving and where he is moving to should be sufficient. A complimentary note about his achievements is always welcome, but make sure it is sincere and fitting for the person, otherwise it may be seen as 'damning with faint praise'.

PARKER
Glass Ltd

Unit 27 Willow Park
Christchurch, Dorset BH23 6MM
Tel: 01202 109111
Fax: 01202 109112

Reg. No: England 962578762
VAT No: 9120564

1 May 2005

To all staff

Resignation of David Scannell

I am sorry to announce the resignation of David Scannell as Head of Sales.

David will be leaving us on 18 May and, after a short holiday, will be taking up his new position as Sales Director with Courtnay Breece Ltd. We shall be looking to appoint his successor within the next three to four weeks.

During the six years that he has been with us, David has presided over a growth in sales which has made us the envy of all our rivals. For this, and for his irrepressible good humour in the face of any crisis, he will be sadly missed.

There will be an opportunity for all staff to say farewell at a gathering at 1.30–2.30pm on 18 May in the Function Suite. Light refreshments will be available.

Peter Cox
Personnel Director

NOTICES TO INDIVIDUAL EMPLOYEES
Letter 156: Notifying an employee of her entitlement to sick pay

Conscientious employees who are off sick for long periods will be concerned about what the company thinks about their time off. This type of letter needs to blend the personal message of sympathy with the 'corporate line'.

The expressions of concern for the employee's health are sandwiched between the regulations on sick pay, but they help to bring the correspondence on to a more personal and sympathetic footing. Phrases such as 'I do hope that you make a swift recovery...' and '...wish you well' are good ones to remember when writing these letters.

RPP Holdings Plc
35/38 New Road, Paignton, Devon TQ3 4UU
Tel: 01803 175653 Fax: 01803 187908
Reg. No: England 1976143

Mrs Sarah Thompson
27 Beacon Close
Paignton
Devon
TQ3 6UJ

14 June 2005

Dear Sarah,

I am very sorry to hear that you are still not making a good enough recovery to be able to return to work.

I have heard in the meantime from your doctor, who says that she does not think you will be fit enough to return to work for at least six months, although she would, obviously, like to keep the situation under review.

You asked me how this news affects your entitlement to pay. In case you do not know about the sickness regulations, you are only entitled to statutory sick pay for the first 28 weeks of your absence through sickness. After that you must claim incapacity benefit.

I do hope that you make a swift recovery and may perhaps be able to return to work sooner than anticipated. You are already being missed by your colleagues, who also wish you well.

Yours sincerely,

Ian Goodge
General Manager

NOTICES TO INDIVIDUAL EMPLOYEES
Letter 157: Refusing to allow a leave of absence with pay

This is a formal letter from someone further up the line, who clearly has no day-to-day dealings with the employee. The tone is very impersonal and cold. Phrases such as 'I am in receipt of...' and 'You will be aware...' create this impression.

At the outset, one might imagine the letter to be uncompromising in its refusal. However, a solution is suggested which will probably be acceptable to the reader, in spite of being prefaced with a begrudging 'In the circumstances...'.

IDENDEN INDUSTRIES
A division of Idenden Plc
Porter House, Hull HU7 4RF, England

Tel 01482 119087 Fax 01482 119088
Registered in England No: 1218943

Mr P Townsend
56 Dockland Avenue
Hull
HU7 1KJ

1 July 2005

Mr Townsend,

Proposed Leave of Absence

I am in receipt of your letter requesting leave of absence with pay from 13 July to 14 July inclusive. In your letter you state your reasons as being that you are moving house.

You will be aware from your letter of appointment and from notices on the notice board of the conditions under which leave of absence with pay are ordinarily granted. Moving house is not covered by these conditions and we regret, therefore, that we are unable to grant you leave of absence with pay.

In the circumstances, however, we are prepared to grant leave of absence for the two days in question, without pay, if this arrangement is acceptable to you.

Perhaps you would telephone my secretary as soon as possible to let me know what you decide.

Yours sincerely,

J P Stone
Personnel Department

NOTICES TO INDIVIDUAL EMPLOYEES
Letter 158: Notifying an employee about a company loan

This letter is a standard company letter for all employees requiring a season-ticket loan. It has a matter-of-fact corporate tone that sticks to the essentials.

It is important, when writing these letters, not to omit details such as how the employee is expected to repay the amount to the company, and how any unused amounts of the loan must be reimbursed, if the employee leaves the company.

Charles Cunningham Ltd

29 Baker Street, LONDON N34 6GH, England
Tel: (020) 7015 1290 Fax: (020) 7015 1271
Reg. No: England 1104398135 VAT No: 82108643

Mr David Hobbs
23 Heather Close
Cambridge
CB2 7HJ

25 January 2005

Dear David,

Company Loan

I am pleased to inform you that the company agrees to make an interest-free loan available to you for £2,566, so that you can purchase an annual season ticket for travel to and from work. The amount will be deducted from your salary in 12 equal monthly instalments.

If, at any time during the course of the next 12 months, you leave the employment of the company, you will be required to reimburse us for the outstanding amount of the loan.

I would be grateful if you could sign and date the enclosed form so that a cheque can be raised.

Yours sincerely,

Kevin Gibson
Finance Manager

NOTICES TO INDIVIDUAL EMPLOYEES
Letter 159: Confirming to an employee the termination of her employment

Terminating someone's contract is never pleasant but, if it can be done on amicable terms, so much the better. The employee and the employer in this case have mutually agreed to part company and the tone adopted is friendly and fits the occasion. It begins on an official note in the first paragraph but soon moves on to a more personal level.

The letter cleverly mixes compliments, praising the attributes of the employee, with a recognition that she does not have an aptitude for cold-calling, which is always going to be '...an uphill struggle for you'. The phrases that praise are worth noting and include '...you would certainly be considered for such a post' and '...we shall be only too happy to provide [a reference] for your satisfactory good character and conduct', which reinforce the good terms and mutually agreed nature of the termination.

Wilson Smith Ltd
A wholly owned subsidiary of The Wilson Group PLC
16 Willow Walk, Retford, Nottingham NG6 8WS
Tel: (01777) 121211 Fax: (01777) 121233
Reg. No: England 1212298762

Ms Christine Edwards
24 Princes Avenue
Nottingham
NG4 7JU

10 September 2005

Dear Christine,

As we agreed this morning, I would like to confirm our mutual decision not to continue your employment beyond the end of next month. Your last day of employment will be 30 October.

I would not wish you to attribute any personal blame to the fact that we are not able to extend your contract beyond your three-month probationary period. The task of selling advertising space by telephone is never an easy one and, although you have made a determined effort, it seems that this field is always going to be an uphill struggle for you. I certainly think that your suggestion of seeking a job in a marketing-oriented field, where there will be less cold-call selling, is likely to be more suited to your skills and aspirations. I only wish we had a vacancy for a marketing position here, as you would certainly be considered for such a post.

If you require a reference, we shall be only too happy to provide one for your satisfactory good character and conduct. You will understand that we would have to include in any reference the caveat that we would not consider cold-call telephone selling to be appropriate employment for you.

I would like to take this opportunity to wish you every success in your future.

Yours sincerely,

Alice Pope
Marketing Director

MATERNITY AND OTHER LEAVE
Letter 160: Notifying an employee of her entitlement to maternity pay

The rules concerning ordinary and additional maternity leave are complex and should be checked carefully before a letter like this is written.

Given the complexity of the law and the need to assess each case individually, it is difficult not to sound too official when writing this letter, but the aim should be to include a mixture of congratulations with 'and these are the rules'.

The warm congratulatory tone is here reserved for the opening, which helps to counteract the colder, more businesslike message of the maternity pay regulations.

Tyler & Piper Associates

76 Whites Lane, Stevenage, Herts SG1 8JP, England
Tel: (01438) 186465 Fax: (01438) 164323

Mrs M Joseph
149 Bronsbury Park
Stevenage
Herts
SG1 7KJ

26 June 2003

Dear Mary,

Statutory Maternity Pay

Thank you for letting me know about your pregnancy – I am delighted for you and do hope everything goes well.

You asked whether you qualified for statutory maternity pay. I have checked the rules on this and they are as follows:

1. You must have been continuously employed by us for at least 26 weeks by the start of the 14th week before the expected week of childbirth (i.e. your 26th week of pregnancy).

2. Your average weekly earnings must also not be less than the lower earnings limit for the payment of National Insurance, which I can confirm is the case in your instance.

3. You must have reached the start of the 11th week before the week the baby is due (or have had the baby by this time).

You will receive maternity pay at 90 per cent of your average weekly earnings for the first six weeks. Thereafter you will receive maternity pay at the flat rate of £106.

Should you choose to return to work before the end of the 26-week ordinary maternity leave period, you must give me 28 days' notice of the date you intend to return on.

I hope this explains the position but if you have any other queries, please do ask.

Yours sincerely

Harry Law
Personnel Manager

Partners: DA Tyler BA & SR Piper MA

MATERNITY AND OTHER LEAVE
Letter 161: Confirming that an employee is not entitled to receive maternity pay

This letter is tricky because of the element of bad news that has to be given. The employee may already know what the rules are, but if she doesn't, she is likely to feel annoyed towards the company, even though the company is simply following the regulations as they stand.

Note how the writer tries to empathise with the employee's predicament: 'I am sorry if you are disappointed...' and 'We will do everything we can to help....' The writer also takes pains to explain that there is nothing he can do: '...you are not entitled by law...' and 'We have no control over these regulations...', which should help to dissipate any anger that is felt towards the company.

Tyler & Piper Associates

76 Whites Lane, Stevenage, Herts SG1 8JP, England
Tel: (01438) 186465 Fax: (01438) 164323

Mrs M Joseph
149 Bronsbury Park
Stevenage
Herts
SG1 7KJ

26 June 2005

Dear Mary,

Re: Statutory Maternity Pay
Firstly, Mary, I would like to say how delighted I am for you at your news – I do hope everything goes well for you.

As I mentioned to you, to qualify for statutory maternity pay you must have been continuously employed by us for at least 26 weeks by the beginning of the 14th week before the expected week of childbirth (i.e. your 26th week of pregnancy).

Your expected week of confinement is the week commencing 16 October. Your qualifying week is the week commencing 10 July. To qualify for statutory maternity pay you would have had to commence your employment with us by 8 January. Unfortunately, because you did not join us until the 19 February you are not entitled by law to receive statutory maternity pay.

We have no control over these regulations and you will understand that, as a company, we are bound by them. However, I have discovered you will be able to claim maternity allowance. I will find out for you how to claim this allowance and the amount you will be entitled to receive.

I hope this clarifies the rules for you – I know it is not easy to take in when you haven't got the dates down on paper. I am sorry if you are disappointed to have missed the qualifying date by such a narrow margin. We will do everything we can to help and, if you would like to return to work following the birth of your child, we shall be delighted to welcome you back.

Yours sincerely,

Harry Law
Personnel Manager

Partners: DA Tyler BA & SR Piper MA

MATERNITY AND OTHER LEAVE
Letter 162: Wishing an employee a speedy recovery

Conscientious employees often feel badly about taking large amounts of time off, even when they are seriously unwell. It is important that the employee is not made to feel guilty about his illness. Coming back too early may only make matters worse.

This letter sets a reassuring tone and implies that everything is under control. A pleasantly informal note is struck by phrases like '...willingly stepped into the breach...' and '...will try to confine it to a small hill...'.

The style of the last sentence is worth noting for other letters: the three instructions have a rhythmic flow that has a lot of impact, making for a memorable and impressive, yet friendly and informal, warm-hearted, close.

 Kelso Limited
16 Abbots Road, Luton, Bedfordshire MK44 7YT
Tel: (01234) 136953 Fax: (01234) 136422
Registered in England No: 9126719 VAT No: 91523489 76

Peter Frost
45 Burgess Avenue
Luton
Bedfordshire
MK43 8RE

13 August 2005

Dear Peter,

Thank you for sending your medical certificate to us confirming that your doctor has advised you to rest for the next three weeks following your terrible bout of 'flu.

I am very sorry that this bug has hit you so hard. John and Harry have willingly stepped into the breach to help out in the intervening period, so please don't worry about returning to a mountain of paper on your desk. They will try to confine it to a small hill and generally keep things ticking over until you return.

Put your feet up, drink plenty of fluids and get well soon.

Best wishes,

Charles Edwards
General Manager

MOTIVATING STAFF
Letter 163: Motivating an employee whose performance has deteriorated

Sometimes, obstructive elements can reduce a person's ability to perform successfully.

Here, a manager is developing solutions to a problem that is preventing an employee from performing at his peak. Being seen to make these kinds of changes can go a long way to improving someone's morale. What might seem fairly trivial problems to the manager can appear as insuperable obstacles to the employee, particularly if the solution is beyond that person's control.

It is often worthwhile spending some time building your employee's confidence up again. This is achieved here in expressions such as: 'You have a great deal to contribute...'; '...I am confident...there will be considerable opportunities to increase your responsibilities' and 'I know you will do your utmost...'.

PARKER
Glass Ltd

Unit 27 Willow Park
Christchurch, Dorset BH23 6MM
Tel: 01202 109111
Fax: 01202 109112

Reg. No: England 962578762
VAT No: 9120564

Mr J Randall
Sales and Marketing Co-ordinator

22 February 2005

Dear John,

Thank you for being so frank and open about the difficulties that you have faced in the last few months. I hope that we may be able to reduce some of the conflicts that you have experienced and create a more fulfilling job for you. You have a great deal to contribute to the sales and marketing team and I am confident that, in the coming months, there will be considerable opportunities to increase your responsibilities.

In your role as Sales and Marketing Co-ordinator, you are, at present, reporting to two people: myself and the Sales Director. I recognise that this can create difficulties, especially when both of us demand a task to be performed at the same time and to the same deadline. From now on, you will report solely to me, and any tasks that the Sales Director requires will come through me. That way, I can monitor the flow of work and prevent one of the sources of conflict.

You should also not be afraid to raise problems (however minor) at an early stage with me. If you are not sure how to perform a particular task or if there seem a number of ways for achieving the goal that has been given to you, please feel free to discuss them with me at any time. Two heads are often better than one when it comes to solving difficult issues.

I agree that we should hold more regular feedback sessions and I suggest that we meet in a month's time to review how the changes are working. Obviously, the prime issue is to achieve the sales targets that we have set ourselves. I know you will do your utmost to achieve the results we need.

Yours sincerely,

T J Squires
Marketing Director

MOTIVATING STAFF
Letter 164: Using a promotion to motivate an employee

Writing a letter that motivates is not easy. It must sound sincere, so the recipient takes it seriously. Money is only one way of rewarding people.

Here, money is not mentioned and instead the writer capitalises on other motivational factors, such as recognition for a job well done: '...made such a positive contribution...'; rewarding with greater responsibility: '...I would like you to become fully responsible for...' and setting challenging goals to be attained: '...ensure that the targets which we have identified are achieved'.

Note how the person expresses confidence in the employee: '...I know you are very capable of accomplishing successfully'.

 Kelso Limited
16 Abbots Road, Luton, Bedfordshire MK44 7YT
Tel: (01234) 136953 Fax: (01234) 136422
Registered in England No: 9126719 VAT No: 91523489 76

Mr J Edmonds
Despatch Department

29 June 2005

Dear James,

I think it was very useful to talk through your performance over the last six months and I wanted to confirm some of the points that were discussed. We are pleased with the way you have so quickly become a key member of the warehouse team and made such a positive contribution from the beginning. You are a conscientious worker and we are very keen for you to build upon the skills that you have developed so far.

As we discussed, from 1 July I would like you to become fully responsible for the following areas and ensure that the goals which we have identified are achieved.

Responsibility	Goal
1. Receive and check deliveries of new stock.	Same day unpacking, storage and notifying the relevant department of arrival.
2. Timely despatch of all goods.	75% of orders despatched the same day. The remainder to be despatched the following day.
3. Management of the warehouse.	Implement an efficient location and picking system for all stock.

I would like to monitor your performance on a monthly basis, to ensure that these targets are achieved and that any difficulties are ironed out at the earliest opportunity. I hope you enjoy the challenge that this role represents and which I know you are very capable of accomplishing successfully.

Yours sincerely,

J Granger
General Manager

MOTIVATING STAFF
Letter 165: Motivating a team to achieve a goal

This letter contains many of the ingredients of a successful motivational letter.

Using rhetorical questions helps to focus the mind on a particular point – here the bonus and how far the company has come in three years. It also deploys another tactic to engage people's interests – using 'we' and 'you' to focus attention on the audience and gain its commitment. If the letter had been peppered with many 'I's', the reader's attention would be focused more on the writer and its impact would be much reduced.

SIMPSON & MARTIN

39 TOP STREET
STOKE-ON-TRENT
ST2 3DR, UNITED KINGDOM
Tel: (01782) 156232 Fax: (01782) 120899
Reg. No: England 96223978 VAT No: 91210674

Miss Karen Davis
Sales Administration

12 June 2005

Dear Karen,

The strategy which we briefed you on this morning is the key to our success. If these targets are achieved, you can look forward to a bonus at the end of next year of over £1,500. Now, isn't that something worth working towards?

Do you remember how, three years ago, we were just one of many suppliers? While we have grown, our old competitors have shrunk away from us. Each one of you has made a marvellous contribution so far to the success of this company. But in every success story are the seeds of failure, and there is no room for complacency. We must be alert to new competitors and what they are doing. We must seize the opportunities that present themselves and make sure not one of them is missed. We must continue to talk to our customers and find out what our competitors are up to. If we are to be number one in three years' time, we must have the resolve, guts, determination and drive to succeed.

We have a superb team, the goal is in view, and the foundations are laid. I know you can achieve what we are asking. All I ask is that you give it your all.

Yours sincerely,

D B Fenton
Sales Director

OFFERING CONGRATULATIONS
Letter 166: Announcing a performance award

The keynote here is to convey enthusiasm and echo the success and achievement that a winner of a performance award should feel.

You should always praise the achievement – this is one of the occasions when the management can freely give recognition, and it will be appreciated by the recipient. Try to make it as personal as possible, as in the phrase: 'It gives me great personal pleasure to recognise...'. Making the result seem close gives the impression that the competition was tough.

Note some of the phrases that are useful in similar letters: '...although it was a very close-run thing...'; '...it is a tribute to your hard work...' and '...a well-earned prize...'.

Charles Cunningham Ltd

29 Baker Street, LONDON N34 6GH England
Tel: (020) 7015 1290 Fax: (020) 7015 1271
Reg. No: England 1104398135 VAT No: 82108643

Ms Jan Hancock
Marketing Department

28 November 2005

Dear Jan,

Outstanding Employee of the Year Award 2005
I am delighted to confirm that you are this year's winner of the Outstanding Employee of the Year Award.

The competition to achieve this accolade was considerable, but I am delighted to say that, although it was a very close-run thing, your dedication to the task combined with your record-breaking output were the winning factors that gave you the edge over the other candidates.

I know that you have been a previous contender for the position, and it is a tribute to your hard work and constancy that, year after year, you have been able to turn out results which anyone here would be proud of achieving.

It gives me great personal pleasure to recognise this achievement with the accolade of the Outstanding Employee of the Year and a well-earned prize of £500, which will be added to your salary this month.

Congratulations, and I hope you will go on to defend your title for many years to come.

Yours sincerely,

T J Ward
Managing Director

OFFERING CONGRATULATIONS
Letter 167: Appreciating an employee's special effort

Appreciating someone unexpectedly can be an extremely powerful tool for motivating him.

With performance awards, there is a sense that the appreciation is obligatory and slightly forced, because someone has to win. This can reduce the motivational benefit. But when a note of appreciation is unannounced and sincerely felt, its impact can be extremely rewarding.

This letter is a good example of the tone and feeling to aim for – particularly recognising areas where there was considerable resistance and achievements which, at the time, may have appeared to go unnoticed.

GKT Products Ltd, Unit 10, Castleway Lane, Alloway, Ayr, KA7 4BE
Telephone (01292) 177900 Fax (01292) 199855   Reg. No: 17964583 VAT No: 679845

David Holmes
General Manager

18 June 2005

Dear David,

The recent achievement of obtaining ISO 9001 has been one that the whole company has won by pulling together, but without the driving force of a few individuals firmly at the helm, I know the project would have had very little chance of even getting off the ground, let alone earning the rewards which are so richly deserved.

I recognise that in the early stages of the project, you experienced considerable resistance to it from both management and employees alike. But, with your determination and hard work, you had the foresight to look ahead to today and convince all of us of the benefits we would be able to reap.

I know that this achievement is as much your special effort as it is the company's and I would like to say a very big personal 'thank you'. You have raised our profile in the eyes of our competitors, our parent company and amongst the other divisions. Well done.

Yours sincerely,

Ron Blake
Director

OFFERING CONGRATULATIONS
Letter 168: Congratulating the winner of a business award

This letter brings out a hoard of useful congratulatory phrases: '...prestigious award...'; '...wonderful achievement...' and 'It means a great deal to me personally...'.

The last sentence has a good ring to it, achieved by mirroring the first half of the sentence in the second half: '...and set the style for our age – a style which, I hope,...' – making it more memorable for the reader.

IDENDEN INDUSTRIES
A division of Idenden Plc
Porter House, Hull HU7 4RF, England

Tel 01482 119087 Fax 01482 119088
Registered in England No: 1218943

Stephen Turner
Design Manager

27 May 2005

Dear Stephen,

Designer of the Year

I was delighted to hear you have won the designer of the year award for the best-produced annual report. Many congratulations.

This is the first time that someone from our firm has won this prestigious award and it is a wonderful achievement, both personally and professionally. I am doubly delighted because this award is a 'sock in the face' to our competitors, who have, for too long, been resting on their laurels. It means a great deal to me personally and to the firm. I am already looking forward to the many new clients who will be beating a path to our door.

Your designs have become a landmark for the industry, and set the style for our age – a style which, I hope, will continue for some time to come.

Yours sincerely,

Ray Hooper
Technical Director

HEALTH AND SAFETY
Letter 169: Reminding staff about the health and safety policy

Health and safety is often one of those areas that falls to the bottom of a company's list of priorities, but every company must ensure it is complying adequately with the regulations. Health and Safety Inspectors are entitled to call unannounced. This letter aims to bring the topic to everyone's attention. It combines a further message about security issues, to prevent unwanted intruders. The tone is clear but fairly formal. 'Please take two minutes to read it...' is a better way of saying 'please read it' as it suggests it will take a very short time and can be easily absorbed. More employees may be encouraged to take note of it instead of filing it away unread. Note the fairly emphatic tone used: 'It is vital...'; 'For his own safety...'; '...do accompany them...'; 'For security reasons...'; '...don't be afraid to ask...' and '...do bring it to the attention of...' – each one designed to give everyone clear, unambiguous instructions.

GKT Products Ltd, Unit 10, Castleway Lane, Alloway, Ayr, KA7 4BE
Telephone (01292) 177900 Fax (01292) 199855   Reg. No: 17964583 VAT No: 679845

14 June 2005

To all members of staff

Health and Safety
Following the recent accident involving a visitor to our premises, I would like to remind everyone of our health and safety policy. A copy of the policy is attached. Please take two minutes to read it and remind yourself of the main points.

It is vital, for safety and security reasons, that if you have a visitor to the building you are responsible for him at all times. For his own safety he should not be allowed to wander freely around the building Remember, the layout can be disorientating to visitors so if your visitors need to use the toilets, do accompany them and escort them back.

For security reasons, if you should see someone you do not recognise wandering about the building unaccompanied, do not be afraid to ask him politely why he is here, whom the visitor is seeing and if that person knows the visitor has arrived.

All employees have a responsibility to take reasonable care of themselves and others and to achieve a healthy and safe workplace. If you notice any hazard or potential hazard, do bring it to the attention of the Health and Safety Manager, John Fish, who will investigate the situation.

Thank you for your co-operation with this policy.

Yours sincerely,

Karl Jones
Health & Safety Officer

HEALTH AND SAFETY
Letter 170: Reporting a death to the Health and Safety Executive

Just as certain accidents and diseases have to be reported, so do deaths, even if they occur several months later, for example, following an accident.

The regulations require that the responsible person (usually the employer) notifies the Health and Safety Executive by the quickest means practicable, which could be 'phone or fax. Initially, you need only give the basic information – subsequently, a form giving more specific details will have to be filled in.

H J KINGSLEY (NORWICH) LTD
Kingsley House, Morris Street, Norwich NR6 7JM
Tel: (01603) 117097 Fax: (01603) 117099 Reg. No: England 12086215 VAT No: 8793519

Fax Message

To:
Name: Mr H T Taylor
Company: Health and Safety Executive
Fax No: 01353 112039

Message From: Tom Frost
Date: 16 March 2005

Please let us know by 'phone or fax immediately if any page is missing or garbled in transmission

---

Dear Mr Taylor,

We have just learned about the death of John Smith, a former employee, who was living at 34 Castle End, Midsham, Cambs and, in accordance with statutory requirements, we are writing to notify you of the fact.

We understand from his wife that his death was a direct result of an accident sustained while working here and which we notified you about on 30 October last year.

Yours sincerely,

Mr Tom Frost
Health and Safety Officer

HOLIDAY POLICY
Letter 171: Announcing extra holiday entitlement

With this kind of change, there are always going to be instant winners and those who will have to wait until they can benefit from the change. Introducing it has the twin benefit that it acts as a reward for those who have been with the company longer and as an incentive to stay for those who have not yet reached the date.

BELLS OF BASILDON

Bells of Basildon Ltd, Unit 12, Way Park, Basildon SS12 6DE
Tel: 01268 109 9954 Fax: 01268 109 5576 Reg. No: England 13078453 VAT No: 75698764

Mr R Norman
General Manager

13 December 2005

Dear Roy,

Holidays
We have decided to change the holiday policy of the company.

From 1 January 2006, all employees who have been with the company for five years will be entitled to an extra two days' holiday a year, in addition to their normal entitlement.

Those of you who have been with the company for less than five years must serve a full five years by 1 January to qualify for two extra days in that year. So, if your fifth anniversary arrives in June, you will not be entitled to take two extra days until the following 1 January.

I hope this clarifies the new policy, but if you have any queries, please do not hesitate to ask me personally.

Yours sincerely,

David O'Brian
Director

HOLIDAY POLICY
Letter 172: Announcing the carrying over of outstanding holiday entitlement

When changing the rules of the company, it is vital to be clear about what the changes mean for people and to set the boundaries of what is permitted.

Here, a fairly simple amendment gives rise to additional questions that the writer has tried to anticipate. Note how the letter begins with a statement of what the existing holiday policy is, so everyone is clear about how the changes differ.

IDENDEN INDUSTRIES
A division of Idenden Plc
Porter House, Hull HU7 4RF, England

Tel 01482 119087 Fax 01482 119088
Registered in England No: 1218943

3 December 2005

To all heads of department

Holidays

Until now, it has been a requirement of the company that everyone takes their holiday within one calendar year, and the right to any holiday not taken by 31 December has lapsed.

It has now been decided to amend the rule, to give everyone the opportunity to be more flexible with their holidays. From today, anyone who has up to a week's holiday entitlement outstanding at 31 December must use it up by 31 March in the following year. The entitlement to any days that are not used by 31 March will lapse. Unused holiday may not be converted to pay. The entitlement to holiday is, of course, still subject to agreement with your manager. It must take into account the business and operational needs of the company and, especially, avoid clashes with other people if this means that a job would be left uncovered.

If you have any queries about this new policy, please see Jemima Denoon.

Yours sincerely,

A K Oakman
Personnel Executive

OFFERING SINCERE CONDOLENCES
Letter 173: Offering condolences to a bereaved wife

Letters of condolence are always difficult to write. No amount of words can help to replace the loss. All that can be hoped for is that the small words of comfort will help to alleviate the grief.

The letter wants to be brief and, above all, sincere. If you can say a few personal words of tribute to the departed person or remember some of his characteristics, this will help to lift the letter, increase the impact of your message and be appreciated by the grieving relative.

Hart & Tucker Ltd
19 Green Street, Maidstone, Kent ME41 1TJ
Telephone: (01622) 109109
Facsimile: (01622) 108106
Reg. No: England 96223978 VAT No: 91210674

Mrs P Burnett
35 Masons Avenue
Maidstone
Kent
ME41 7UJ

16 August 2005

Dear Mrs Burnett,

I was very sorry to hear your sad news.

Although I only knew Alex briefly, I thoroughly enjoyed working with him and found his professionalism and dedication to his consultancy second to none. When Alex broke the news to me of his cancer, I was amazed at the way he was able to continue working, providing answers to our enquiries and checking details throughout the project, and, true to his dedication, always keeping to the timescales that were requested.

The successful completion of the project gave Alex a great sense of pride and I hope it will be a source of comfort to you to know that, as a tribute to him, we would like to name the last building which he designed the Alex Burnett Building. I hope it will be a source of comfort to know that Alex's work will be remembered in this way.

Please accept the most sincere condolences and deepest sympathy from all at Hart & Tucker Ltd.

Yours sincerely,

J P Smith
Managing Director

OFFERING SINCERE CONDOLENCES
Letter 174: Offering condolences to the parents on the sudden loss of a son

A sudden and tragic death can make the task of writing a condolence letter all the more difficult. The opening sentence here is a good one to use, when a letter like this is required. It has the right mix of empathy and sincerity, even though the level of shock felt by the writer will always be less than the grieving relative.

The rule of being brief and sincere still applies. Note the clutch of phrases that can be used for similar condolence letters: 'We were deeply shocked...'; '...it will be very difficult for us to forget...'; 'We will miss him sorely' and 'Please accept our sincere sympathy....'

Thomas King
& Palmer Ltd
serving the world

24 Fuller Road, Welling,
Kent DA16 7JP
Tel: (01322) 100132
Fax: (01322) 100178

Reg. No: England 1212298762
VAT No: 92905643

Mr & Mrs P Strong
34 Kelvin Drive
Welling
Kent
DA16 5GP

26 September 2005

Dear Mr and Mrs Strong,

We were deeply shocked by John's untimely death and I am writing to extend our heartfelt condolences to you both at this painful time.

John was an outstanding member of his team and an extremely loyal and conscientious employee. He always went about his work so willingly and cheerfully and it will be very difficult for us to forget his bubbly personality, which lifted everyone's spirits so much. We will miss him sorely.

Please accept our sincere sympathy on your loss. If there is anything we can do, please let us know.

Yours sincerely,

Andrew Rogers
Managing Director

CHAPTER 6

Banking, insurance and property

What you'll find in this chapter

✔ Managing an account
✔ Loans and overdrafts
✔ Insurance
✔ Property
✔ Finance documentation

This chapter focuses on letters that are ancillary to many core business activities but which are no less important to the smooth running of a business. Everything from dealing with an estate agent, insurance broker to bank is considered. Indeed, if a business does not enjoy good relations with its bank, it may find it hard to survive at all.

Banking letters

The routine letters to a bank illustrate opening an account, closing an account and declining an offer to open an account. Letters 181–182 show the kind of information that banks like to see when they ask to be put in the picture about the financial situation.

Insurance

The letters here deal with requests for insurance and for a revised quotation.

Property

When making offers to estate agents it is important to confirm what is included, to avoid misunderstandings at a later stage. The letters here show how to handle it. When purchasing property you will also need to arrange for surveys to be done. Letters 185–186 show how to instruct a surveyor.

Finance documentation

Pressing a debtor to pay in a foreign country is likely to be difficult, if the customer defaults on payment. It is far better to make sure that payment is secure before the goods are despatched. Letter 189 deals with asking a bank to pay on the presentation of a letter of credit.

MANAGING AN ACCOUNT
Letter 175: Opening a current account

When opening a current account, a bank will need to know some basic information before it accepts you as a customer. The customer here is already known to the bank, so it is able to dispense with the usual formalities. Don't forget, a bank will want to know who the signatories to an account will be, whether the account is 'both to sign' or 'either to sign' and what name the account should be in.

PARKER
Glass Ltd

Unit 27 Willow Park
Christchurch, Dorset BH23 6MM
Tel: 01202 109111
Fax: 01202 109112

Reg. No: England 962578762
VAT No: 9120564

Mr F Turner
Manager
RSH Bank PLC
73 Main Street
Dorset
BH23 6MM

3 May 2005

Dear Mr Turner,

We are reorganising the administration of our accounts department and wish to open another current account, from which all our suppliers will be paid. Our existing Current Account No. 629523 will be used for all other transactions.

I would be grateful if you could arrange for £10,000 to be transferred from Account No. 629523 to the new account. The signatories for the new account will be myself and Mary Martin. You already have my specimen signature on file and I enclose a sample of Mary Martin's signature. Both signatures will be required on all cheques. The account should be in the name of Parker Enterprises.

I look forward to receiving a chequebook for the new account.

Yours sincerely,

A Parker
Finance Director

MANAGING AN ACCOUNT
Letter 176: Cancelling a cheque

Occasionally, cheques will go astray or get lost in the post. If this happens, you should cancel the cheque by 'phone and confirm it in writing. This will stop anyone else cashing the cheque if it falls into the wrong hands.

Don't forget to give precise details about the cheque (its payee, amount, number and date written).

It will be a help to identify the replacement cheque that has been sent, in case the bank looks for the cheque by amount or otherwise confuses the new cheque with the old.

SIMPSON & MARTIN

39 TOP STREET
STOKE-ON-TRENT
ST2 3DR, UNITED KINGDOM
Tel: (01782) 156232 Fax: (01782) 120899
Reg. No: England 96223978 VAT No: 91210674

J W Cross
Manager
RSH Bank PLC
3 Main Street
Stoke-on-Trent
ST2 3RF

7 May 2005

Dear Mr Cross,

Our Cheque No. 107348

I am writing to confirm that we would like to cancel Cheque No. 107348 (dated 2 April 2005) for £2,745.89, which was in favour of John C Smith Ltd. I understand there is a charge of £7 for stopping a cheque, which will be debited from our account. .

As I mentioned on the telephone this morning, it appears to have been lost in the post and we are issuing a replacement cheque (No. 107399).

Please confirm that the cheque has been stopped.

Yours sincerely,

John Herbert
Finance Director

MANAGING AN ACCOUNT
Letter 177: Notifying a bank about a change of signature for cheques

If a signatory to a cheque leaves the company, you will have to notify the bank of the changes: which account is affected; the name of the old and new signatory; the date when the signature will be accepted from and an example of the new signature for the bank's reference.

Taylor Taylor & Shaw
Benton House, Clifton, Bristol BS16 7LJ
Tel: (0117) 1089254   Fax: (0117) 1089211

Brian Fowler
Branch Manager
RSH Bank PLC
16 Main Street
Clifton
Bristol
BS16 7JJ

15 August 2005

Dear Mr Fowler,

Account No. 5497610
With the departure of our accountant, Stanley Pritchard, the two signatures that will appear on the cheques drawn on Account No. 5497610 will be mine and that of John Barclay, who is replacing Stanley. This will take effect from 1 September.

I enclose a sample of John's signature for your file and would be grateful if you could confirm safe receipt.

Yours sincerely,

A W Taylor

Partners: AW Taylor & GS Taylor

MANAGING AN ACCOUNT
Letter 178: Closing an account

Banks will usually require instructions about closing accounts to be made in writing. A simple letter like this one is all that is required. Don't forget to include details of where you want the remaining balance of the account to go to.

Tyler & Piper Associates

76 Whites Lane, Stevenage, Herts SG1 8JP, England
Tel: (01438) 186465 Fax: (01438) 164323

Mr K Foster
Manager
Martins Bank PLC
54 High Street
Stevenage
Herts
SG1 8JP

17 April 2005

Dear Mr Foster,

Account No. 354896
We no longer need our Account No. 354896 and I would be grateful if it could be closed immediately.

Please transfer the remaining balance to Account No. 729491.

Yours sincerely,

S R Piper
Finance Manager/Partner

Partners: DA Tyler BA & SR Piper MA

LOANS AND OVERDRAFTS
Letter 179: Declining an offer to open an account

A company has been offered terms to open an account, but it has decided to shop around for a better rate. A bank will always appreciate knowing why you are not opening an account. Don't forget to keep your letter courteous – you never know when you may need the services of that bank again in the future.

Grange & Turner Ltd

32 WESTBOURN ROAD, WITNEY, OXON OX6 7HY

Telephone (01993) 107888
Fax (01993) 107843

Reg. No: England 13078453
VAT No: 75698764

Mrs Y Norman
Business Manager
Barkers Bank plc
23 High Street
Witney
Oxon
OX6 7HY

20 June 2005

Dear Mrs Norman,

Thank you for your letter of 12 June, outlining the terms on which you are willing to provide us with an overdraft and current account.

We have considered your offer, but regret that we shall not be opening an account with you, as we have been able to secure an overdraft rate with Macaulays Bank which is 0.5 per cent lower.

Thank you for your time considering our application and I hope we may have an opportunity to do business in future.

Yours sincerely,

DG Edwards
Director

LOANS AND OVERDRAFTS
Letter 180: Following up an application for a business loan

If you visit a bank manager seeking funds for a project, he is very unlikely to commit at the meeting to grant you the funds requested. Instead, he will want to take a day or two to consider your proposal and perhaps put it in front of his credit committee. Note how the company uses the time to go back to the bank with a positive statement, which should help tip the balance in your favour, if the bank is undecided whether to lend the money.

BELLS OF BASILDON

Bells of Basildon Ltd, Unit 12, Way Park, Basildon SS12 6DE
Tel: 01268 109 9954 Fax: 01268 109 5576 Reg. No: England 13078453 VAT No: 75698764

Richard Hobbs
Small Business Manager
Barkers Bank plc
27 High Street
Basildon
SS12 6DF

30 April 2005

Dear Richard,

Re: Our Application for a Business Loan

Thank you for your time on Tuesday concerning our application for a business loan. We are pleased that your initial reaction to our plan is positive, and that you feel our proposition is viable. We appreciate that you require a few days to consider the plan in detail.

Since our meeting, I am delighted to report that we have finalised the details of the contract to supply Galestreet supermarket, which gives us a guaranteed monthly cash-flow of £20,000 per month, £4,000 more than the amount we originally anticipated. We are aiming to sign the contract on Friday 27 May and it would be reassuring to know that the finance will be in place to fund the capital-equipment purchase, which is necessary to accommodate the increased output.

I realise this does not give you a lot of time to consider the plan. Nevertheless, I hope it is sufficient for you to give us a response before we sign the contract.

Yours sincerely,

Simon Frost
Managing Director

LOANS AND OVERDRAFTS
Letter 181: Informing a bank of your positive current position

As part of the management of a business account, banks often want to be kept regularly informed about the financial progress of a company. What they are usually most interested in is the state of the current order book and how that translates into a forecast for the coming months.

This letter focuses on the headline figures (which is all the bank will be interested in at present). You can always submit the evidence to support the figures in subsequent documentation.

Note how the letter keeps its attention on figures – it doesn't try to gloss over the picture with a more general statement. This is the kind of approach which will satisfy a bank. If you do attempt to give a general gloss, the bank will be quick to see through this and may come down heavily on you with some penetrating questions.

H J KINGSLEY (NORWICH) LTD
Kingsley House, Morris Street, Norwich NR6 7JM
Tel: (01603) 117097 Fax: (01603) 117099 Reg. No: England 12086215 VAT No: 8793519

Mr Peter Edwards
Barkers Bank plc
14 North Street
Norwich
NR6 6JM

10 April 2005

Dear Mr Edwards,

Re: Quarterly Review of H J Kingsley (Norwich) Ltd
I promised to let you have details of our order book as part of the quarterly review.

I am pleased to say that our current orders are 15 per cent up on the comparable period last year, at just over £250,000. Enquiries for which we have quoted total £850,000. Historically, we convert 73 per cent of quotes to firm orders. Based on those figures, our projected sales turnover for the year, as depicted in the cash-flow forecast, of £1.75 million is a prudent assessment of the company's likely performance for the current financial year.

I hope this provides you with the information that you need. If you require any further information, please do not hesitate to ask.

Yours sincerely,

Colin North
Director

LOANS AND OVERDRAFTS
Letter 182: Informing a bank of your deteriorating position

If the financial picture is positive, you will not be concerned about giving information to the bank. However, if the picture is less than good, it may be tempting to disguise what is happening in the hope that the situation will improve. But this would be the wrong step to take. It may buy you a temporary reprieve, but what if the picture does not improve? You will end up digging yourself into an even bigger hole.

It is far better to face up to the circumstances and find both a way of managing it and of convincing the bank that your strategy will produce the results that are needed. Note how this letter takes a positive approach, even though the news is not good: '...we do have a strategy in place to manage the decline....which will more than compensate and put us ten per cent ahead of the value of our current order book....'.

H J KINGSLEY (NORWICH) LTD
Kingsley House, Morris Street, Norwich NR6 7JM
Tel: (01603) 117097 Fax: (01603) 117099 Reg. No: England 12086215 VAT No: 8793519

Mr Peter Edwards
Barkers Bank plc
14 North Street
Norwich
NR6 6JM

10 September 2005

Dear Mr Edwards,

Re: Review of H J Kingsley (Norwich) Ltd

I promised to let you have details of our current position since our review last month. As I indicated over the 'phone, the situation has not improved, but we do have a strategy in place to manage the decline.

Our current orders are, frankly, disappointing. As at last night, the figure was £203,000, which is four per cent down on the same period last year. As a consequence, we have trimmed our expenditure by six per cent and conducted a detailed analysis of what our customers require. This has produced the evidence that their tastes are moving from the need for a low-cost functional product to a middle-of-the-range quality item. We have redesigned both the product and the packaging to reflect this changing taste, and we plan to have it on the shelves by the end of this year. Although we forecast a fall in the volume of orders, the profitability per item will increase, which will more than compensate and put us ten per cent ahead of the value of our current order book within the next six months.

I hope this strategy meets with your approval and we shall be able to maintain our overdraft at current levels.

Yours sincerely,

Colin North
Director

INSURANCE
Letter 183: Requesting insurance

Insurance on property should be effected from the moment that you become responsible for it, not from the date of occupation.

This letter requests a company to arrange insurance cover for a building that has just been purchased. To insure the building, the insurer needs to know the address of the property, the date from when insurance needs to take effect, the value of the property (which the building valuation report will provide) and the type of policy required.

Fenner & Sons

16 George Street, Woodbridge,
Suffolk IP3 7KL
Tel: (01394) 198423
Fax: (01394) 198444
Registered in England: 91221299
VAT No: 919129075 80

Mr Kevin Little
Barker Insurance Brokers
24 Middle Street
Ipswich
IP2 3TY

20 March 2005

Dear Kevin,

Re: Buildings Insurance for 45 Edmunds Street, Bury

We are about to acquire a detached property at 45 Edmunds Street, Bury which we shall be using as commercial premises. We anticipate signing the purchase contract towards the end of next month.

The premises will not be occupied for two months, so we are concerned to insure the building only at this stage. I enclose a copy of the valuation report on the building, which estimates the rebuilding cost at £105,000.

We would like to effect an all-risks policy and I would be grateful if you could let me have your quotation for the most favourable rates.

Yours sincerely,

George Rose
Director

INSURANCE

Letter 184: Asking an insurance broker for a revised quotation

It is important that life insurance and pension arrangements are reviewed periodically. If there are discrepancies between policies, make sure these are investigated adequately. This letter is asking for revised quotations to vary the benefits.

Taylor Taylor & Shaw

Benton House, Clifton, Bristol BS16 7LJ
Tel: (0117) 1089254   Fax: (0117) 1089211

Mr R Denny
Shipleys Insurance Brokers
11 Wallace Road
Bristol
BS4 5FD

14 March 2005

Dear Bob,

Re: Pension Scheme
I have just been reviewing our pension scheme and my wife is concerned that her scheme does not appear to have a 'death in service' benefit, although mine does. Please advise what the additional cost of this benefit would be.

I am also considering increasing the life assurance that is attached to my pension, from £150,000 to £250,000. Please also advise me what difference this would make to the monthly premium.

Yours sincerely,

A W Taylor

Partners: AW Taylor & GS Taylor

PROPERTY
Letter 185: Asking for a quote to survey a property

Before instructing a surveyor to inspect a property, ask him for a quotation for carrying out the work. He will want to know some basic information about the property and what its value is. It may be best to send him the estate agent's details, so he can see how large the property is and how much work is involved. He will usually also want to know the age of the property, which may have a bearing on the amount of work.

Thomas King
& Palmer Ltd
serving the world

24 Fuller Road, Welling,
Kent DA16 7JP
Tel: (01322) 100132
Fax: (01322) 100178

Reg. No: England 1212298762
VAT No: 92905643

Mr J R Holt
W B Webster & Son
6 High Street
Dartford
Kent
DA1 2OB

14 July 2005

Dear Mr Holt,

12a High Street, Welling
Further to our telephone conversation today, I enclose, as requested, the estate agent's particulars regarding the above property.

I would be grateful if you could give me a quotation for carrying out a full structural survey on the property and how soon you would be able to make your inspection.

We have made an offer on the property, although we are waiting to hear whether it has been accepted.

Yours sincerely,

F G York
Director

PROPERTY
Letter 186: Instructing a surveyor to inspect a property

If you notice specific defects in a property that require remedial work when instructing a surveyor to inspect a property, it is worth asking him to make a specific comment on the nature and extent of those defects. You may obtain more detailed advice and a more thorough inspection of the faults, even though you would expect them to be covered in the surveyor's report, together with additional points which you had not noticed. Note the confirmation of the quotation, to prevent any misunderstanding about its cost.

Thomas King
& Palmer Ltd
serving the world

24 Fuller Road, Welling,
Kent DA16 7JP
Tel: (01322) 100132
Fax: (01322) 100178

Reg. No: England 1212298762
VAT No: 92905643

Mr J R Holt
W B Webster & Son
6 Bishops Croft
Dartford
Kent
DA1 2OB

14 July 2005

Dear Mr Holt,

12a High Street, Welling

Just to let you know that our offer to purchase the above freehold property for £76,000 has now been accepted and, as I mentioned on the 'phone the other day, I would be grateful if you could carry out a full structural survey. A copy of the estate agent's particulars is enclosed. I understand the fully inclusive cost of the survey will be £327.

I am a little concerned about some of the defects to the property. I am sure that you will pick them up anyway but I thought I should mention them. The small office at the back of the property seems to have an excessively damp smell. I gather it has not been used for some time, but I would appreciate if you could investigate any repairs that may be necessary. Also, water appears at some time to have come through into the upstairs front office, next to the chimney breast. Is this a current problem or does it appear as if repairs have been carried out but redecoration has not been done?

I look forward to receiving your report.

Yours sincerely,

F G York
Director

PROPERTY
Letter 187: Making an offer on a property to an estate agent

If you make an offer on a property, the estate agent will confirm it with you in writing. It is advisable that you also confirm the price that has been agreed and any other items that are to be included in the sale, such as carpets and blinds.

It is easy for misunderstandings to occur over the 'phone and if the agent has it in writing from you, it will save arguments later on.

Heading your letter 'subject to contract' under English law does not bind you to the sale until contracts have been signed and exchanged.

Thomas King
& Palmer Ltd
serving the world

24 Fuller Road, Welling,
Kent DA16 7JP
Tel: (01322) 100132
Fax: (01322) 100178

Reg. No: England 1212298762
VAT No: 92905643

Mr Eddie Wright
Hope Taylor & Moore
35 Lion Row
Dartford
Kent
DA3 2ON

14 May 2005

Subject to Contract

Dear Mr Wright,

12a High Street, Welling

Further to our telephone conversation this morning, I am writing to confirm our offer of £76,000 to purchase the above property.

This offer is to include all carpets, blinds, fixtures and fittings at the premises.

Yours sincerely,

F G York
Director

PROPERTY
Letter 188: Confirming an offer to an estate agent

If you decide to make an offer that is subject to certain conditions, it is important that you spell out exactly what those conditions are. This letter is applying pressure on the sellers to move out sooner than they initially wanted and to have a local authority easement (right of access over the property) released.

The penultimate paragraph (notifying the agent about instructing a solicitor and arranging for a valuation) is designed to convey confidence to the agent and seller about your seriousness in going through with the sale.

H J KINGSLEY (NORWICH) LTD
Kingsley House, Morris Street, Norwich NR6 7JM
Tel: (01603) 117097 Fax: (01603) 117099 Reg. No: England 12086215 VAT No: 8793519

Mr S Clark
Foster & Clark
56 Baker Street
Norwich
NR3 1QA

20 April 2005

Subject to Contract

Dear Simon,

15 Forest Row, Norwich
Just to confirm our discussion today.

We undertake to increase our offer from £120,000 to £125,000 for the purchase of 15 Forest Row, Norwich. This additional sum is offered on the basis that The Stone Partnership undertake to have the local authority easement released, prior to exchange of contracts. Any costs relating to having the easement released shall be the responsibility of the Stone Partnership. We do not wish to delay completion until mid-July as suggested to you by Mr Jones of the Stone Partnership (for which the lesser sum of £120,000 would have been payable). This additional sum of £5,000 is also being offered on the basis that The Stone Partnership aim to exchange contracts with us at the earliest practicable date, which we anticipate being in the week beginning 17 April, with completion occurring three weeks later, in the week beginning 8 May.

I understand that The Stone Partnership has accepted this arrangement and these timescales should be realistic, allowing sufficient time for all the paperwork to be completed and for the easement to be released. I have, therefore, instructed our solicitor to continue with the sale and am making arrangements for the valuation on the property to be carried out.

I trust this is a satisfactory summary of our conversation and that the sale will proceed smoothly.

Yours sincerely,

Peter Hills
Director

FINANCE DOCUMENTATION
Letter 189: Asking the bank to pay on the presentation of a letter of credit

Before a bank will pay out against an Irrevocable Letter of Credit, it will demand that all the documentation is correct. The exact documentation required will vary depending on the countries the goods are going to and from.

Setting the documents out as a list will help you to check that nothing has been omitted and enable the bank to check more easily that it has received all the items that you declare are enclosed.

IDENDEN INDUSTRIES
A division of Idenden Plc
Porter House, Hull HU7 4RF, England

Tel 01482 119087 Fax 01482 119088
Registered in England No: 1218943

A & A Bank
Bills and Credits Department
Mint House
PO Box 10
Monting Court
London WE1 9DP

Dear Sirs,

Your Ref: E54000/1002

Re: Irrevocable Documentary Credit No: 92000026 for $21,640.00
From: Bank of Ghana Limited, Accra
Consignee: Hellpack Industries Limited, Accra

With regard to the above, we enclose your original credit documents, together with the following:

1. 3 copies original-certificate of value
2. 3 copies commercial invoice
3. Full set less 1 original plus 2 non-negotiable copies of bill of lading
4. Original clean report of findings plus embossed and signed invoice
5. 2 copies packing list
6. Our certification that we have sent the appropriate copies of the documents to the opener
7. Our draft to the value of $17,800.00
8. 2 copies certificate of analysis

I trust that everything is in order and we would ask you to pay this directly to our account as follows and notify us accordingly:

Barkers Bank plc
Overseas Financial Services
10 Blair Street
London E1 8BL

Account Name: Idenden Industries
Account No: 3156974582

Many thanks for your co-operation.

Yours faithfully,

John Foster
International Sales

Business and the community | **207**

CHAPTER 7

Business and the community

What you'll find in this chapter
- ✔ Requests and invitations
- ✔ Declining requests and invitations
- ✔ Objections – making and handling

All businesses will, to some extent, have dealings with the community in which they are involved. The letters in this chapter (190–199) deal with requests for charitable donations, an invitation to present an award, invitations to speak at meetings, handling a request to serve on a local committee and dealing with local residents on planning issues.

Requests and invitations

Handling requests from charities for donations that you are going to accept is easier than declining requests. You have to counter the impression of being mean-minded and uncharitable and finding a good reason is not always easy. The letters here (194–197) show how to approach such requests and the right words to choose if you want to decline.

Handling objections

Letter 198 shows how to react to a controversial development and what to do if you find yourself in the hot seat, up against some potentially angry local residents. It has some good phrases which will help mollify the objections. Letter 199 deals with making an objection to a local authority about a planned development and gives hints on how to put your message across in the strongest terms, to make the maximum impact.

REQUESTS AND INVITATIONS
Letter 190: Accepting a request for a donation

Supporting a charity venture can be good for developing relations with the local community. If you consider helping in this way, with a little thought and planning you may be able to use the opportunity to get the press involved and turn it into a PR opportunity, for both your company and the charity.

Hart & Tucker Ltd
19 Green Street, Maidstone, Kent ME41 1TJ
Telephone: (01622) 109109
Facsimile: (01622) 108106
Reg. No: England 96223978 VAT No: 91210674

Martin Foster
Kids in the Sun
34 Barton Close
Maidstone
Kent
ME41 1JK

16 June 2005

Dear Mr Foster,

Thank you for your letter of 15 June telling us about your plans to give disabled children the chance to go on holiday.

I think the work that you are doing in this area is tremendous and we would be delighted to donate £2,500 towards the cause. In return, I wonder if it might be possible to arrange for a small handing-over ceremony of the cheque with a photographer and perhaps with some of the children who will benefit? We enjoy very good relations with the local press and I believe a photo in the paper would present a excellent opportunity to promote both our causes.

Please let me know what you think about this idea and all the very best of luck in achieving your target of £20,000.

Yours sincerely,

Helen Jones
Director

REQUESTS AND INVITATIONS
Letter 191: Invitation to present an award at a ceremony

When persuading someone to attend a ceremony, keep the letter as brief as possible. Give the reader sufficient information to understand what the ceremony is for, enough background about the award and when the ceremony will be, but make sure the information is kept relevant and concise. A little bit of flattery will go a long way, as here: 'It will be a tremendous honour...'.

RPP Holdings Plc
35/38 New Road, Paignton, Devon TQ3 4UU
Tel: 01803 175653 Fax: 01803 187908
Reg. No: England 1976143

Mrs Ann Connor
Chairwoman
Chamber of Commerce
The Town Hall
Clarke St
Paignton
TQ3 4UN

8 May 2005

Dear Mrs Connor,

This week we have been awarded registration to ISO 9001, the standard which gives our customers quality guarantees. Obtaining registration to ISO 9001 is a major achievement for our company. It has taken over two years to implement our Quality Management System, something to which the entire workforce of 50 has contributed. It is also a source of great pride that we are the first binder manufacturer in the country to be granted ISO 9001 registration.

To mark the occasion, we are planning to hold a short award ceremony, and I am writing to ask if you would be willing to present the award to us at this unique event. The ceremony will be held at 11.45am on 15 July, at our premises. The ceremony will be followed by a luncheon.

It will be a tremendous honour for us if you are able to accept this invitation and I look forward to hearing from you.

Yours sincerely,

John Herbert
Director

REQUESTS AND INVITATIONS
Letter 192: Offering support for a community venture

This letter is a response to a request for financial help towards a children's hospice. The company is responding positively to the request, with both financial and practical help. The practical help in this instance will be appreciated as much as the purely financial.

 Kelso Limited
16 Abbots Road, Luton, Bedfordshire MK44 7YT
Tel: (01234) 136953 Fax: (01234) 136422
Registered in England No: 9126719 VAT No: 91523489 76

Ms J Parish
Churchill House
Saffron Close
Luton
Bedfordshire
MK44 7YH

28 July 2005

Dear Ms Parish,

Thank you for your letter of 14 July about your plans for a children's hospice in Luton.

It is not normally our policy to make charitable donations, but we were so moved by the plight of the children that you care for that we have decided to make an exception. I am delighted to enclose a cheque for £1,000 on behalf of everyone at Kelso Limited.

In addition, I would also like to offer more practical help with the building conversion. As one of the leading builders in Luton, we are willing to release three of our men for a week to help you with any aspect of the building work. We have skills in bricklaying, plastering, tiling and other general structural changes and I would be pleased to discuss ways in which we may be able to make a contribution.

Yours sincerely,

Tony Southgate
Director

REQUESTS AND INVITATIONS
Letter 193: Accepting an invitation to speak at a meeting

If you are asked to give a presentation or talk, it pays to do as much research as you can. If you are not clear about the type of people attending and what their interests are, find out, so your talk can be tailored to their needs. You will also need to know how long the talk should be, and whether the right technical equipment is available.

If you can, always request to be one of the earlier speakers in the day: your audience will be more alert and inclined to listen then. After lunch is a bad time, as is the last slot of the day, because your audience may be itching to leave and the other speakers may have overrun on their time, leaving you with less time than you have prepared for, to get your message across.

PARKER
Glass Ltd
Unit 27 Willow Park
Christchurch, Dorset BH23 6MM
Tel: 01202 109111
Fax: 01202 109112

Reg. No: England 962578762
VAT No: 9120564

David Firth
Christchurch Business Club
19 Buttercup Gardens
Christchurch
Dorset
BH23 5MM

28 July 2005

Dear David,

Re: Presentation to the Christchurch Business Club
Thank you for your letter of 20 July about the Christchurch Business Club meeting on 10 October.

I confirm that I will be available to give a short presentation on how we do business and the successful team behind our venture. I would appreciate it, though, if you could indicate how many people you expect to attend; how long the presentation is expected to last and how many other presentations there will be. I would expect to accompany my talk with a few slides. Can you also confirm if there is a 35mm slide projector and screen available?

I would also like, if possible, to be one of the earlier speakers in the event.

I look forward to hearing from you.

Yours sincerely,

Roger Crabb
Marketing Director

DECLINING REQUESTS AND INVITATIONS
Letter 194: Declining a request for a donation – pre-existing commitment

The charity will be able to appreciate the reason for declining here because the company has a pre-existing policy towards donations and is keen to make '...a more significant contribution...'. The tone is formal but polite: 'For this reason, I regret we must decline your invitation...'.

Offering to have a collecting tin will help take some of the disappointment out of not receiving a corporate donation and make the reader feel that it was worthwhile writing the letter.

Fenner & Sons

16 George Street, Woodbridge,
Suffolk IP3 7KL
Tel: (01394) 198423
Fax: (01394) 198444
Registered in England: 91221299
VAT No: 919129075 80

Mr Paul Middleton
H.D.S.C.F.
14 Franklin Gardens
Mildenhall
Suffolk
IP28 7JU

30 July 2005

Dear Mr Middleton,

Your letter of 13 July to John Yippley has been passed to me to reply.

Each year, one per cent of our revenue is allocated to charitable ventures. Last year, we took the decision to commit ourselves to five causes for the next three years. That way, we felt we would be able to make a more significant contribution than if our donations were spread more thinly across many causes. For this reason, I regret we must decline your invitation, but I would like to wish you every success in raising funds for your cause.

If it would be of any help, we would be prepared to keep a collecting tin at our reception so that we may collect donations from both members of staff and visitors to our site. Please let me know if this is of interest.

Yours sincerely,

J P Turner
Director

DECLINING REQUESTS AND INVITATIONS
Letter 195: Declining a request for a donation – criterion not met

A letter declining to give a donation is not easy to write. But not replying at all is discourteous and bad for your public relations. Remember, the person writing to you may also be a customer. The problem with declining a donation is that it is easy to appear mean-minded and uncharitable. This letter provides a good reason that will be understood by the charity.

Tyler & Piper Associates

76 Whites Lane, Stevenage, Herts SG1 8JP, England
Tel: (01438) 186465 Fax: (01438) 164323

Mr Paul Middleton
H.D.S.C.F.
14 Franklin Gardens
Mildenhall
Suffolk
IP28 7JU

3 February 2005

Dear Mr Middleton,

Thank you for your letter about your extremely worthy cause, offering holidays to disabled children in Suffolk.

As a small company employing only 20 people, we have only limited funds available for charitable donations each year. As such, we have to set down strict criteria for the causes to which we will donate. One of the prime considerations is the area which the cause will benefit. I understand that the holidays are for children in the Suffolk area and I regret that this is outside the region in which we have decided to concentrate our charitable work and we must, therefore, regretfully decline your invitation.

I am sorry for the disappointment this will undoubtedly cause, but I do hope you understand our reasons. We do, however, hope your venture succeeds and I would like to take this opportunity to wish you every success.

Yours sincerely,

SR Piper

Partners: DA Tyler BA & SR Piper MA

DECLINING REQUESTS AND INVITATIONS
Letter 196: Declining a request to speak at a meeting

If you are unable to attend a function that offers a good public-relations opportunity, try to nominate someone else to take your place. You won't be letting the organiser down or missing out on the chance to tell people about your business.

PARKER
Glass Ltd

Reg. No: England 962578762
VAT No: 9120564

Unit 27 Willow Park
Christchurch, Dorset BH23 6MM
Tel: 01202 109111
Fax: 01202 109112

David Firth
Christchurch Business Club
19 Buttercup Gardens
Christchurch
Dorset
BH23 5MM

28 May 2005

Dear David,

Thank you very much for your invitation to speak at your business club meeting on 10 June.

Unfortunately, I shall be away on holiday when your meeting is planned and unavailable to speak personally. However, my colleague and fellow director, David Harvey (who knows our business intimately), would be willing to speak in my place.

May I suggest you call him on 01202 109111 to discuss the arrangements?

Yours sincerely,

Roger Crabb
Marketing Director

DECLINING REQUESTS AND INVITATIONS
Letter 197: Declining a request to serve on a local committee

This is another potentially tricky letter, but it is better to turn the idea down than to half-heartedly carry out the responsibilities that any committee post inevitably calls for.

The reply here is fairly vague but seems genuine, so is unlikely to provoke a counter-request. Note the use of the phrase '...additional outside responsibilities', suggesting that your obligations are not simply '...business commitments...'.

PARKER
Glass Ltd

Unit 27 Willow Park
Christchurch, Dorset BH23 6MM
Tel: 01202 109111
Fax: 01202 109112

Reg. No: England 962578762
VAT No: 9120564

David Firth
Christchurch Business Club
19 Buttercup Gardens
Christchurch
Dorset
BH23 5MM

18 July 2005

Dear David,

Thank you for your letter of 15 July asking if I would like to sit on the committee representing the interests of the members of the local business club.

I have enjoyed membership of the club. However, my business commitments for the foreseeable future preclude me from taking on any additional outside responsibilities.

I am sorry that I am unable to assist on this occasion and hope you are successful in finding an alternative member who is able to help.

Yours sincerely,

Roger Crabb
Marketing Director

OBJECTIONS – MAKING AND HANDLING
Letter 198: Responding to local residents about a potential disruption

A letter to a wider local community on a controversial topic needs careful thought before being sent. Feelings could be running high and you may have to work hard to make residents appreciate that their interests have been taken into account and not ignored.

Note the way the letter empathises with the reader from the start: 'As residents ourselves, we all understand the depth of feeling...'. And note the frank way this letter ends: inviting people to pick up the 'phone helps to portray a picture of honesty and openness that is disarming.

IDENDEN INDUSTRIES
A division of Idenden Plc
Porter House, Hull HU7 4RF England

Tel 01482 119087 Fax 01482 119088
Registered in England No: 1218943

13 April 2005

Dear Resident,

I am writing to you all directly concerning the plans for the quarry at the end of Stone Road in your village. As residents ourselves, we all understand the depth of feeling about this development. We are as concerned as you to ensure that the character of Littlegreen village is not damaged and I would like to reassure you of our commitment to this.

I know you are concerned about the increase in lorry traffic that this development may cause. In our consultation with the local planning authorities, we have given a commitment that all lorries will use a designated route to minimise the impact caused and to keep the environment as safe as possible for residents. The lorries will travel only between Stone Road and the A113. They will, therefore, avoid the heart of the village and, apart from the houses on Stone Road, none of the residential areas will be affected. The lorries will be strictly limited in the hours at which they can be driven, to between 7.30am and 7.30pm. Night-time traffic and noise will therefore be avoided.

It is anticipated that the quarry will have a working life of around ten years. As part of the planning agreement, we are committed to returning the quarry to a natural environment when it ceases to have any further commercial use. Indeed, we believe that the plans in hand for a wildlife and waterfowl reserve will enhance the environment tremendously, particularly in an area that has few wetland habitats of this type.

I hope this letter clarifies for many of you the principal issues of concern to you. However, if any of you have any other concerns about the development that you would like to discuss, please pick up the 'phone and call me on the above number or write to me at the address given.

Yours sincerely,

Peter Hand
Director

OBJECTIONS – MAKING AND HANDLING
Letter 199: Objecting to a planning application

Objections to an authority like this must be supported by strong factual reasons why your objection is justified, if you are to have any sway with the deciding authority. 'Because we don't like it' will not be sufficient.

Note how the company adds weight to the objection by making it seem as if Shortly's already has insufficient car parking space which is being abused, as the company has '...already had to make several representations...'.

The strongest argument is saved until the end: pointing out that the application does not conform to the local regulations. These arguments give credibility to the strength of the opening phrase of the final paragraph: 'We object in the strongest terms...'.

Hart & Tucker Ltd
19 Green Street, Maidstone, Kent ME41 1TJ
Telephone: (01622) 109109
Facsimile: (01622) 108106
Reg. No: England 96223978   VAT No: 91210674

Kent County Council
Council Chambers
Maidstone
Kent
ME41 3OD

For the attention of the Planning Officer:

24 May 2005

Dear Sirs,

Re: Planning Application for Shortly's Building in Green Street
We are in receipt of the application for a new factory building for Shortly Ltd on Green Street.

On inspecting the plans, we are extremely concerned to find that insufficient provision appears to have been made for the additional car parking that will be necessary for the increase in staff, deliveries and visitors that the new building will generate. Our concern is amplified by the fact that, at present, we operate a shared car park with Shortly's and have already had to make several representations to them for using spaces which are allocated to us.

We understand from the announcements in the press that the building is required because they are relocating their Witchbury site to the Green Street operation. We understand that there will be no job losses resulting from this relocation and the same number of staff will be working in Green Street as were employed in Witchbury. I understand the Witchbury operation had provision for over 100 car parking spaces, yet the additional number allowed for here is only 60 spaces. We also understand that the local regulations state that there should be at least one car parking space for each 50 square metres of office space. With just over 5,000 square metres of new office space there should be a minimum of 100 extra spaces provided for.

We object in the strongest terms to the application as it stands and would ask you to reconsider the plan in the light of these points, which clearly do not conform to current local planning requirements.

Yours sincerely,

Tony Kidd
Director

APPENDIX 1

Ways to start your letter

As discussed ... requested ... agreed ...

As discussed, will you please send ...

As discussed, I enclose samples of ...

As discussed, I am very sorry for the delay in sending you ...

As requested, I enclose ...

As we agreed this morning, I would like to confirm our mutual decision ...

At our last meeting, it was agreed that ...

As you are aware ...

As I am sure you are aware, ...

As I have previously explained to you, ...

As you are aware, under our holiday policy, the company reserves the right ...

As you are no doubt aware, there are certain confidential and personal files ...

As you are no doubt aware, the recent events in ...

As you know, we deal with a number of different suppliers ...

As you know, we have been working ...

Congratulations ...

Congratulations.

Congratulations on winning ...

Firstly, Mary, I would like to say how delighted I am for you at your news ...

Many congratulations on the birth of your son.

May I be the first to offer you our congratulations on ...

I was delighted to hear you have won ...

I would like to offer you my personal congratulations ...

I am sorry ...

Firstly, apologies for the delay in replying to your fax, which was caused by ...

First of all, my sincere apologies for not responding to your enquiries ...

Firstly, I would like to say how sorry we are that you have had to wait so long ...

I am sorry if this messes you around but our client has just notified us that ...

I am sorry that you feel that you have not received the level of service expected.

I am sorry that you feel the price of ...

I am sorry to hear that you are unable to trace ...

I am sorry to learn of your recent bereavement.

I am very sorry that you were left waiting ...

I am very sorry to hear that you are still not making a good enough recovery ...

I am very sorry.

What can I say? Sorry.

Oops! We've made a real clanger.

We were all very saddened to learn about the sudden death of your wife ...

We were deeply shocked by John's untimely death ...

We were shocked and saddened to hear of Howard Green's fatal accident.

I was very sorry to hear your sad news.

I write as one of Howard's new customers to say how very, very sad we were ...

Following ...

Following our conversation this morning, I am delighted to confirm our offer ...

Following our telephone conversation ...

Following the recent accident involving ...

Following the staff meeting this morning, I am writing to confirm that ...

Following your claim for ...

Further to ...

Further to our recent discussion, I have pleasure in enclosing ...

Further to our recent telephone conversation, I have pleasure in enclosing ...

Further to our telephone conversation, I am writing to introduce you to our ...

Further to your fax this morning: at the moment I am feeling very let down by your ...

Further to your recent conversation with ...

Further to your request for ...

I ...

I note from my diary that you have an appointment to see me on ...

I promised to let you have details of ...

I realise that I should not have ...

I recently saw details of your company's range of ...

I telephoned your office last week for a revised quotation ...

I think it was very useful to talk through your performance over the last six months ...

I don't dispute that other customers have accepted ...

I wrote to you on 16 September chasing the above order for ...

I am surprised ... disappointed ...

Bob, you personally gave me your word and I trusted you to pay promptly ...

I am surprised to have had no response to my fax dated ...

I am surprised to have received no reply to our previous letter ...

I am afraid that our Financial Director has put these orders on hold ...

I am at a loss to understand why you have not paid us the monies which you owe.

I am extremely disappointed that I find myself having to write to you yet again.

I am now getting very concerned that we have heard nothing from you ...

I am very disappointed that you have not remitted the sum of ...

I am very disappointed with you.

I hoped that I would not have to write to you about ...

I have now sent you a number of fax messages and am disappointed ...

We regret to note that you have failed to respond to our previous reminders ...

I am pleased ...

I am pleased to confirm your appointment as agent for ...

I am pleased to inform you that the company agrees to ...

I am pleased to quote you ex-works prices for the items, as requested.

I am delighted to confirm that you are this year's winner of ...

I am delighted to report that we have had an excellent year ...

I am delighted to say that our sales are ahead of expectations ...

It was a pleasure to meet you and Richard in February ...

It was a pleasure to meet you yesterday ...

It was great to meet you and your team last week.

I have received ...

I have received a consignment of ...

I have received in the post this morning your invoice no. ...

I have received your catalogue of ...

I am in receipt of your fax of 10 February.

I am in receipt of your letter of 30 June, asking for a reference for ...

I received a copy of your autumn catalogue, giving details of ...

I received, this morning, your invoice no. ...

Yesterday, we received ...

We received your delivery of ...

We today received from you ...

We have received an application from ...

I am writing ...

I am writing concerning your request for a refund ...

I am writing on a matter that is causing ...

I am writing to advise you of a change in our terms and conditions ...

I am writing to clarify the position about the ...

I am writing to confirm our telephone conversation, regarding ...

I am writing to express my growing dissatisfaction of the service we are receiving ...

I am writing to let you know that we have decided not to renew your contract ...

I am writing to thank you for recommending me to ...

I am writing to you because I want you to know of our experience ...

I am responding to the idea that you put forward ...

I confirm ...

I confirm our faxed quotation for ...

I confirm our quote of ...

I confirm that, as of today, we are amending your terms of contract ...

I confirm the points we discussed at our meeting on ...

Just a note to confirm our conversation today ...

Just a quick note to confirm the deal agreed ...

I would just like to confirm that we have considered your request to ...

I write to confirm our order for ...

Confirming my telephone call and your return fax, ...

This is to confirm our meeting at your offices at 10.30am tomorrow, 25 January.

This is to confirm the details and the key terms of the offer we have accepted ...

I enclose ...

I enclose, herewith, a draft copy of ...

I enclose our purchase order for ...

Please find enclosed our cheque to the value of ...

Please find enclosed our statement as at 31 July for £2,903.86.

It is ...

It is not often I receive such an abusive letter. In spite of your rude tone ...

It is with a tinge of sadness that I have to announce ...

It is with regret that I tender my resignation as ...

It has come to my attention that you ...

It was useful to review your progress to date ...

I have ...

I have been advised by ...

I have been given your name by ...

I have checked my records and realise that ...

I have considered your letter of 21 January and your assertion that ...

I have just been reviewing ...

I have just come across a product that is so good ...

I have just received your ...

I have just returned from a visit to ...

I have now reviewed your proposal to ...

I hope ...

I hope the last order we supplied to you was satisfactory and met your expectations.

I hope you and Joshua are well and that you are not having too many sleepless nights.

I refer to ...

I refer to our order dated ...

I refer to our order for ...

I refer to our telephone conversation this morning.

I refer to your letter of 11 February.

I refer to your letter of 23 April 2005 about a consignment of ...

I trust ...

I trust that you enjoyed your break.

I trust that you received our consignment ...

I trust that you have received my previous correspondence.

I understand ...

I understand from my colleague ...

I understand from our Mr Davies that you are considering moving ...

I understand that, to obtain the price that is right for us, you have asked us to take ...

I understand that you are concerned about the amount of time you have been given ...

We understand that ...

I was appalled ... astonished ... concerned ...

I was appalled to learn that our consignment had not arrived on time with you.

I was astonished when I telephoned your accounts department this morning ...

I was extremely concerned to hear that you have not received ...

I was most disturbed to receive your letter of 20 April, informing me of ...

I was very disturbed to receive your letter, concerning ...

I was given your verbal assurances on Tuesday that you would have no problem ...

I would like to ...

I would like to correct a factual error in your ...

I would like to place a firm order for ...

I would like to remind you of our agreement ...

I would like to tackle a problem that we have come across ...

Many thanks for ...

Many thanks for agreeing to act as our ...

Many thanks for the cheque for £...., received this morning.

Many thanks for the letters received from both John and yourself, concerning ...

Many thanks for your enquiry for ...

Many thanks for your excellent talk, which ...

Many thanks for your latest offerings.

Many thanks for your letter, asking if we are prepared to offer ...

Many thanks for your letter of 13 January.

Many thanks for your order, received today.

Please ...

Please arrange for the consignment of ...

Please let me have a price on Tuesday 5 April for ...

Please find enclosed our cheque to the value of ...

Please find enclosed our statement as at 31 July for £2,903.86.

Please find attached our order for ...

Please find our cheque to the value of £1,123.60 to cover our order ...

Please supply a quotation for the following: ....

Please supply and deliver as follows: ...

Thanks for ...

Thanks for coming in to see me last week.

Thanks for coming to put the ...

Thanks for looking into the possibility of arranging ...

Thanks for sending through the latest price changes.

Thanks for your delivery of ...

Thanks for your quotation for ...

Thanks for your fax of 9 May. Sorry that I have sat on it for so long ...

Thank you ....

I felt I had to write to you to say how delighted I have been with ...

Just a note to say thank you for the cheque.

Just a quick note to thank you very much for your time the other day ...

Thank you for allowing me time to assess the above product.

Thank you for applying for a Credit Account with us.

Thank you for asking if we would be interested in buying ...

Thank you for attending the interview last week for the post of ...

Thank you for being so frank and open about the difficulties that you have ...

Thank you for bringing the lower than expected performance to my attention.

Thank you for buying ...

Thank you for coming to see me last ...

Thank you for contacting me about ...

Thank you for letting me know about ...

Thank you for returning the ...

Thank you for sending ...

Thank you for taking the trouble to clarify the situation for me.

Thank you for the business which you have brought to us.

Thank you for the courtesy extended to me during my visit to ...

Thank you very much indeed for your extremely pleasant letter ...

Thank you very much for arranging a most enjoyable day for me.

Thank you for your ...

Thank you for your application for a credit account.

Thank you for your application for the post of ...

Thank you for your cheque for £1,500 in part settlement of your account.

Thank you for your comments on our proposed discount.

Thank you for your completed application form for the position of ...

Thank you for your enquiry about the price of ...

Thank you for your fax, which I received this morning, asking if ...

Thank you for your fax, regarding payment for your orders.

Thank you for your invoice no. ...

Thank you for your kind invitation to ...

Thank you for your latest delivery, received today.

Thank you for your letter dated 17 February, addressed to our Managing Director, which has been brought to my attention.

Thank you for your letter dated 9 September, addressed to our Managing Director, who has passed this to me for my attention.

Thank you for your letter expressing concern about the service you are receiving ...

Thank you for your letter of 11 September and for the samples ...

Thank you for your letter of 12 June, concerning the carriage charge on our invoice.

Thank you for your letter of 12 June, outlining the terms ...

Thank you for your letter of 15 July, notifying us that ...

Thank you for your letter of 20 June, regarding ...

Thank you for your letter of 21 May, advising us ...

Thank you for your letter of 24 June, applying for the post of ...

Thank you for your letter of 26 January, asking about the terms for ...

Thank you for your letter of 3 June, enquiring if we have any vacancies for ...

Thank you for your letter of 30 April in response to our order ...

Thank you for your letter of 3 December and for your kind comments.

Thank you for your letter of 7 March, which reached me today.

Thank you for your letter of 5 July, expressing concern over ...

Thank you for your letter, querying the price of ...

Thank you for your order against our quotation no. ...

Thank you for your payment of £..., which, I note, was credited to our account ...

Thank you for your prices, received this morning.

Thank you for your proposed price ...

Thank you for your recent enquiry.

Thank you for your recent faxes. I apologise for the delay in replying.

Thank you for your recent order for the enclosed ...

Thank you for your recent order. I am afraid that we have temporarily sold out of ...

Thank you for your recent telephone call, regarding ...

Thank you for your request for a reference for ...

Thank you for your suggestion that we ...

Thank you for your telephone call today.

Thank you for your time on Tuesday, concerning ...

Thank you very much for your letter about ...

We...

We are a small company, specialising in ...

We are currently seeking to be registered ...

We are in receipt of your cheque for ...

We are intending to trade with ...

We are interested in ...

We are pleased to announce the appointment of ...

We are reorganising the administration of our accounts department ...

We have an outstanding debt of ...

We have been notified by ...

We have considered your request to operate an agency ...

We have decided to change the holiday policy of the company.

We have just learned about the death of ...

We have just secured an unexpectedly large order ...

We have noticed some abuses of the telephone for private calls ...

We have recently received the enclosed statement from you.

We have reviewed the price changes to our products for the next 12 months.

We have supplied you with items on four separate occasions to the value of ...

We met at the Multimedia 99 show (on the Wednesday) and you showed me ...

We no longer need ...

We note that you have failed to respond to our previous demands to settle ...

We wish to obtain ...

We would like to carry out some amendments to ...

With reference to ...

With reference to our recent telephone conversation, ...

With reference to our telephone conversation, I have pleasure in introducing ...

With reference to the above, we have received ...

With regard to the above, we enclose ...

Re: your fax to our accounts manager of ...

Re: your recommendation of ...

You ...

You have been issued with ...

You have been specially selected to receive one of our star prizes ...

You have received two written warnings about ...

You may have heard rumours circulating ...

You supplied us with a new ...

Your ...

Your account has been passed to me for attention ...

Your account with us is now SERIOUSLY OVERDUE.

Your company has opened a credit account with us.

Your customer ... has applied to us for a credit account ...

Your subscription to ... will be expiring within the next three months.

More notes to start on ...

A week ago, you arranged for ...

According to my records, you still owe ...

As a company committed to providing a quality service, ...

As you are a valued customer, we want every pound you spend with us to save you money.

Having arrived back safely, ...

Here is our ...

In April this year, you ordered ...

In case you failed to receive the details we sent last month of our fabulous ...

In conversation with your colleague, Mary, yesterday, it emerged that ...

In response to your telephone enquiry this morning, I am writing to announce that ...

Just a quick note to let you know that ...

On 30 September, we placed an order for ...

On 6 August, we received from you a consignment of ...

On a recent visit to your company, I left our company brochure for your attention ...

Our agreement of 20 January stipulates that you undertake to supply us with ...

Payment for this order was due in ...

The response to our advertisement for an Office Manager has exceeded ...

Since we have acquired ...

Something very peculiar appears to have been happening with ...

Until now, it has been a requirement of the company that everyone ...

With the departure of ...

APPENDIX 2

Nice turns of phrase

This appendix selects over 200 of the best phrases for you to choose from. It concentrates on phrases with mood and emotion so, whether you are having to write a letter of condolence, persuade someone to your way of thinking or bring a supplier up sharply, you are certain to find the right phrase to fit the moment.

Stern phrases

I trust our purchase order instructions will be rigidly adhered to in future.

As they have not been received by the due date, we are exercising our right under the agreement to cancel the order forthwith.

I was surprised to see a carriage charge included for ...

No mention was made of this charge ...

Our purchase order referred expressly to the fact that delivery was to be included in the price ...

You may recall that when I placed the order, you granted us a special discount ...

... it should be little more than an extension of what your current practices are ...

We expect our suppliers to give us the service that we demand ...

It will certainly make us think twice about using you in the future ...

Unless you can agree to do our printing profitably within the price agreed, we will probably have to agree to part company.

I expect a full refund by return.

We shall have no option but to seek an alternative supplier.

I am therefore bound to advise you that ...

Please give it your most urgent attention.

It is time this matter was brought to a close.

... we shall not hesitate in disallowing the commission payment ...

... it is naturally disconcerting ...

It is also particularly disappointing ...

You have not had the authority ...

I was led to believe that this was included in your quotation.

... your failure to notify us ...

Your conduct in this matter has been extremely disappointing ...

I was very disturbed ...

... we have already had to make several representations ...

We object in the strongest terms ...

I hope this makes our position clear ...

We expect you to accomplish it within the agreed deadline and budget.

We must have a solution if you are to retain our custom.

I regard this behaviour as totally unprofessional.

I am not satisfied that the goods are of merchantable quality.

Since the goods are not fit for the purpose intended ...

I must stress that, in placing this order with you, ...

... it was absolutely conditional on your ability to meet our deadline.

... for which we shall seek compensation.

I was astounded to find that ...

... we shall be seeking recompense for any losses that we incur.

... the occasion was a shambolic disaster from start to finish.

I strongly sense that you are taking us for granted ...

... the entire job is simply unacceptable ...

I am particularly irritated that, once again, you are blaming ...

I am hoping that you will take these issues more seriously than your colleagues appear to ...

Contractual phrases

Under the terms of our agreement ...

... I trust that you will abide by the terms of our agreement.

I would like to draw your attention to the agreement ...

Our agreement expressly forbids you ...

... in full and final settlement ...

... it was a condition of our contract ...

As you have not kept to the terms of your contract ...

... failure to comply with our terms ...

... we shall have no option but to terminate ...

... we are exercising our right not to pay ...

... we undertake to rectify ...

... we have made good the defect ...

... we have honoured our contract to you ...

Letting someone down lightly

At the moment, it does not fit in comfortably with our plans for the immediate future ...

I am afraid I must say 'Thanks but no thanks'.

Our decision was arrived at after a great deal of discussion and thought.

It was not an easy decision to make ...

While I believe that your experience is right for us, ...

I am confident that you would be able to secure a good number of orders for our business but ...

... it would not be fair to either of us ...

Phrases that trigger people's emotional responses

You will understand that, as a business, we put a high premium on reliability.

I am feeling very let down by your company ...

... don't have a moral leg to stand upon ...

... really should know better ...

It was not we who caused this problem ...

Phrases that charm customers

... as a special favour ...

... enclosed is the guarantee which sets out our promises and your rights ...

We look forward to a long and happy association with your business.

Should we fall short of your high expectations in any matter ...

... please contact me personally.

... and trust that this helps in compensating you for your dissatisfaction.

We are, of course, concerned to offer you the best possible service ...

... as you are a highly valued customer ...

Anticipating that this arrangement will be acceptable to you, I have pleasure in enclosing ...

... you have been specially chosen ...

... we are asking a select group of our customers ...

... you will avoid immeasurable hassle ...

Making a gentle request

... we will have to ask you ...

... I do not consider it unreasonable to ask you to ...

I don't want to put you to any trouble, but it would be enormously helpful ...

I appreciate this is a busy time for you, but I wonder if ...

It therefore does not seem unreasonable to request ...

Phrases that aim to reassure

I confirm that we are happy to stand by our original quotation.

I assure you it is perfectly normal and will not impede its function.

... it does not fulfil the high standard that we demand and you, as a customer, expect.

... would not dream of stepping beyond the powers ...

I am appalled at how you have been treated ...

I was most disturbed to receive your letter ...

... the intention is not to squeeze a quart out of a pint pot.

... before you come running to us crying 'foul' ...

I know how frustrating it is to be left high and dry ...

I trust everything is in order ...

Making sincere apologies

If I could perhaps explain the circumstances that occurred, not as an excuse, but so you can see the exceptional and unexpected difficulties that we faced.

I am deeply sorry that we have let you and your client down ...

This unfortunate event has highlighted a gap in our procedures.

I am extremely sorry this has occurred ...

This is a very rare occurrence (it happens about once a year) ...

Please accept our unreserved apologies.

I have made enquiries and have discovered that in this instance one of our internal procedural systems failed.

I do hope that this will go some way to restoring your faith in us.

It seems you have been plagued by gremlins on this occasion.

I have pushed you to the front of the waiting list ...

We are all real people in this company, who try very hard indeed to give a fast and efficient service.

I am sorry that you feel that you have not received the level of service expected.

I am confident that you should not experience the same level of disruption now.

I am sorry for any inconvenience caused.

I apologise for this oversight ...

Refusing and rejecting

I regret that we are unable to assist you further in this matter.

For this reason, I regret we must decline your kind invitation ...

I am sorry that we cannot be more helpful on this occasion.

Although, as is clear, I do not agree with much of your letter ...

... I very much regret that we must insist ...

While we do not like to impose unnecessary restrictions ...

I regret that we have decided not to take your application further on this occasion.

I have to be completely honest and say that there is no way we can pay ...

... I wish to deny in the strongest terms possible ...

... we refute your claim.

... I cannot think of any circumstance in which I would dream of agreeing ...

I do not accept your assertions ...

Persuasive phrases

... the charge reflects a contribution only towards the final cost ...

... we do everything we can to keep the charges as competitive as possible ...

... all our suppliers accept it, without exception ...

... we shall have no option but to seek an alternative supplier.

... I guarantee that you will experience the best ...

... we have striven to keep the price increases to an absolute minimum ...

... we see this as a modest contribution towards our continued mutual success ...

... it would not be in our best interests ...

... we are taking on the chin the cost of inflation and the increased cost of ...

Chasing payment

We have now decided to take legal advice on this matter, with a view to the recovery of our money ...

... instructions will be issued to our solicitors to proceed against you.

... please arrange immediate settlement.

... this thorny issue of payment ...

... remit this by return ...

... in view of the one-sided nature of our correspondence ...

... the matter will be passed into other hands in seven days.

... I hope you will render this action unnecessary ...

If you have sent your remittance in the last few days, please disregard this letter.

No further reminders will be issued.

We appreciate this act of good faith ...

... despite our best efforts to obtain payment from you ...

Responding to requests for payment

The reasons for the delay are both tedious and convoluted.

Should any future invoices slip through the net ...

I am extremely embarrassed about the long delay ...

Praise, flattery and recognition

... because you are the best person for the job ...

I will respect your decision, whatever it is.

... thank you personally for all the hard work ...

Thank you once again for your major contribution ...

... the best minds are devoted to this project ...

... I am delighted to announce that you are eligible to receive ...

Congratulations on taking the initiative ...

... I am very impressed by their versatility ...

Your role in this is, of course, pivotal.

... I applaud your enthusiasm for not missing a sale ...

It will be a tremendous honour ...

It gives me great personal pleasure to recognise ...

Threatening to take legal action

While we have no quarrel with your business ...

... we intend to take legal action against ...

... unless she agrees to abide by the terms of our agreement ...

... we shall commence legal proceedings against her.

Warnings

I must warn you ...

... we find it inexcusable ...

... failure to do so ...

You have been given every opportunity ...

As you have chosen to ignore all the warnings ...

... we have no alternative ...

... you must not undertake ...

... you were unable to give us a satisfactory reason ...

Offering help and assistance

... we shall be only too happy to provide ...

We will do everything we can to help ...

... I shall be keeping my fingers crossed.

Motivational

... I know you will be very capable of successfully accomplishing ...

You have a great deal to contribute ...

I am confident that there will be considerable opportunities to increase your responsibilities.

I know you will do your utmost ...

I know you will be able to make a major contribution ...

... it is a tribute to your hard work ...

It means a great deal to me, personally, ...

Condolence

We were deeply shocked ...

... it will be very difficult for us to forget ...

We will miss him sorely.

Please accept our sincere sympathy.

We were shocked and saddened ...

Selling phrases

... will cut a swathe through the tasks ...

By far the best, ever.

... that makes the guide, for me, utterly irresistible.

... quickly and confidently ...

Do have a look at it ...

... a return that is absolutely guaranteed.

... you do not, absolutely not, have to buy anything from us ...

What do you have to lose?

I have just come across ...

... we felt it essential to let you know about it ...

Just complete the fax-back acceptance offer ... before everyone else does.

... outstanding value for money ...

Appealing for donations

... go a little way to help ...

... find the heart to help ...

... It's not a lot to ask ...

Keeping your options open

Your payment terms are subject to the timing of our payment runs.

However, we reserve the right to return ...

Keeping a supplier firmly on the hook

I accept this as a gesture of apology but not as a satisfactory recompense for the late delivery.

Exaggerating a point slightly

It has cost us up to £400 more a month ...

Preparing the ground for bad news

I very much regret that, as from 1 May, we must increase prices of this product ...

APPENDIX 3

Ways to finish your letter

Best ...

Best regards.

Best wishes.

Best wishes and good luck.

Best wishes from myself and all at ...

I ...

I am grateful that you took the trouble to write ...

I am returning the item with this letter and expect a full refund of ...

I am sorry for any inconvenience caused.

I am sorry that we cannot be more helpful on this occasion.

I do hope that this will go some way to restoring your faith in us.

I enclose a stamped addressed envelope for your convenience when you reply.

I have pleasure in enclosing ...

I have pleasure in returning the product as required ...

I must insist that, from now on, we are given priority treatment.

I regret that we are unable to assist you further in this matter.

I therefore look forward to your immediate reassurance ...

I very much regret that we shall be unable to offer you a refund.

I hope ...

I hope that we continue to be of benefit to you in the future.

I hope they are a success for you.

I hope this arrangement is acceptable to you.

I hope this arrangement is satisfactory.

I hope this explains the position but, if you have any other queries, please do ask.

I hope this information helps you.

I hope this makes our position clear.

I hope this matter can now be closed.

I hope this plan meets with your approval.

I hope this proposal will be of interest to you.

I hope you are willing to help us in this matter.

I hope you have a very successful and prosperous New Year.

I hope you will be able to agree to this proposal.

I look forward to ...

I look forward to a long, fruitful and communicative business relationship.

I look forward to a long and prosperous association with your company.

I look forward to continuing a close relationship with your business in the future.

I look forward to hearing from you and, of course, to receiving your order.

I look forward to hearing from you at your earliest convenience.

I look forward to hearing from you shortly.

I look forward to hearing from you, with regard to ...

I look forward to hearing from you.

I look forward to meeting you all again soon.

I look forward to meeting you.

I look forward to receiving confirmation of your order.

I look forward to receiving your remittances by return.

I look forward to receiving your reply.

I look forward to seeing you again shortly.

I look forward to seeing you on your next visit to the UK.

I look forward to your advice on this matter.

I look forward to your further enquiries.

I look forward to your immediate response.

I trust ...

I trust that further action will now be taken and look forward to your response.

I trust that you find these of interest.

I trust that you will abide by the terms of our agreement.

I trust this gives you the information that you require.

I trust this is a satisfactory summary of our conversation.

I trust this is all in order and hope that you are satisfied with the goods as supplied.

I trust this summarises our conversation satisfactorily.

I trust you will take the above into account.

I would ...

I would appreciate it if you could amend your records accordingly.

I would appreciate it if you could settle the account by the end of this month.

I would be grateful if one of your representatives could telephone me ...

I would be grateful if you could arrange for ....

I would be grateful if you could confirm safe receipt.

I would like to take this opportunity to wish you every success in your future.

If ...

If anyone has any queries about this new policy, please come and see me at any time.

If I can be of any further assistance to you, please do not hesitate to contact me.

If not, please arrange immediate settlement.

If there is anything we can do, please let us know.

If this is of interest, let me know.

If you ...

If you are interested in any of these, do give me a call.

If you are still unable to locate the item, please let me know.

If you do not receive the items by next Tuesday, please let me know.

If you have any further queries on this matter, please contact me again.

If you have any further questions, please do not hesitate to contact me.

If you have any more queries, please do not hesitate to contact me.

If you have any queries, please give me a call.

If you have any queries, please contact me on ...

If you have any questions, or need any further information, please give me a call.

If you have sent your remittance in the last few days, please disregard this letter.

If you need further information, please do not hesitate to contact us.

If you require any further information, please do not hesitate to ask.

If you would like further information, please ring us on ...

In the meantime ...

In the meantime, please could you arrange for ...

In the meantime, I shall ensure that ...

In the meantime, if you have any queries, please give me a ring.

It ...

It is essential that these instructions are adhered to, strictly.

It is time this matter was brought to a close.

It would be appreciated if you could let me know, by return.

Kind ...

Kind regards,

Kindest regards,

Let me know ...

Let me know if this is of interest to you.

Let me know if you find out any details and, once again, many thanks for your help.

Let me know what you decide. I will respect your decision, whichever way it goes.

Let me know your thoughts.

Many thanks for ...

Many thanks for your co-operation.

Many thanks for your help.

Many thanks for your prompt and courteous attention to this matter.

Many thanks for your time and effort on our behalf.

Once again, ...

Once again, please accept our sincerest apologies.

Once again, please accept our apologies.

Once again, my sincere apologies.

Once again, thank you very much indeed for taking the trouble to write to me.

Please accept ...

Please accept my apologies for this delay.

Please accept our most sincere condolences and deepest sympathy, from all at ...

Please accept our sincere apologies for the distress caused.

Please accept our sincere apologies for this slight deterioration in service.

Please accept our sincere sympathy for your loss.

Please accept our unreserved apologies.

Please ...

Please advise me of ...

Please call me back urgently, so we can discuss this.

Please cancel ...

Please come back to me if it does not solve the problem.

Please confirm whether this time is convenient for you.

Please arrange for the balance to be supplied as soon as possible.

Please give this matter your most urgent attention.

Please let me know if anything goes wrong again.

Please do not hesitate to call me, should there be any issue that you want to discuss.

Please do not hesitate to contact us, should you need any further information.

Please do not hesitate to get in contact, if we can be of further assistance.

Please find enclosed a copy of our current price list, as requested.

Please give me a call if you would like to set up a meeting.

Please give me a ring if anything is unclear.

Please let me know if this arrangement is of interest.

Please let me know if you think this outline plan is suitable.

Please let me know when these samples will be sent.

Please, please, please supply us with the missing items ASAP.

Please telephone me on receipt of this letter, to let me know ...

Please transfer the remaining balance to account no. ...

Please try to answer these queries quickly, to enable us to ...

Should you ...

Should you be uncertain about any aspect of it, please do not hesitate to give us a call.

Should you have any urgent enquiries, please do not hesitate to contact me personally.

Should you require any further information, please do not hesitate to contact us.

Sorry ...

Sorry for any inconvenience caused by this matter.

Sorry for any trouble caused.

Thank you ...

Thank you again for your assistance, and all good wishes for a successful ...

Thank you for the interest you have shown in our company.

Thank you for your assistance in this matter.

Thank you for your attention to this matter.

Thank you for your co-operation with this policy.

Thank you for your co-operation in this matter.

Thank you for your help with this matter.

Thank you for your interest in our range of products.

Thank you for your interest.

Thank you for your kind attention.

Thank you for your time and efforts on our behalf.

Thank you in advance for your co-operation.

Thank you, once again, for your kindness.

Thank you once again.

Thank you very much indeed for taking the trouble to write to reassure me.

Thanking you in advance.

Thanking you in anticipation of your assistance in this matter.

We hope ...

We hope never to hear from you again.

We hope you find the package of value and look forward to your future custom.

We look forward ...

We look forward to a long and happy association with your business.

We look forward to hearing from you.

We look forward to helping you save money throughout the coming year.

We look forward to receiving your payment.

We look forward to seeing you then.

We look forward to welcoming you as a customer.

We look forward to your valued, continued support.

We look forward to receiving your cheque by return.

We ...

We regret, therefore, that we must decline your kind offer.

We shall keep you informed, as and when developments occur.

We thank you for this order and look forward to your further enquiries.

We very much appreciate your help in this matter.

We would appreciate your quotation by fax and at the latest by Thursday 16 June.

With ...

With kind regards,

With very best wishes,

Would you ...

Would you kindly acknowledge receipt of this letter and confirm ...

Would you kindly arrange for someone to come and ...

Would you please confirm that ...

Your ...

Your immediate response (and payment) would be appreciated.

Your order will be dispatched as soon as we receive your remittance.

More notes to end on ...

A quick reply would be much appreciated.

Any future orders will have to be paid for in advance.

As stated, we will be having no further dealings with your company.

Do let me know what you decide and I shall be keeping my fingers crossed.

Finally, I enclose the form duly completed and signed.

Give me a call to let me know when you are coming.

Hope to speak to you soon.

Just tick the box on the enclosed reply-paid envelope and send it back to us.

May we take this opportunity of thanking you for your valued support during ...

Regards,

The agenda for this meeting is attached.

This does not help to foster confidence in our business together.

To find out how we can help you, call me now on ...

Whatever the cause of the delay may be, we must have a solution ...

Index

A
abusive customer (handling) 68
accepting *see* Index of Letters by Type
account management (banking) 191–4
accounts
   opening 135–6
   overdue 71, 123–34
acknowledging 56, 153
   see also Index of Letters by Type
addresses (layout) 21
advertisements 116–19
advising *see* Index of Letters by Type
agency/agents
   changes notified 113, 114
   commission queries 109–12
   performance/conduct 103–8
   requests for 98–102
amending
   orders 10–11
   see also correcting/corrective action; Index of Letters by Type
announcing
   to employees 167–9
   see also Index of Letters by Type
apologising *see* Index of Letters by Type
appealing *see* Index of Letters by Type
appointments
   changed/missed 62
   of General Manager 80

appreciating 181
   see also congratulating; thanking; Index of Letters by Type
asking *see* Index of Letters by Type
awards 180, 182, 210

B
banking 189
   loans and overdrafts 195, 197–8
   managing an account 191–3
bereavement 150, 187–8
blacklisting 67
bonus announcement 167
breach of contract 70
buildings insurance 199
business
   associate (thanking for referral) 79
   awards 180, 182, 210
   community and *see* community relations
   contracts *see* contracts
   going under (payment from) 132

C
cancelling *see* Index of Letters by Type
candidates (interviews/offers) 151–7
carriage charge 16–17
chasing *see* Index of Letters by Type
cheques 192–3
clarifying *see* Index of Letters by Type
commission 111–12, 126
committee membership (declining) 216
community relations
   company policy 185
   objections (making) 208, 217–18
   requests and invitations 207, 209, 211–16
company loan (for employees) 172
company policy 186
competition (between clients) 53
competitor, agent working for 106, 108

complaining *see* Index of Letters by Type
condolences 150, 187–8
confirming *see* Index of Letters by Type
congratulating 180–2
   see also appreciating; thanking; Index of Letters by Type
consoling *see* Index of Letters by Type
consultancy/consultant 19, 162
'contra' invoices 144
contracts
   breach of 70
   of employment 161–2
   termination of employment 162, 173
   verbal assurances 39, 65
correcting/corrective action 47–8
   see also amending; Index of Letters by Type
cost
   carriage charge 16–17
councils (local) 217–18
court proceedings 134
credit
   granting 135–8
   letters of 51–2, 205
   notes 14, 16–17
   refusing 140–2
   terms 13, 125, 141
current account (opening) 191
current financial position 197
customers
   apologising to *see* Index Letters of Type
   blacklisting 67
   complaining *see* Index of Letters by Type
   handling awkward 67–70
   keeping informed 80, 81–4
   lapsed (reviving) 82, 84
   market research 83
   negotiating with *see* Index of Letters by Type
   quotations (refusing) 71–4
   quotations to 45–8

responding to enquiries 49–57
thanking 75–9
see also credit; debt collection; payment

D
deaths 150, 184, 187–8
debt collection
   demands for payment 123–6
   demands for payment (strong) 127–30
   final demands 131–4
   involving lawyers 148
   queries and disputes 143–5
   requests for payment 146–7
debt, writing off 142
declining *see* Index of Letters by Type
defective goods 41, 64
   complaints 37
defective work 29, 33
delays
   in deliveries 34–5, 56, 63, 66
   in payments *see* debt collection
delivery
   carriage charge 16–17
   delays *see* delays
   incorrect consignments 27–8
   instructions 8, 10
   missed items 30, 31
   non-delivery 34–5, 56, 67
demands for payment 123–6
   final 131–4
   stronger 127, 130
denying
   liability 69–70
   see also Index of Letters by Type
discounts 104
   prompt payment 66, 137
dismissing
   agents 108

employees 166

see also Index of Letters by Type

disputing 13, 16–17, 40, 143–6

see also Index of Letters by Type

distributor 98, 100–2, 114

documentation

finance (international) 190, 205

transport (international) 55

donations 209, 211, 213–4

E

employment/employees

announcements/notices 167–9

appointment of 80–1

condolences 150, 187–8

congratulations to 178, 180, 182

contracts and terms 161–2

dismissals 166

health and safety 183–4

interviews and offers 151–7

maternity and other leave 174–6

motivating staff 177–9

notices to individuals 170–3

references 150, 158–60

resignations 115, 161, 169

sales representatives 36

warnings 150, 163, 166

work policies 185–6

enclosing *see* Index of Letters by Type

encouraging *see* Index of Letters by Type

errors 54

liability denied 69

estate agent (property offer to) 203

explaining *see* Index of Letters by Type

ex-works quotation 45

F

failing company, payment from 132

feedback 83
finance 189
    insurance 199–200
    see also banking
finance documentation 190, 205
financial position, current 197
finishing a letter 243–51
following up *see* Index of Letters by Type
force-free trial 89

G
general announcements (to employees) 167–9
General Manager appointment 80
giving *see* Index of Letters by Type
goals (team motivating) 179
goods
    incorrect consignment 14, 27–8
    missing 30, 31
    non-delivery 34–5, 56, 67
    see also defective goods; delivery; orders; payment; product(s); refunds

H
handling *see* Index of Letters by Type
health and safety policy 183–4
holidays 185–6
hospitality, thanking for 76

I
information
    advising *see* Index of Letters by Type
    requests 18–19
informing and telling *see* Index of Letters by Type
instructing *see* Index of Letters by Type
insurance 199–200
international trade
    finance documentation 190, 205
    payment 147
    quotes and orders 51–2
    transport documentation 55

interviews (for employment) 151–7
invitations and requests 207, 209–12
  declining 213–16
inviting *see* Index of Letters by Type
invoices 143–4
  carriage charge 16–17
  proforma 139–40
  querying 15–17
  unpaid *see* debt collection
Irrevocable Letter of Credit 51

J
job applicants 151–7

K
key persons (resignation) 115

L
lawyers (debt collection) 148
leave of absence 171, 176
legal action (debt collection) 134, 148
letters of credit 51–2, 205
liability denied 69–70
loans 172, 195–8

M
mailing lists 58–9
management
  of bank accounts 191–4
  see also sales and marketing management
market research 83
maternity pay/leave 174–5
media coverage (public relations) 115
meetings 97
  invitation to speak at 212
misconduct (warnings) 150, 163–6
motivating 104, 177–9
  see also Index of Letters by Type

N

negotiating *see* Index of Letters by Type
non-delivery of goods 34–5, 56, 67
non-payment 71, 142
notices to employees 167–73
notifying *see* Index of Letters by Type

O

objecting 208, 217–18
    see also Index of Letters by Type
offering *see* Index of Letters by Type
office relocation 168
opening *see* Index of Letters by Type
orders 54
    acknowledgements 56
    delays 34–5, 56
    incorrect consignment 14, 27–8
    non-supply (payment outstanding) 71, 142
    placing/amending 8–11, 57, 73
    purchase orders 8, 12–13, 21, 27
    terms and conditions 12–14
    see also delays; delivery; goods; product(s); quotations
outlining *see* Index of Letters by Type
Outstanding Employee of the Year Award 180
overdraft facilities 195

P

packing list 55
payment
    demands for 123–34
    international trade 190, 205
    non-payment 71, 142
    queries 15–17, 143–5
    requests for 146–7
    of wages/salaries 171
    see also credit; debt collection; discounts; goods; product(s)
pensions 200
performance awards 180, 182

performances
  of agents 103–108
  unsatisfactory 177
personal approach 81, 91, 94
phrases 233–42
placing *see* Index of Letters by Type
planning applications 217–18
policy changes (explaining) 22
prices
  changes 7, 109–10, 114
  errors (correcting) 47–8
  negotiation 24, 53
  see also discounts; quotations
product(s)
  benefits of 92
  information 18, 46
  quality 37, 64, 69
  unsuitability of 25
  see also goods; orders
profit-sharing schemes 167
proforma invoice 139–40
promotion (used to motivate) 178
prompt payment discount 137
property 190, 201–2, 204
public relations 115
purchase order 8, 12–13, 21, 27

Q
quality of products 37, 64, 69
quality of services 32, 38, 60
querying *see* Index of Letters by Type
quotations 200–1
  giving 46, 48
  international trade 51–2
  querying 6–7
  requesting 4–5, 148
quoting *see* Index of Letters by Type

R

recommending *see* Index of Letters by Type
recruitment policies 151–7
reference numbers 15
references (employment) 150, 158–60
referrals 79, 91
refunds 17, 41, 74
refusing *see* Index of Letters by Type
rejecting *see* Index of Letters by Type
relocation policies 168
reminding *see* Index of Letters by Type
repairs 29, 33
replying *see* Index of Letters by Type
reporting *see* Index of Letters by Type
reprimanding 12, 36, 106
    see also Index of Letters by Type
requesting *see* Index of Letters by Type
requests and invitations 207, 209–12
    declining 213–16
resignations 115, 161, 169
responding *see* Index of Letters by Type
returning
    goods 27–8
    see also Index of Letters by Type
reviving *see* Index of Letters by Type

S

safety 163–5, 183–4
sales and marketing management 85, 87
    advertising agencies 116–19
    agent's commission 109–12
    agent's performance/conduct 103–8
    notifying changes to agent 113–14
    requesting an agency 98–102
sales letters 85–6, 87–97
sales representatives 36
samples 89
seeking *see* Index of Letters by Type

selling *see* Index of Letters by Type
sending *see* Index of Letters by Type
services 18–19, 46, 50, 84, 96
   quality of 32, 38, 60
sick pay/leave 170, 176
signature change (on cheques) 193
solicitors 134, 148
speaking at meeting 212, 215
starting a letter 219–31
statements (querying) 145
story-telling (sales tactic) 95
'subject to contract' 203–4
subscription renewal 96
summary dismissal 166
suppliers
   complaints 29–41
   errors/goods missing 27–8
   invoices/statements 14–17
   negotiating arrangements 22–3, 25–6
   orders 8–13
   quotations (querying) 6–7
   quotations (requesting) 4–5
   requests/instructions 18–21
surcharges 114, 138
surveying 201–2 *see also* Index of Letters by Type
system changes (explanation) 22

T
teamwork (motivating) 179
telling and informing *see* Index of Letters by Type
terminating
   consultants' contract 162
   employment 173
   see also Index of Letters by Type
terms 51
   agency agreement 100–1, 105–6, 108, 191–2
   credit 13, 125, 141
   employment contract 161–2

terms and conditions 136
  amendment 20, 23
  breach of 70
  supplier's 12–13
testimonials 93
thanking 76–9, 103
  see also appreciating; congratulating; Index of Letters by Type
trading account (new) 136
transport documentation (international trade) 55
trial samples 89

U
unjustified complaints 69
unwanted mail 58–9
using *see* Index of Letters by Type

V
verbal assurances 39, 65

W
warning
  safety code breach 163–5
  see also Index of Letters by Type
welcoming
  new customers 49–50
  see also Index of Letters by Type
work policies 185–6
writing off a debt 142